Literature
Philosophy
Religion

Critical Essays on Mark Twain, 1910–1980

Critical Essays on Mark Twain, 1910–1980

1–1710

Louis J. Budd

G.K. Hall & Co. • Boston, Massachusetts

1 – 1710

Library of Congress Cataloging in Publication Data
Main entry under title:

Critical essays on Mark Twain, 1910-1980.

(Critical essays on American literature)
Includes index.
1. Twain, Mark, 1835-1910—Addresses, essays, lectures.
2. Authors, American—19th century—Biography—Addresses, essays,
lectures.   I. Budd, Louis J.   II. Title.   III. Series.
PS1331.C76   1983   818'.409   83-4400
ISBN 0-8161-8652-9

This publication is printed on permanent/durable acid-free paper
MANUFACTURED IN THE UNITED STATES OF
AMERICA

CRITICAL ESSAYS ON AMERICAN LITERATURE

This series seeks to publish the most important reprinted criticism on writers and topics in American literature along with, in various volumes, original essays, interviews, bibliographies, letters, manuscript sections, and other materials brought to public attention for the first time. The second volume of Louis J. Budd's collection on Mark Twain anthologizes thirty essays published between 1910–1980, materials valuable not only for their interpretive insight but for their historical influence as well. In addition, Professor Budd has written a substantial introduction that puts each of the articles into its position in the long debate about Twain's proper place in American letters. Among the materials collected are statements by Owen Wister, Herman Wouk, and William Dean Howells, classic essays by H. L. Mencken, Carl Van Doren, and Fred Lewis Pattee, and modern scholarship by Newton Arvin, John C. Gerber, and Judith Fetterley. We are happy to welcome this volume to the series, and we are confident that it will make a lasting contribution to American literary study.

JAMES NAGEL, GENERAL EDITOR

Northeastern University

CONTENTS

INTRODUCTION

I

This volume continues or joins *Critical Essays on Mark Twain, 1867–1910*. For even before Mark Twain's death, his personality as well as his oeuvre had achieved an enduring, magical force apart from the physical man who wore out at the age of seventy-five. Of course nobody insisted on the distinction before time enforced it. But by 1899 the then official literary passport to immortality had been issued: the first collected edition of Twain's work. Privately and ironically but exultantly, he agreed with his daughter in 1906 that he was a "recognized immortal genius." For a while, posthumous works arranged by his literary executor prolonged the impression of an active writer and thus blurred the line from the other side. Likewise, up into the 1930s a few critics could reminisce vividly about knowing him. In fact, Brander Matthews (whose essay is reprinted here) could have claimed a much closer friendship than he implied. While venerating the artistry of Twain's writings, his crony William Dean Howells understandably centered on the glow of their author's presence. This focus was confirmed by Alvin Johnson's judgment in 1920 that, along with the "scattered proofs of titanic power" in Twain's texts, the "oral tradition reveals a personality far greater."

Of course, a change in Twain's standing and the ways of discussing it did begin to operate in 1910. A probably jealous observer, hostile toward "humor with a nasal twang to it," gloated:

> It will not be long before the real Mark Twain will be distinguished from the fictitious celebrity created by the truly wonderful advertising skill of his publishers. Indeed, in the ability he displayed in adapting himself to the advertising campaign so perfectly planned and carried out by them, there was more genius than shown in any of his writings for many years. His literary output long ago ceased to be spontaneous, yet he was always kept prominently before the public.[1]

To put the matter more sympathetically, Twain had finally stopped expanding the reach of his fascinating persona and enriching its polyphonic

1

effects through interviews, triumphs at banquets, or apparently candid revelations of his moods, habits, and strategies. Between 1899 and 1910 he had regularly stirred suspense about late writings too fiery to appear while the author was around to bear the heat, and critical hedging against surprises lingers on, if now more in hope than anxiety. However, it became safer and safer to talk about a rounded, fixed career. Then, at some indeterminable point, Twain changed from a recent contemporary into an ancestor formed by a distinctly earlier era and therefore an era by definition less threatened but also less insightful than the tormented present. The humanistic challenge for criticism remains: to appreciate what Twain offered on his own terms and yet to press beyond antiquarianism and serve current needs.

After the burst of overdone eulogies in 1910 Twain's literary reputation shows a surprising consistency. The drama of highlighting the later battles among critics can blur three steadier patterns. First, the gulf between highbrow and lowbrow demands on his books was noticed from the first or, more precisely, so far back as 1885, perhaps sooner in England. Second, through critical storm and lull his popularity—and the provocation that poses to some intellectuals—has never wavered. Archibald Henderson, himself more learned than the run of the campus scholar while enough of a maverick to write the first biography of George Bernard Shaw, exulted at how Twain's humor had gone

> everywhere making warm and lifelong friends of folk of all nationalities who have never known Mark Twain in the flesh. The stevedore on the dock, the motorman on the street-car, the newsboy on the street, the riverman on the Mississippi—all speak with exuberant affection of this quaint figure in his white suit, ever wreathed in clouds of tobacco smoke. . . . It is Mark Twain's imperishable glory, not simply that his name is more widely known than that of any other living man, but that it is remembered with infinite and irrepressible zest.[2]

Third, better than most writers in the academic canon, Twain, perhaps because he often overrode the boundaries of genre, has survived the cycles of rigid theory. Inevitably, the structuralists and deconstructionists have turned to his texts, but more dutifully than hungrily; furthermore, the graduates rather than the doyens of those schools have done the prospecting. To be sure, the perfectly shaped anthology will carry every school in fair measure, and continuity will meet discontinuity in a lasting synthesis. But with the recent breakneck mutation in systems of criticism, who can predict what from the contemporary forum will strike 1990 as memorable or instructive?

The tireless interest that the public takes in Twain's personality has a counterpoint that Twain, no kinder toward professional critics than the typical author, would have been tempted to burlesque. Especially before the surprising breadth of tributes that the centennial of his birth evoked in

1935, the predictions that his legend was about to fade away sounded less sorry than relieved. While a leader of the first group to bring American literature squarely into the curriculum, Fred Lewis Pattee (reprinted here) sounded almost gratified:

> The elements that most contributed to the phenomenal contemporary fame of Mark Twain for the most part have vanished. His inimitable presence we no longer can feel. The world for which he wrote has passed utterly. The circle of friends who knew him and loved him and sustained him is growing small. To the majority of readers today he is but a set of books. The real ordeal of Mark Twain is at hand now.

The romantic faith that the one noble stairway to immortality must build on recorded works of art—Keats's "high piled books in charactry"—hangs on among critics too sophisticated to confess it openly. But Twain's presence has soared past the grave, boosted at first by Henderson and Albert Bigelow Paine and in the 1930s by Bernard DeVoto, who traveled "in a gang all by himself" (to borrow a figure Twain liked).

No matter who feels qualified to condescend to Hal Holbrook, he is turning out the strongest booster of all. Though he was not the first impersonator—the breed may go back as far as 1868, and it swarmed into vaudeville during the season after Twain's death—Richard Schickel's review should convince anybody to give Holbrook credit for quality. His success overshadows the other sources and proofs of Twain's indelible legend—the Broadway musicals, movies, advertisements, television specials, and "fillers" in the printed media. Such material hardly rates as an "essay" in the modern use of the word, but it affects the critical wars, just as every teacher of British and American literature is pushed toward disdain, perplexity, headpatting, or gratitude by the signs of Twain's appeal. The reach of that appeal generates more essays than bibliographers can track down in newspapers, popular magazines (*Redbook* or *Armchair Detective*), and journals off the beat of literary scholars (*Architectural Review* or *Conservationist*). Since at least 1885 both amateurish and accomplished poems have addressed Twain respectfully; Alexander Pope would have let a few of them pass as essays. With the media hungering for content, used up quicker every year, Twain's legend seems bound to survive. That white suit may be more famous now than ever.

Actually, the formalists keep a sharper eye on personality than they admit or perhaps recognize, and Twain is one of those authors like Byron, Poe, Baudelaire, Tolstoy, or Mailer who soon distract the vigilance toward ideological rigor. The New Critics quietly played the biographical card against Twain, and Freudians feel compelled to confront him either with his naive self-betrayal of compulsions, as Leslie Fiedler sees it, or with his burrowing psyche, dragged into harsh daylight again by Justin Kaplan. His grittiness had patches of basaltic gloom that now suits the modernist temper. The paperback *Letters from the Earth*, bought by more traveling salesmen than Van Wyck Brooks would find believable, meets the most sophisticated standards for pessimism, and the "Mysterious Stranger" manuscripts have turned into a puzzle that ranks with "The Turn of the Screw" (rather than "The Lady or the Tiger?"). Critics establishing a genealogy for the Southern literary renaissance have claimed Twain as a native, too soon an exile but never a renegade despite *Adventures of Huckleberry Finn*. This anthology, if larger, would have included the relevant essays by Arlin Turner and Louis D. Rubin, Jr.[3] Even so, those included show that his character usually elbows into any discussion of his artistry.

In the last few years, penetrating essays have demonstrated that a fresh cycle of biographical analysis has started.[4] Now that the complete edition of Twain's letters is about to back its promises with three volumes, his outward character will attract more study, in the process compounding its charm because his spontaneity and wit radiate through the letters more irresistibly than anywhere else. Likewise, his autobiography will get close attention as a shaggy-dog problem in the genre that has suddenly commanded debate about its rationale. Only a prophet can tell whether the feminist school will decide that Twain was particularly rewarding (or insensitive) and whether the onrolling sexual revolution will judge him an early liberator with the now swarming editions of *1601* or merely another Victorian sniggering at a stag party. An essay too long to include here has finally looked into the commonplace that he was the latter-day Rabelais.[5] Anybody should predict, however, that more historians of science fiction will discuss him among those rare nineteenth-century intellects who contemplated the cosmos, not just the Darwinian struggle, and framed man against the immensity of light-years. Overall, no matter what flaws are magnified to belittle Twain's old appeal, another side of his character or mind spins into impressive view.

No debunker goes so far as to deny the tenacious popularity of his writings. Any banning of *Huckleberry Finn* makes news, followed by chiding editorials and letters from a "shocked citizen." The net effect is a reaffirmation, with a shot of antitoxin for the danger of becoming a bland classic. During the Great Depression, when a librarian tabulated the strength of Twain fans, their amplifying comments did not confess to using him simply as an escape though Newton Arvin, another distinguished pioneer in teaching American literature, made that charge anyway.[6] The key point is that appreciation of his range of abrasive, even threatening ideas has worked down to the core of his audience. When *Newsweek* gave him major space (by its standards) in 1960, it faced up to his dark sides. Furthermore, it clearly assumed that his readership reached far beyond campuses. As Hamlin Hill has shown best, Twain aimed at the biggest possible sales;[7] he would gloat today at being displayed on spinning racks in airports and drugstores and would admire the covers designed to lure the eye. His mass audience, pleased to have its judgment confirmed, respects the fact that he has serious standing, proved sometimes in startling ways, such as the news that Pope John Paul I was a devotee. At home Twain heads the trio—rounded out by Poe and Frost—who have some degree of both popular and highbrow status as authors.

Today, the demotic audience still feels no need to box off its zest for Twain's personality from his writings. He wove himself—often by name—into his pages so aggressively that only the strictest theoretician can insist on the separation for a band of believers. A middle ground presents Twain as raconteur, as a gregarious soul with roots in folksay who enlivened formal or casual occasions, popping one-liners, spinning yarns, building from cues on the spot. We circulate a fund of Twainisms whose moment of birth or even authenticity can baffle the experts. Many semiliterates know somehow that Twain dazzled the age with his anecdotes, as Owen Wister fondly recalled as late as 1935 and Edgar Lee Masters jealously conceded. While communal memory stays clear on the point, "no one has undertaken an assessment of the enormous number of after-dinner and occasional speeches, toasts, and offhand remarks as an art form as important to Mark Twain as the memorized lecture-circuit performances."[8] Is it philistine to add: more important to his public than many of his books?

That public expects his quips and anecdotes to leave a fallout of wisdom. The easy explanation can go back to the tradition of the cracker-barrel, front-porch philosopher. But Alan Gribben's research into Twain's reading warns us that he often thought and drolled at an obviously informed level.[9] Eventually he appealed as much to the attitude of his times that encouraged tomes on the intellectual and moral system of Tennyson or Browning or, starting in the 1890s, liked testimony from businessmen on how Ralph Waldo Emerson had sustained their climb upward. Wilbur Marshall Urban, a Leipzig doctor of philosophy who had already published a 433-page treatise entitled *Valuation*, found it worthwhile to gauge Twain's caliber since humor is the "one moral invention" by Americans and Twain is "the Edison of our spiritual life."[10] In 1940 his ideas on "education" were codified with total solemnity. While his "maxims" keep passing around, the reprintings at some disciple's expense dwindled after the 1920s, and the clever witticisms are outlasting those with a savage thrust. Still, many an admirer thinks of Twain as more shrewd than funny. An author who survives outside the research libraries after his or her vogue has waned must offer truths that the ordinary reader will try to live by though the mandarins of culture label them simplistic and the semioticians disassemble them. The best omen for Robert Frost's immortality on this earth is that some of his lines, however elusive under explication, get quoted in the mass media.

Learned commentators prefer to discuss not the impact of Twain's values but his reputation—both its relative standing and its prospects.

Ultimately, all criticism keeps reshaping the canon—the list nowhere legislated but widely accepted, even by literary terrorists, as the authority for who is a major artist.[11] Maintaining the canon exerts discrimination in almost the civil-rights sense; the insistence on judging relative worth can unwittingly assume that writers fall into two classes, innately separate and harmed by any miscegenation. The reviewers of a book about Twain or of a posthumous collection have seldom stuck to the immediate point. This drift toward projecting the final verdict strengthened during the 1920s when American literature graduated into a field of scholarship whose pioneers were pulled between asserting overdue claims and proving their sensitivity to the British canon. Even today some of their Ph.D.'s feel obliged to sound sterner than elitist colleagues. In the classroom the Great Tradition has to cope with constant reminders that Twain is widely known and liked. After some honored names draw at best a blank, his arouses warmth so noticeable that comment on pecking order seems mandatory. Of course many academics support Twain's prestige, and their essays in this volume try to nudge it higher. Others concede that it is holding up as mysteriously as the national solvency. But, on balance, he is too often treated like a rich-for-the-day prospector or a stockmarket bull who may panhandle tomorrow under the skyscraper he owned yesterday. Twainians cannot yet feel certain that he will stare from the academic Mount Rushmore.

Until 1940 or so there was in fact a continuing effort to swear off respect for his works. Urban's essay became a fuzzy on-the-other-handing from a professional logician. While not demonstrably hostile to popular culture, Urban, destined to produce a heavily assigned textbook in ethics, exemplified the lingering genteelist urge to elevate the masses. Just as vacillating, F. L. Pattee's essay recalls now a tagline of the 1970s: Was that a yes or a no? Owen Wister, whose own good time had passed long ago and who had fallen back on his Eastern status, held a reluctant undertone in his cheerleading for the centennial of Twain's birth.[12] After the lull of World War II, Twain has suffered, not alone, from the tendency of some critics to sound superior to whomever they examine, implying they could have made the novel or poem on trial more symmetrical in ideas and tighter in symbolism. Since they did not get around to inventing a hedonistic fallacy, it is allowable to suggest their intellect cannot sanction the Twain qualities that first attracted them. The latter part of this collection lacks enough essays in the vein of H. L. Mencken and DeVoto, especially their observant delight with his viscerality and irreverence that C. Merton Babcock does echo. As a truly sophisticated problem, our deepening grasp of Twain's mind and the society that shaped it requires superhuman balance in order to define his autonomy within the deterministic forces he overemphasized himself. Before we reach the stage of believing we can account for him convincingly, the suspicion arises that the quintessential Twain is being submerged.

For the shaky present, programmatic criticism climaxes the academics' reaction to the rise of demotic literature and soothes the humanists' eagerness to stake out their turf in the specialization of learning. Critics with an imposing methodology backed by facts from patient researchers are cowing the Sunday essayist who could reverse the sequence of *The Prince and the Pauper* (1882) and *A Connecticut Yankee in King Arthur's Court* (1889). But a new wave of informed interest has swelled up anyhow. On average the many Mark Twain doubles, who perform mostly as amateurs though a few semipros doubtlessly dream of livable incomes, hit a solid level of authenticity. The results of scholarship have trickled down better than any benefits of tax cuts for the wealthy, and adaptations for Public Broadcasting hire expert consultants, partly because the audience will catch bloopers or basic distortions of Twain's career.

II

The cycle of explication is still expanding if only because it made a later start with Twain than any other classic figure. Along with raising student opinion of his aesthetic weight, its collective result has magnified the importance of two or three texts (novels rather than books of travel) and of a few sketches and stories, actually less vital to Twain than his polemical essays by the 1890s. Furthermore, explication has focused on his latent abstractions rather than his humor, which is particularly hard to systematize.[13] Recent volumes like this one have favored close analyses of his artistry and of the motifs most appealing to literary specialists.[14] Of course, *Adventures of Huckleberry Finn* gets the most space by far.[15] Yet *The Adventures of Tom Sawyer* may run third behind *Pudd'nhead Wilson*, which is looser in structure but better haunted with false corridors. Lately, *A Connecticut Yankee* has attracted subtle readings of its plot as well as its imagery, and others are exploring the "Great Dark" manuscripts.[16] My volume could fill itself with eloquent and penetrating explications.

Nevertheless, it would still have to choose among essays that contradict each other because rigorous theory does not lead any more firmly to consensus than the impressionism of the 1910s and 1920s. For its nonthematic approach, therefore, Janet H. McKay's essay is used to represent the mountain of explication that almost overshadows *Huckleberry Finn* itself. She has the specific value of demonstrating its verbal magic, one of the few achievements granted Twain by carping Edgar Lee Masters and treated reverentially after Ernest Hemingway exaggerated its influence on American writers. At the other academic pole, this anthology could not find room for a pure specimen of scholarship that adds to the substantive knowledge about Twain texts or biography. Since 1963 the annual chapter in *American Literary Scholarship* has tried to point out such

Some may feel this collection should have given the center ring to the Brooks-DeVoto debate. Its partisans overrate, however, the interest that the reader dedicated to primary texts takes in the fury among critics who are—at least traditionally—serving under those texts. Furthermore, it only deepened the old cleavage between those who would have changed Twain fundamentally if they could and those who respect him as a marvel of uniqueness. Still, there is no use understating the debate either. It did set off a chain reaction, which Lewis Leary traces perceptively in his introduction for *Mark Twain's Wound*. Ideas stimulated by Brooks and DeVoto reappear throughout the later part of my volume, often with praise for both of them; their impact will continue to matter. A recent essay, not available for reprinting, reevaluates it incisively.[19]

The space saved from well chewed subjects has gone to four underdeveloped perspectives. First, beneath Twain's downhome tang he belongs firmly to transatlantic culture. This collection has favored essays from that viewpoint, and I wish it could have made room for a full discussion of Cervantes and Twain or Caroline Gordon's surprising bridge between him and Dante. The more predictable approaches to him as crypto-Victorian would also have gone into a bigger volume.[20] Second, my pattern of selection tries to suggest better his importance for writers who came after him.[21] Mencken's enthusiasm was immediate and lusty while Robert Herrick, almost a generation older, waited until the end of his career to state or perhaps recognize Twain's liberating effects. A replete anthology would involve at least Sherwood Anderson, John Steinbeck, J. D. Salinger, and Norman Mailer.[22] The heart of the matter lies in affinity and inspiration, not the "influence" proved by source hunting or the line Hemingway drew to his special needs. Third, this collection has therefore welcomed estimates from Twain's guild, starting inevitably with Howells but bypassing the familiar "Mark the Double Twain" by Theodore Dreiser and the crotchets of Masters to leave space for Mencken, Wister, Herrick, Herman Wouk, Kenneth Rexroth, and Edward Field though not Wright Morris, Kurt Vonnegut, Jr., or still other writers. Finally, this collection values Twain's appeal for the less self-conscious kinds of culture—the folk, oral, mythic, and visual modes.[23] To repeat: it hopes to encapsulate his significances for Western society since 1910. Actually, regimes under all ideologies have welcomed some of his works into every major language; for example, at least five translations of a Twain book have appeared in Albania since the mid 1950s, and many more in mainland China. Before reaching for the global Twain, however, we need a rounded grasp closer to home.

Chronologically, my choices aim to ensure fair weight for the criticism between 1910 and 1940, partly to scotch any implication that we have attained a definitive wisdom since then. Unimpeachable judgment can come only with some kind of Doomsday. Meanwhile, it is helpful to relearn that Paine's biography won an enthusiastic reception without which Brooks would have aroused much fainter notice in 1920. Understandably, the centennial of Twain's birth stirred up stocktaking in 1935. The next wave in 1960 seized the fiftieth anniversary of his death as a pretext; the centennial of *Huckleberry Finn* will bring another, narrowed crest. So far the lusty course of Twain's fame makes any talk of a revival sound melodramatic. Still, because academic publishing has boomed, this volume uses six essays from 1976 and after. We do not have to believe in the latest annual model of scholarship to find a growth in knowledge and insight that absorbs preceding decades of work.[24] But this collection stops at 1980 to tone down what pollsters call the "recency" effect or what fashion magazines worship as "au courant" glitter. Certainly 1980 cannot pass for a culmination just as the two editions of the Mark Twain Project have caught their second wind.

Readers of this introduction might expect the dutiful point that the varying responses to Twain tell as much about the critics and the often unexamined values of their own day. That is true. But Twain's strength can bend his remaker instead. At the risk of looking idolatrous, this collection offers essentially positive essays because they fit better the reality of his staying power.

III

As already mentioned, the format of the *Critical Essays* series limited the pages available and so excluded many significant items. Fortunately, the cost of permission for reprinting did not control any choices. I was surprised by the magnanimity of the authors and the publishers of magazines and journals. Twain would have understood stiff fees.

Having been educated by the Center for Editions of American Authors, the Committee on Scholarly Editions, and the Association for Documentary Editing, I state that each text is reprinted without tampering. Only slips of typesetting have been corrected. Some errors of fact remain, useful markers for the rising level of precision on matters Twainian.

Louis J. Budd

Duke University

Notes

1. From *The Lotus*, an undated monthly brochure from the Authors' Bureau (Babylon, New York); seen in Mark Twain collection of Beinecke Library, Yale University.

2. "Mark Twain," *Harper's Monthly*, 118 (May, 1909), 949.

3. Turner, "Mark Twain and the South: An Affair of Love and Anger," *Southern Review*, NS 4 (April, 1968), 493–519; Rubin has addressed the subject several times, most recently and richly in "Mark Twain's South: Tom and Huck," in *The American South: Portrait of a Culture*, ed. Rubin (Baton Rouge: Louisiana State Univ. Press, 1980), pp. 190–205. The essay by Leland Krauth, reprinted here, bears on this sprawling subject.

4. For example, Stephen Fender, " 'The Prodigal in a Far Country Chawing of Husks': Mark Twain's Search for a Style in the West," *Modern Language Review*, 71 (October, 1976), 737–56; Forrest G. Robinson, "Why I Killed My Brother: An Essay on Mark Twain," *Literature and Psychology*, 30, Nos. 3–4 (1980), 168–81; and, besides the essay by Leland Krauth reprinted here, his "The Proper Pilot: A New Look at 'Old Times on the Mississippi'," *Western Illinois Regional Studies*, 2 (Spring, 1979), 52–69.

5. Sholom J. Kahn, "Mark Twain as American Rabelais," *Hebrew University Studies in Literature*, 1 (Spring, 1973), 47–75.

6. Charles H. Compton, "Who Reads Mark Twain?" *American Mercury*, 31 (April, 1934), 465–71; also as pp. 15–40 in his *Who Reads What? Essays on the Readers of Mark Twain, Hardy, Sandburg, Shaw, William James, The Greek Classics* (New York: H. W. Wilson, 1935). Arvin's essay is reprinted here.

7. "Mark Twain: Audience and Artistry," *American Quarterly*, 15 (Spring, 1963), 25–40.

8. Hamlin Hill, "Who Killed Mark Twain?" *American Literary Realism, 1870–1910*, 7 (Spring, 1974), 123. Since this judgment, Paul Fatout has published *Mark Twain Speaking* (Iowa City: Univ. of Iowa Press, 1976). Masters' essay, "Mark Twain: Son of the Frontier," ran in *American Mercury*, 36 (September, 1935), 67–76.

9. Especially Gribben's commentary in *Mark Twain's Library: A Reconstruction*, 2 vols. (Boston: G. K. Hall, 1980). His related articles are too numerous to list; see for example, " 'I Detest Novels, Poetry & Theology': Origin of a Fiction Concerning Mark Twain's Reading," *Tennessee Studies in Literature*, 22 (1977), 154–61.

10. "Mark Twain, Pure Fooling," *Neale's Monthly*, 1 (May, 1913), 515–22. Robert T. Oliver's tribute to Twain as educationist is reprinted here.

11. See Alvin B. Kernan, *The Imaginary Library: An Essay on Literature and Society* (Princeton: Princeton Univ. Press, 1982), p. 68. "Canon-making never stops, and it can be considered the major business of all writing about literature. . . ."

12. Reprinted here. For a perspective on how a critic of Twain bends to private partialities, see Ben M. Vorpahl, " 'Very Much Like a Fire-Cracker': Owen Wister on Mark Twain," *Western American Literature*, 6 (Summer, 1971), 83–98.

13. I regret especially that limits on space did not allow including David Karnath, "Mark Twain's Implicit Theory of the Comic," *Mosaic*, 9 (Summer, 1976), 207–18.

14. We have, in chronological order, Arthur L. Scott, *Mark Twain: Selected Criticism* (Dallas: Southern Methodist Univ. Press, 1955; rev. 1967); Lewis Leary, *Mark Twain's Wound* (New York: Crowell, 1962); Guy A. Cardwell, *Discussions of Mark Twain* (Boston: Heath, 1963); Henry Nash Smith, *Mark Twain: A Collection of Critical Essays* (Englewood Cliffs, N.J.: Prentice-Hall, 1963); Justin Kaplan, *Mark Twain: A Profile* (New York: Hill and Wang, 1967); Frederick Anderson, *Mark Twain: The Critical Heritage* (London: Routledge and Kegan Paul, 1971); David B. Kesterson, *Critics on Mark Twain* (Coral Gables: Univ. of Miami Press, 1973); Dean Morgan Schmitter, *Mark Twain: A Collection of Criticism* (New York: McGraw-Hill, 1974). The Anderson, Kaplan, and Smith collections are perhaps the most interesting. Sharon K. Hall, ed., *Twentieth-Century Literary Criticism, Vol. 6* (Detroit: Gale, 1982), has representative excerpts of criticism from 1867 to 1980. Finally, see Elizabeth MacMahan, *Critical Approaches to Mark Twain's Short Stories* (Port Washington, N.Y.: Kennikat, 1981).

15. See Barry A. Marks's volume in the Problems in American Civilization Series (Boston: Heath, 1959); Kenneth S. Lynn, *"Huckleberry Finn": Text, Sources and Criticism* (New York: Harcourt, Brace, 1961); Richard Lettis et al., *Huck Finn and His Critics* (New York: Macmillan, 1962); Claude M. Simpson, in the Twentieth-Century Interpretations Series (Englewood Cliffs, N.J.: Prentice-Hall, 1968); Hamlin Hill and Walter Blair, *The Art of "Huckleberry Finn,"* 2nd ed. (San Francisco: Chandler, 1969)—contains a facsimile of the first edition of the novel; James K. Bowen and Richard VanDerBeets (Glenview, Ill.: Scott,

Foresman, 1970)—"With Abstracts of Twenty Years of Criticism"; John C. Gerber, *Studies in "Huckleberry Finn"* (Columbus, Ohio: Charles E. Merrill, 1971); Sculley Bradley et al., *Adventures of Huckleberry Finn*, 2nd ed. (New York: Norton Critical Editions, 1977). Also of special interest: Henry Nash Smith's Riverside Edition (Boston: Houghton Mifflin, 1958); Leo Marx's edition with annotations (Indianapolis: Bobbs-Merrill, 1967); Michael Patrick Hearn, *The Annotated Huckleberry Finn* (New York: Clarkson N. Potter, 1981).

16. This interest builds on the two edited volumes John S. Tuckey has drawn from the Mark Twain Papers. In turn he has selected the most interesting material from those volumes for *The Devil's Race-Track / Mark Twain's Great Dark Writings / The Best from "Which Was the Dream?" and "Fables of Man"* (Berkeley: Univ. of California Press, 1981).

17. Roger Asselineau, *The Literary Reputation of Mark Twain from 1910 to 1950: A Critical Essay and a Bibliography* (Paris: Librairie Marcel Didier, 1954), pays full attention to European critics. Thomas A. Tenney, *Mark Twain: A Reference Guide* (Boston: G. K. Hall, 1977) adds many items (and also supplies the bibliographical details on any essay mentioned in my Introduction). In *Mark Twain International: A Bibliography and Interpretation of His Worldwide Popularity* (Westport, Conn.: Greenwood Press, 1982), Robert M. Rodney concentrates on reprintings and translations. However, his long introduction draws many insights from his bibliographies.

18. Charles Neider declined to grant permission for using material in *Mark Twain and the Russians: An Exchange of Views* (New York: Hill and Wang, 1960). Two representative sociopolitical essays I would have included if space allowed are Edith Wyatt, "An Inspired Critic," *North American Review*, 205 (April, 1917), 603–15, and Arthur L. Scott, "Mark Twain: Critic of Conquest," *Dalhousie Review*, 35 (Spring, 1955), 45–53.

19. Guy A. Cardwell, "Mark Twain: The Metaphoric Hero as Battleground," *ESQ: A Journal of the American Renaissance*, 23 (1st Quarter, 1977), 52–66; also relevant is his "The Bowdlerizing of Mark Twain," *ESQ*, 21 (3rd Quarter, 1975), 179–93. More generally helpful is Alan Gribben's two-part "Removing Mark Twain's Mask: A Decade of Criticism and Scholarship," *ESQ*, 26 (2nd–3rd Quarter, 1980), 100–108, 149–71.

20. See Dennis Welland, "Mark Twain the Great Victorian," *Chicago Review*, 9 (Fall, 1955), 101–09; Roger B. Salomon, "Mark Twain and Victorian Nostalgia," pp. 73–91 in *Patterns of Commitment in American Literature*, ed. Marston LaFrance (Toronto: Univ. of Toronto Press, 1967). For Gordon see "The Shape of the River," *Michigan Quarterly Review*, 12 (Winter, 1973), 1–10.

21. See Edwin Fussell, "Hemingway and Mark Twain," *Accent*, 14 (Summer, 1954), 199–206. Jesse Bier, "A Note on Twain and Hemingway," *Midwest Quarterly*, 21 (Winter, 1980), 261–65, sums up the stylistic connection with fitting cogency.

22. See especially Edgar M. Branch, "Mark Twain and J. D. Salinger: A Study in Literary Continuity," *American Quarterly*, 9 (Summer, 1957), 144–58; Sydney J. Krause, "Steinbeck and Mark Twain," *Steinbeck Quarterly*, 6 (Fall, 1973), 104–11; Robert Taylor, "Sounding the Trumpets of Defiance: Mark Twain and Norman Mailer," *Mark Twain Journal*, 16 (Winter, 1972), 1–14.

23. Besides Glauco Cambon's essay on Twain and Charlie Chaplin (reprinted here), I would have liked especially to find room for St. George Tucker Arnold, Jr., "The Twain Bestiary: Mark Twain's Critters and the Tradition of Animal Portraiture in Humor of the Old Southwest," *Southern Folklore Quarterly*, 41 (1977), 195–211.

24. Besides Arthur G. Pettit (reprinted here), another critic who synthesizes recent biography with other scholarship and criticism is Nadia Khouri, "From Eden to the Dark Ages: Images of History in Mark Twain," *Canadian Review of American Studies*, 11 (Fall, 1980), 151–74.

ESSAYS AND REVIEWS

The International Fame of Mark Twain

Archibald Henderson*

"Art transmitting the simplest feelings of common life, but such always as
are accessible to all men in the whole world—the art of common life—the
art of a people—universal art."

Tolstoy: "What Is Art?"

It is a mark of the democratic independence of America that she has
betrayed a singular indifference to the appraisal of her literature at the
hands of foreign criticism. Upon her writers who have exhibited derivative genius—Irving, Hawthorne, Emerson, Longfellow—American criticism has lavished the most extravagant eulogiums. The three geniuses
who have made permanent contributions to world literature, who have
either embodied in the completest degree the spirit of American democracy or who have won the widest following of imitators and admirers in
foreign countries, still await their final and just deserts at the hands of
critical opinion in their own land. The genius of Edgar Allan Poe gave rise
to schools of literature in France and on the continent of Europe; yet in
America his name remained until now debarred from inclusion in a so-
called Hall of Fame! Walt Whitman and Mark Twain, the two great
interpreters and embodiments of America, represent the supreme contribution of democracy to universal literature. In so far as it is legitimate
for any one to be denominated a "self-made man" in literature, these two
men are justly entitled to that characterization. They owe nothing to
European literature—their genius is transcendently original, native,
democratic. The case of Mark Twain is a literary phenomenon which imposes upon criticism, peculiarly upon American criticism, the distinct
obligation of tracing the steps in his unhalting climb to an eminence completely international in character. Mark Twain achieved that eminence
by the sole power of brain and personality. In this sense his career is
unprecedented and unparalleled in the history of American literature.
Criticism must define those signal qualities, traits, characteristics—
individual, literary, social, racial, national—which encompassed his

*Reprinted with permission from *North American Review*, 192 (December, 1910), 805–15.

world-wide fame. For if it be true that the judgment of foreign nations is virtually the judgment of posterity, then is Mark Twain already a classic.

Upon the continent of Europe, Mark Twain first received notable critical recognition in France at the hands of that brilliant woman, Mme. Blanc ("Th. Bentzon"), who devoted her energies in such great measure to the popularization of American literature in Europe. The essay on Mark Twain, in the series which she wrote, under the general title "The American Humorists," appeared in the *Revue des Deux Mondes* in 1872 (July 15th). In addition to a remarkably accurate translation of "The Jumping Frog" into faultless French, this essay contained a minute analysis of *The Innocents Abroad*; and at this time Mme. Blanc was contemplating a translation of *The Innocents Abroad* into French. There is no cause for surprise in the discovery that a scholarly Frenchwoman, reared on classic models and confined by rigid canons of art, should stand aghast at this boisterous, barbaric, irreverent jester from the Western wilds of America. When one reflects that Mark Twain began his career as one of the sage-brush writers and gave free play to his democratic disregard of the traditional and the classic as such, it is not to be wondered at that Mme. Blanc, while honoring him with elaborate interpretation in the most authoritative literary journal in the world, could not conceal an expression of amazement over his enthusiastic acceptance in English-speaking countries:

> Mark Twain's "Jumping Frog" should be mentioned, in the first place, as one of his most popular little stories—almost a type of the rest. It is, nevertheless, rather difficult for us to understand, while reading the story, the "roars of laughter" that it excited in Australia and in India, in New York and in London; the numerous editions of it which appeared; the epithet of "inimitable" that the critics of the English press have unanimously awarded to it. . . .
>
> We may remark that a Persian of Montesquieu, a Huron of Voltaire, even a simple Peruvian woman of Madame de Graffigny, reasons much more wisely about European civilization than an American of San Francisco. The fact is that it is not sufficient to have wit or even natural taste in order to appreciate works of art.
>
> It is the right of humorists to be extravagant; but still common sense, although carefully hidden, ought *sometimes* to make itself apparent. . . .
>
> In Mark Twain the Protestant is enraged against the pagan worship of broken marble statues—the democrat denies that there was any poetic feeling in the Middle Ages. . . .
>
> In the course of this voyage with Mark Twain (*The Innocents Abroad*), we at length discover, under his good-fellowship and apparent ingenuousness, faults which we should never have expected. He has in the highest degree that fault of appearing astonished at nothing—common, we may say, to all savages. He confesses himself that one of his great pleasures is to horrify the guides by his indifference and stupidity. He is, too, decidedly envious. . . . We could willingly pardon him his patriotic

self-love, often wounded by the ignorance of Europeans, above all, in what concerns the New World, if only the national pride were without mixture of personal vanity. . . .

Taking the "Pleasure Trip on the Continent" altogether, does it merit the success it enjoys? In spite of the indulgence that we cannot but show to the judgments of a foreigner; while recollecting that those amongst us who have visited America have fallen, doubtless, under the influence of prejudices almost as dangerous as ignorance, into errors quite as bad—in spite of the wit with which certain pages sparkle—we must say that this voyage is very far below the less celebrated excursions of the same author in his own country.

It is only too patent that the humor of Mark Twain, the very qualities which won him his immense and sudden popularity, make no appeal to Mme. Blanc. She conscientiously and painstakingly upbraids him *au grand sérieux* for those features of his work most thoroughly surcharged with *vis comica*. Three years later Mme. Blanc returns to the criticism of Mark Twain, in an essay in the *Revue des Deux Mondes* (March 15th, 1875), entitled *"L'Age Doré en Amérique"*—an exhaustive review and analysis of *The Gilded Age*. The savage charm and genuine simplicity of Mark Twain are not devoid of attraction even to her sophisticated intelligence; and she is inclined to infer that jovial irony and animal spirits are qualities sufficient for the amusement of a young nation of people such as are the Americans, since they do not pique themselves upon being *blasés*. According to her judgment, Mark Twain and Charles Dudley Warner are lacking in the requisite mental grasp for the "stupendous task of interpreting the great tableau of the American scene." Nor does she regard their effort at collaboration as a success from the standpoint of art: "From this association of two very dissimilar minds arises a work very difficult to read; at every moment we see the pen pass from one hand to the other and the romancer call the humorist to order, only too often call him in vain. . . . Do not expect of Mark Twain either tact or delicacy, but count upon him for honest and outspoken shrewdness. . . ."

The charm of Colonel Sellers wholly escapes her, for she cannot understand the truly loving appreciation with which this genial burlesque of the later American industrial brigand was greeted by the American people. The remarkable talents of Mark Twain as a reporter impress her most favorably; but she is repelled by "that mixture of good sense with mad folly—disorder," the wilful exaggeration of the characters, and the jests which are so elaborately constructed that "the very theme itself disappears under the mass of embroidery which overlays it." "The audacities of a Bret Harte, the temerities of a Mark Twain still astonish us," she concludes; "but soon we shall become accustomed to an American language whose savory freshness is not to be disdained in lieu of still more delicate and refined qualities that time will doubtless bring."

In translating "The Jumping Frog" (giving Mark Twain the opportunity for re-translating it—"clawing it back"—into English which furnished amusement for thousands), in elaborately reviewing, with long citations, *The Innocents Abroad* and *The Gilded Age*, Mme. Blanc rendered a genuine service to Mark Twain, introducing him to the literary world of France and Europe. In 1881 Emile Blémont still further enhanced the fame of Mark Twain in France by publishing in free French translation a number of his slighter sketches, under the title *Esquisses Américaines de Mark Twain*. In 1884 and again in 1886 appeared editions of *Les Aventures de Tom Sawyer*, translated by W. L. Hughes. In 1886 Eugène Forgues published in the *Revue des Deux Mondes* (February 15th) an exhaustive review, with lengthy citations, of *Life on the Mississippi*, under the title *Les Caravanes d'un Humoriste*. His prefatory remarks in regard to Mark Twain's fame in France at this time may be accepted as authoritative. He called attention to the commendable efforts of French scholars to popularize these "transatlantic gayeties." But the result of all the efforts to import into France a new mode of comic entertainment was an almost complete check. There was one notable exception; for *The Adventures of Tom Sawyer* was really appreciated and praised as—an "exquisite idyll"! The peculiar twist of national character, the specialized conception of the *vis comica* revealed in Mark Twain's works, tended to confine them to a restricted *milieu*. To the French taste, Mark Twain's pleasantry appeared *macabre*, his wit brutal, his temperament dry to excess. By some, indeed, his exaggerations were regarded as "symptoms of mental alienation"; and the originality of his verve did not conceal from French eyes the "incoherence of his conceptions."

> "It has been said," remarks M. Forgues, "that an academician slumbers in the depths of every Frenchman; and this it was which militated against the success of Mark Twain in France. Humor, with us, has its laws and its restrictions. So the French public saw in Mark Twain a gross jester, incessantly beating upon a tom-tom to attract the attention of the crowd. They were tenacious in resisting all such blandishments. . . . *As a humorist* Mark Twain has never been appreciated in France. The appreciation he has ultimately secured—an appreciation by no means inconsiderable, but in no sense comparable to that won in Anglo-Saxon and Germanic countries—was due to his shrewdness and penetration as an observer, and to his marvellous faculty for evoking scenes and situations by the clever use of the novel and the *imprévu*. There was, even to the French, a certain lively appeal in an intelligence absolutely free of convention, sophistication or reverence for traditionary views *qua* traditionary."

Although at first the salt of Mark Twain's humor seemed to be lacking in the Attic flavor, the leisurely exposition of the genially naive American in time won its way with the *blasé* Parisians. It is needless to cite those works of his which were subsequently translated into the French language. It has been recorded that tourists who could find no copy of the Bible in the street book-stalls of Paris were confronted on every hand with copies of *Roughing It*! When the English edition of Mark Twain's collected works appeared (Chatto and Windus: London), that authoritative French journal, the *Mercure de France* (December, 1899), paid him this distinguished tribute:

> His public is as varied as possible, because of the versatility and suppleness of his talent which addresses itself successively to all classes of readers. He has been called the greatest humorist in the world, and that is doubtless the truth; but he is also a charming and attractive story-teller, an alert romancer, a clever and penetrating observer, a philosopher without pretensions and, therefore, all the more profound, and finally a brilliant essayist.

Perhaps the present writer may be pardoned for mentioning that when an essay of his on Mark Twain appeared in *Harper's Magazine*, in 1909, M. Lux, reviewing it in *L'Indépendence Belge*, says:

> In Mark Twain's writings are to be distinguished, exalted and sublimated by his genius, the typically American qualities of youth and of gayety, of force and of faith. His countrymen love his philosophy, at once practical and high-minded. They are fond of his simple style, animated with verve and spice thanks to which his work is accessible to all classes of readers. . . . He describes his contemporaries with such an art of distinguishing their essential traits, that he manages to evoke, to *create* even, characters and types of eternal verity. The Americans profess for Mark Twain the same sort of vehement admiration that we have in France for Balzac.

In Italy, as in France, Mark Twain was regarded as a remarkable impressionist; and *The Innocents Abroad* had wide popularity in Rome. But with the peculiar *timbre* of Mark Twain's humor his Italian audience was not wholly sympathetic; they never felt themselves thoroughly *au courant* with the spirit of his humor.

> "Translation, however accurate and conscientious," as the Italian critic, Raffaele Simboli, has pointed out, "fails to render the special flavor of his work. And then in Italy, where humorous writing generally either rests on a political basis or depends on *risqué* phrases, Mark Twain's 'Sketches' are not appreciated because the spirit which breathes in them is not always understood. The story of the 'Jumping Frog,' for instance, famous as it is in America and England, has made little impression in France and Italy."

It was rather among the Germanic peoples and those most closely allied to them racially and temperamentally, the Scandinavians, that Mark Twain found most complete and ready response in Europe. At first sight, it seems almost incredible that the writings of Mark Twain, with their occasional slang, their not infrequent colloquialisms, and their local

mine—and almost in the same hour and the same breath"—this, Mark Twain confessed, was the most extraordinary coincidence of his life.

By German critics Mark Twain was hailed as the leading exponent of American humor, not only in the United States, but, in Herr Ludwig Salomon's phrase, "everywhere that culture rules." *Robinson Crusoe* was held to exhibit a limited power of imagination in comparison with the ingenuity and resourcefulness of *Tom Sawyer*. At times the German critics confessed their inability to discover the dividing-line between astounding actuality and humorously fantastic exaggeration. The description of the barbaric state of western America possessed an indescribable fascination for the Europeans. At times Mark Twain's bloody jests froze the laughter on their lips; and his "revolver humor" made their hair stand on end. "Such adventures," one bold critic observes, "are possible only in America—perhaps only in the fancy of an American!" "Mark Twain's greatest strength," says von Thaler, "lies in his little sketches, the literary snapshots. The shorter his work, the more striking it is. He draws directly from life. No other writer has learned to know so many different varieties of men and circumstances, so many strange examples of the *Genus Homo*, as he; no other has taken so strange a course of development."

The deeper elements of Mark Twain's humor did not escape the attention of the Germans, nor fail of appreciation at their hands. In his aphorisms, embodying at once genuine wit and experience of life, they discovered the universal human being; and it is chiefly for this reason that they found these aphorisms worthy of profound and lasting admiration. Franz Sintenis saw in Mark Twain a "living symptom of the youthful joy in existence"—a genius capable at will, "despite his boyish extravagance," of the virile formulation of fertile and suggestive ideas. On the occasion of Mark Twain's seventieth birthday, German Europe united in honoring the man and writer. Able critical reviews of his life and work were published in Germany and Austria—more in German Europe than in America! From these various essays—in such authoritative publications as the *Neue Freie Presse* (Vienna), *Tägliche Rundschau* (Leipzig), *Allgemeine Zeitung* (Munich), *Gymnasium* (Paderborn), and the *Illustrirte Zeitung* (Leipzig) —I select one short passage from the pen of the able critic, Dr. Leon Kellner, of Vienna:

> A bohemian fellow, who is full of mischief without the slightest trace of malice in it, an imaginative story-teller who is always ready to make himself and others ridiculous without coming anywhere near the truth, a fantastic and Johnny-look-in-air who nevertheless never loses the solid ground from under his feet, a vagabond and adventurer, who from crown to sole remains a gentleman and with the grand manner of a Walter Scott keeps his commercial honor unsoiled—that is the writer Mark Twain and the citizen Samuel Langhorne Clemens in one person.

He hails Mark Twain as "the king of humorists"—who understood how to transmute all earthly stuff, such as the negro Jim and the street Arab, Huckleberry Finn, into "the gold of pure literature." At the time of Mark Twain's death, when so many tributes were paid him all over the world, one of his German critics wrote, with genuine insight into the deeper significance of his work: "Although Mark Twain's humor moves us to irresistible laughter, this is not the main feature in his works; like all true humorists, *ist der Witz mit dem Weltschmerz verbunden*, he is a witness to higher thoughts and higher emotions, and his purpose is to expose bad morals and evil circumstances in order to improve and ennoble mankind."

Mark Twain is loved in Germany, the critics pointed out, more than all other humorists, English or French, because his humor "turns fundamentally upon serious and earnest conceptions of life." It is a tremendously significant fact that the works of American literature most widely read today in Germany are the works of—striking conjunction!—Ralph Waldo Emerson and Mark Twain.

"The Jumping Frog" fired the laugh heard round the world; it initiated Mark Twain's international fame. *The Innocents Abroad* won the thoughtful attention of the English people. Since that day Mark Twain has been the adored author of England and the colonies; in lieu of a national author, the English chose Mark Twain for the national author of the English-speaking world. His popularity in England was as great as in America or Germany; all classes read his works with unfeigned delight; critics of the highest authority praised his works in the most glowing terms. The personal ovation to him in 1907, which I witnessed, was the greatest ovation ever given by the English public to a foreign visitor not a crowned head; and Oxford University honored him with her degree.

At that time the oldest of England's periodicals, *The Spectator*, paid Mark Twain this significant and comprehensive tribute:

It is all, surely, the most admirable fun and light-heartedness. But fun, light-heartedness and unrivalled sense of humor are by no means Mark Twain's only, nor even, perhaps, his most commanding, characteristics. He has a peculiar power of presenting pathetic situations without "slush." . . . He is, above all, the fearless upholder of all that is clean, noble, straightforward, innocent and manly. . . . He has his extravagances; some of his public, indeed, would insist on them. But if he is a jester, he jests with the mirth of the happiest of Puritans; he has read much of English knighthood, and translated the best of it into his living pages; and he has assuredly already won a high degree in letters in having added more than any writer since Dickens to the gayety of the Empire of the English language.

It is gratifying to citizens of all nationalities to recall and recapture the pleasure and delight Mark Twain's works have given the world for decades. It is peculiarly gratifying to Americans to rest confident in the belief that, in Mark Twain, America has contributed to the world an international and universal genius—sealed of the tribe of Molière, a congener of Defoe, of Fielding, of Le Sage—a man who will be remembered, as Mr. Howells has said, "with the great humorists of all time, with Cervantes, with Swift, or with any other worthy his company; none of them was his equal in humanity."

Mark Twain's Portrait

Anonymous*

Benjamin Franklin stands for the practical genius of the American; Emerson, for his power of vision; Lincoln, for the romance of the man of slight opportunity; and "Mark Twain," for humor. All these men represented other qualities; but when one thinks of American sagacity, spirituality, opportunity, or humor, this group inevitably come before the imagination. They were all men of the soil; they could not have been produced in any other country. There have been many distinguished Americans who might have grown up in other surroundings and conditions; but not one of this group could have been what he was on any other soil or under any other sky. Mark Twain was all his life an exponent of the pioneer qualities of the Mississippi Valley; the large, free, unconventional, humorous point of view of the men who crossed the Alleghenies, built up the Central West and Southwest, and created in the thirties and forties of the last century a world of their own. They were hardy spirits, divorced from European association, with small access to libraries, with great native energy and power of imagination. They were thoroughgoing Americans in their love of their Government and their pride in it; but they lived their lives with very little governmental interference, and they would have resented any curtailment of what they regarded as their individual rights. In the amplitude of the great valley through which the Mississippi passes there was a sense of opportunity which was so accessible and led so far that it took on the more romantic aspects of adventure. The Mississippi was then, as it has since been, a river of careless habits. It has small respect for private property; and when the floods came, it changed its course without consulting the real estate records. The same spirit of freedom animated those who lived upon it; and Mark Twain appeared on the scene at the moment when to be a pilot on a Mississippi boat was the highest ambition of the boys who lived along the river. It presented a rare combination of exalted position, large responsibilities, and personal independence. It was a thoroughly masculine life. It had much more to do, even among its sober practitioners, with the bar than with the drawing-

*Reprinted from *Outlook*, 102 (November 9, 1912), 528–29; a review of Albert Bigelow Paine, *Mark Twain: A Biography* (New York: Harper, 1912).

room. It was lawless so far as conventions were concerned, and it was not specially deferential to statutes; but it had its own standards, and woe to the man who did not meet them.

In that free and easy life men formed the habit of looking at things in the large, of minimizing discomforts, and of regarding a man's dependence on external conditions as a subject for humor. In fact, all life was looked at with a large and careless eye, and men were judged by the possession of primitive qualities rather than by conformity to accepted standards. Everything rested on elementary bases; the upper ranges of social life were yet to be climbed. But there was the stuff of which heroes are made in the men of the Mississippi Valley. Their courage, buoyancy, and sense of fun set them in striking contrast with the people who live on the Volga as they have been described by Gorky. Good-fellowship, readiness to help, indifference to the opinion of the world but great deference to local opinion, quickness to turn a hand to any occupation, and general resourcefulness were the characteristics of the men with whom Mark Twain had to do in the early days.

He never was in any sense a literary man. It was probably to his advantage that in that early period he read few books, but dealt with life at short range, and used the vocabulary of his contemporaries. It was a very fresh, pictorial, and unconventional vocabulary. A good deal of it would have sounded profane in the ears of any other section. As a matter of fact, it was profane, but it was picturesque, hyperbolical, and, in a rough sense, poetic swearing. It was an age without reverence, but not without respect for the fundamental verities of life. When Mark Twain, commenting on his inability to remember names, said, "I'll forget the Lord's middle name sometime, right in the midst of a storm, when I need all the help I can get," he was not conscious of any irreverence; he was using the most vivid form of words in which he could put a defect which annoyed him.

Mark Twain never had any sense of reverence, any more than he had the sense of reticence or the sense of privacy. The free and easy habits of his early life, the ease with which he took the fundamental attitude towards his fellows without reference to the conventional attitude, remained with him to the end; and he was quite as much at home talking with royalty at a garden party at Windsor Castle as he was talking with his old friends in the pilot-house of a Mississippi steamboat. The whole valley was a big neighborhood. Everybody was more or less interested in everybody else. There was no formality, and any stiffness of social intercourse would have been regarded with as much opprobrium as a dress coat. It was a fresh and, in a sense, an original development of humanity; and Mark Twain arrived on the scene just in time to know it at first hand and to report it in his own speech. For this reason his descriptions of life on the river, his *Tom Sawyer* and *Huckleberry Finn*, will probably form the basis on which his future reputation will rest.

A man with such original force and such indifference to conventions needs an open-minded biographer; and Mark Twain was fortunate in finding such a reporter in Mr. Albert Bigelow Paine, who has drawn a full-length portrait of his subject on a very large canvas. This biography fills three large volumes. It is much too long; but it presents the apology of being interesting from cover to cover; and Mr. Paine is entirely within the truth when he says, commenting on the death of Mark Twain, "Nations have often mourned a hero—and races—but perhaps never before had the entire world really united in tender sorrow for the death of any man." Mark Twain was undoubtedly more widely known than any other American whose reputation rests on what he has written; and if the interest in his work sometimes rested on its contrast with European opinion and standards rather than on its intrinsic vitality and veracity, it remains true that the world had a great respect for the author of *Innocents Abroad*. It did not always approve of him; but it was immensely entertained by him, and it discerned the tenderness of the man's heart and the resolute integrity of his nature. For Mark Twain was also a representative American in his love of his home and his devotion to his wife and children. No man could have been more fortunate than was he in the intimate relationships of his life; and no romance was ever more tender or beautiful than his adoration of his wife, herself a woman of exquisite nature, not unaware of her husband's limitations and defects of taste, but splendidly loyal to the pure gold mingled with the alloy, and year by year, with intense patience and devotion, helping him in his career. And all the world knows how his innate integrity came out when financial misfortune overtook him, and how, on the edge of old age, he set forth on an adventure which might have taxed the energies of a young man, and returned with his debts behind him.

Humor was the very atmosphere of his mind. When he began to observe or to speak, it was inevitable that he took the humorous point of view. Like all other humorists, he was profoundly serious at heart; but when he looked at the world it was bathed in the great liberating atmosphere of a quality which is as much an element of genius as imagination. Sometimes this humor was pictorial, sometimes fantastic; for a time after the death of Mrs. Clemens it was corrosive and destructive. It was often homely. When he returned from his wedding trip and found a house ready for him, completely furnished, the gift of his father-in-law, he promptly invited that gentleman, whenever he was in town, to send his bag there and spend a night or even two nights, remarking that it would not cost him a cent. That was the easy, familiar speech of the old frontier. It was the equivalent of the most elaborate expression of gratitude, and had the great advantage of being both fresh and entertaining.

Mr. Paine's biography will always be a mine for students of the American life and literature of our time. Although it is too long, the material which should have been omitted will be of great service for other uses than that of immediate biography; for it gives at full length the portrait of the most original American representative of a section and a time, the exponent of certain qualities which are not original on this continent but which have here taken on original forms. Read in connection with such a tender tribute as Mr. Howells's "My Mark Twain," this biography recalls one of the most fascinating personalities of the age.

A Literary American

[Stuart P. Sherman]*

The reviewer sat down before these three thick volumes with a determination to do his duty, yet with a distinct apprehension that he should be overtaken by fatigue before he emerged from the two-hundred-and-ninety-sixth chapter and plunged into the twenty-four appendices. He was thinking of Mark Twain as an author of books; and his mind was still irritated by memories of the extravagant admirers who saluted the veteran of a thousand ovations as a superlative artist, a profound moralist, and a grave philosopher. He knew Mark Twain's works tolerably well, greatly admired three or four of them—the others much less—and wished them all shorter. He remembered that Twain had been writing autobiography in one form or another for fifty years, and that the later instalments in the *North American Review* had affected him as painful and terribly prolix. He reflected on the fact that Mr. Paine was a man of Western education and sympathies, that Twain was his literary idol, and that this biography was the fruit of six years' labor, during four of which the subject had offered himself for study and had dictated volumes of recollections. He suspected that these 1,719 pages would constitute a last disproportionate monument under which the old humorist would be buried. Then he opened the book and began to read.

When he left off reading two or three days later, he felt as if he had just returned from an exploration of the world, and were rounding out in tranquility a restless life that had extended over three-quarters of a century. He looked back over a stream of experience of historical breadth and national significance, in which the writing of books had been only an incident. He had been carried back to the days of Andrew Jackson, and, with the hope and hunger of the westward migration, had drifted as the slaveholding John Clemens out of Kentucky into Tennessee and on to Missouri, and there had died, dreaming in poverty of his 75,000 acres of Tennessee land unsalable at 25 cents an acre. He had been born again in the son, half-educated, mischievous, and eager, and had set type for a struggling little journal in Hannibal, Missouri, ten years before the Civil War, and

*Reprinted from *Nation*, 95 (November 14, 1912), 457–59; a review of Albert Bigelow Paine, *Mark Twain: A Biography* (New York: Harper, 1912).

had made his first sensation by printing in his brother's paper a poem inscribed "to Mary in H——l [Hannibal]." He had taken one end of a Testament, his mother the other, and had promised not to "throw a card or drink a drop of liquor," and had set out to see the world, still as printer, in St. Louis, New York, Philadelphia, Keokuk, and Cincinnati. But then he heard the call of the river, and for four years was a pilot, and studied the intricate mysteries of the Mississippi, and laughed and jested with rivermen from St. Louis to New Orleans, till a shell from the Union batteries exploded in front of his pilot-house and ended that chapter. Then for a few days as second lieutenant of an extemporized militia company, he rode a small yellow mule to the aid of the Confederacy. Next, the golden flare in the far West caught his eye, and, couched among the mailbags behind sixteen galloping horses, he swapped yarns across seventeen hundred miles of plains till he reached Carson City, and became a miner, and suffered the quotidian fever of the prospector daily anticipating the yellow nuggets in the bottom of the pan, and filled his trunk with wild-cat stock, and knew the fierce life of frontier saloons and gambling hells. From the unfruitful pick and shovel he passed on into the boisterous, bowie-knife journalism of the *Enterprise*, and thence to vitriolic humor on the *Morning Call* in San Francisco, and he sent his name to the Atlantic Coast with the "Jumping Frog of Calaveras County," and lined his pockets with gold by a great news "scoop" in the Sandwich Islands.

It was 1866, he was thirty-one years old, and his career had just begun. He now entered upon a forty-year engagement as a public lecturer, and competed successfully with Fanny Kemble and P. T. Barnum, and made himself known personally to hundreds of thousands, and convulsed them with laughter. At the same time he became a great traveller, perlustrated the cities of his native land, plundered the vineyards of Greece, presented an address to the Czar, visited Jerusalem with the Innocents, sojourned in England and gossiped with the Prince of Wales, in Germany and dined with the Emperor, in India and was entertained by a native prince in Bombay, interceded with President Krueger for the prisoners of the Jameson Raid, captured the cities of Australia and New Zealand, and exacted tribute from the whole world. Three or four years after the Civil War he began to throw off books as a comet throws off meteors. Then he took up the burdens of a publisher, bargained with Gen. Grant for his memoirs, and sold a quarter of a million copies where the other bidder had planned for a sale of five or ten thousand. His imagination took fire at a dream of magnificent wealth, and he became a great speculator, and in one year invested $100,000 in projects, and sunk a fortune in an unperfected type-setting machine, and went into bankruptcy. Then, at the age of sixty he girded himself anew and made another fortune in three years and repaid his creditors to the last dollar, and in a few years more had accumulated a third fortune for himself, and drew annual royalties equal to the salary of the President of the United States, and built himself splendid mansions, and rested from his labors on an Italian mahogany bed, clad in a dressing-gown of Persian silk. Then the University of Oxford summoned the printer, pilot, miner, reporter, traveller, lecturer, author, publisher, capitalist across the sea, and robed him in scarlet, and made him a Doctor of Letters, and he retired into unofficial public life till the call came to set his course towards the sinking sun.

This is not the biography of an author; it is the prose Odyssey of the American people; and it will continue to be read when half of Mark Twain's writings are forgotten. It will continue to be read because it conveys in relatively brief compass the total effect which he spent a lifetime in producing—with American recklessness and prodigality, with floods of garrulous improvisation. Mr. Paine loiters a little, it is true, through the mild Indian summer of Mark Twain's final prosperity, but that was the period of his personal relations with his hero, and we must forgive him if, like an artist infatuated with his subject, he paints us several portraits differing only slightly in attitude and shading. His first two volumes are really marvels of compression; he disposes, for example, of the trip to Palestine in twenty-odd pages, and of the voyage around the world in less; yet we venture to predict that he tells about as much of those famous expeditions as after the lapse of a hundred years a more sophisticated posterity will stay to hear. From first to last he rejects tempting opportunities to digress into history and overflow into description; he supplies only so much setting as serves to bring the actor into higher relief. He is under an illusion, we believe, as to the value of Mark Twain's theology and philosophy and literature—notably in the case of the "Personal Recollections of Joan of Arc"; but his sense of what we may call biographical value is admirable. His book is full of animated and characteristic phrase, gesture, and attitude. He has extenuated nothing of his hero's weakness or his strength, and has set forth with all possible veracity the process through which the man of the frontier became, without losing his essence and his tang, quite literally the man of the world.

No one recognized more frankly than Mark Twain himself that in a sense he was a raider from the Border. He never pretended to be the thing that he was not, and, on the other hand, he was never ashamed of the thing that he was. He planted himself, according to the Emersonian injunction, squarely upon his instincts, accepted the "society of his contemporaries, the connection of events," and, with a happy faculty for turning everything to account, capitalized his very limitations. It was one of the secrets of his immense personal effect that he never felt nor looked like a scholar or a thought-worn literary person, but rather like a man of affairs—erect, handsome, healthy, debonair—in his earlier years like a prosperous ranchman, later like a financier, a retired field-marshal, an ambassador, or, as his friends would have it, like a king. It was an iron constitution, tempered in the Mississippi and tested in the mining camps of the West, that enabled him to endure the stupendous fatigues of his great lecturing tours, to throw off 100,000 words of a novel in six weeks, to toil—without exercise and smoking heavily—all day and half the night, and, when he was past seventy, to talk copyright for hours with a hundred and fifty different Congressmen and radiate superfluous energy at a dinner in the evening, or to play billiards with his biographer till four o'clock in the morning.

If a kind of unconscious frontier impudence persuaded him of his competency as a Biblical critic, and carried him into the realm of abstract ethics, and led him late in life to add the weight of his authority to the followers of Delia Bacon, it was a kindred and valuable mental innocence that made the first fifty years of his life a perpetual voyage of discovery, sharpened his observation and his appetite for experience, and preserved the vernacular vigor of his speech. Had he undergone in his formative period the discipline of an older and firmly stratified society, he would have been saved from some lapses in taste, but he would have lacked that splendid self-confidence which is born of living among an homogeneous folk, and which in the long run explained his unrivalled power, on the platform and in print, of getting in touch with his public. As pilot, miner, and Nevada journalist he found his most profitable associates among men rather than among women, and there he formed the habit of addressing himself to a robust masculine audience—a habit which gives him an almost unique distinction in American literature, and marks him clearly as belonging to the heroic age. It is a significant fact that he was introduced to his future wife by her brother, who had become a great friend of his on the voyage of the Innocents. It is an equally significant fact that the friendship terminated and the brother departed on a journey when he learned that the humorist intended to marry his sister. If Mark Twain ever became a lion among the ladies, it was because they liked lions, not because he accepted their conventions. He detested Jane Austen, her works, and her world; and unabashed he accounted for his antipathy: "When I take up one of Jane Austen's books, such as *Pride and Prejudice*, I feel like a barkeeper entering the kingdom of heaven." What he thought of the "kingdom of heaven" he has set forth in another place. His religious ideas he had from Tom Paine and Robert Ingersoll—another mark of the spiritual frontier; his finer moral feelings, from his wife and from his mother.

In his rather heavy-handed attack upon Bourget, Mark Twain declared that there is nothing "characteristically American" except drinking ice-water. But on the occasion of a railway accident he wrote to a friend, "It is characteristically American—always trying to get along short-handed and save wages." If the eulogists of Mark Twain's humor could hold themselves to a strict inquisition, they would find themselves praising sometimes his legitimate triumphs and sometimes—with an admiration for success that is characteristically American—his colossal crimes. His humor has many phases, but in the main it depends upon the absolutely reckless release of that speculative temperament and imagination which ruined the pioneers in Tennessee and squandered a fortune in unprofitable inventions. Mark Twain's typical "good story" is something like a Western "good proposition"; it is a magnificent lie with an insignificant kernel of truth. If the truth evaporates entirely, the result may be painful burlesque—such as we find in the low spots of *Huckleberry Finn* and the *Connecticut Yankee*. This Western humor depends also upon a perfectly fearless revelation of the reaction of the pioneer upon an unfamiliar environment. This is the prevailing humor of the *Innocents*, and of some of Mark Twain's confidential communications: "Whenever I enjoy anything in art, it means that it is mighty poor. The private knowledge of this fact has saved me from going to pieces with enthusiasm in front of many and many a chromo." Nothing could be more delightful of its kind, unless it is the confession of a mistake that he made at Oxford after he had received his degree. At a dinner given at one of the colleges he wore evening dress, but found the assembled company clad in their scarlet academic costume: "When I arrived the place was just a conflagration—a kind of human prairie-fire. I looked as out of place as a Presbyterian in hell." But this humor sometimes depends also upon a disregard of the proprieties, and on occasion it consists in nothing but this disregard of the proprieties. An example that pretty well illustrates this type may be found in the one-hundred-and-twenty-third chapter of the biography. The humor on this occasion consisted in reminding Gen. Grant and his veterans of the Army of the Tennessee and the six hundred guests at a great and solemn banquet that once upon a time their grim commander-in-chief was wholly occupied in trying to get his big toe into his mouth—"and if the child is but the father of the man, there are mighty few who will doubt that he succeeded." The house, we are informed, came down with a crash, and Sherman exclaimed, "I don't know how you do it!" But that was what, in the present state of civilization, should be called a crime. It is a crime against taste, colossal and barbaric. It is humor befitting the bronzed revellers in Carson City or the Welsh giants of the "Mabinogion."

Mr. Paine, like some other recent critics, dwells with a kind of retaliatory gusto upon certain Brahminical reservations in the welcome accorded to Mark Twain by members of the older New Englander inner circle; he is sure that the world is now having its laugh at the Brahmins. He reminds us also that, while Twain was still on a kind of nervous probation in America, he had been received with unrestrained delight in England. But the right explanation of the hesitation on this side of the water does not seem to have occurred to him. The fact is that Twain was hailed with jubilation by Englishmen because he answered perfectly to their preconceptions of the American character. They could enjoy him, furthermore, with the same detached curiosity and glee that their

ancestors at the Court of James I felt in the presence of Pocahontas—another typical American who, as we read, received marked attention from the Queen, and accompanied her to the Twelfth Night
revels. We imagine that some gentlemen in Virginia were a little worried
lest it should be thought in England that all their wives were Indians—without deeming it all necessary to apologize for Pocahontas; she
was a lovely barbarian, to be sure, but she was truly representative only
of the dusky background of their civilization. The Brahmins with some
justice looked upon Mark Twain, and will continue to look upon him, as a
robust frontiersman, produced in the remote Jacksonian era, carrying
into the courts of kings the broad laughter of the plains, and only
representing adequately an America that is already historical and almost
fabulous. We would no more condescend to this Herculean humorist than
to any other epic hero; we accept him heartily as we accept Robin Hood
and Charlemagne, the wily Odysseus and Dick Whittington, thrice Lord
Mayor of London. But, surely, in this day, when we are all exalting the
primitive, it should be thought no diminution of his greatness to say that
he would be out of place in the *Divine Comedy* or *Paradise Lost*—to reaf-
firm that he is the hero of what our ballad enthusiasts call a "folk" epic,
and that he wins upon us by the savory earthiness, the naive impudence,
the lucky undisciplined strength of the folk hero.

[Review of A. B. Paine's *Biography*]

[William Dean Howells]*

The question of how long he will last as a humorist, or how long he will dominate all other humorists in the affection of his fellow-men, is something that must have concerned Mark Twain in his life on earth. If he still lives in some other state, the question does not concern him so much, except as he would be loath to see good work forgotten; but, as he once lived here, it must have concerned him intensely because he loved beyond almost any other man to make the world sit up and look and listen. The question of his lasting primacy is something that now remains for us survivors of him to answer, each according to his thinking; and it renews itself in our case with unexpected force from the reading of Mr. Albert Bigelow Paine's story of his personal and literary life.

Of course, if we are moderately honest and candid, we must all try to shirk the question, for it would be a kind of arrogant hypocrisy to pretend that we had any of us a firm conviction on the point. For our own part, the Easy Chair's part, we prefer only to say that if the world ever ceased to love and to value his humor it would do so to its peculiar loss, for, as we have always held, the humor of no other is so mixed with good-will to humanity, and especially to that part of humanity which most needs kindness. Beyond this we should not care to go in prophecy, and in trying to guess Mark Twain's future from the past of other humorists we should not care to be comparative. There are only three or four whom he may be likened with, and, not to begin with the ancients, we may speak in the same breath of Cervantes, of Molière, of Swift, of Dickens, among the moderns. None of these may be compared with him in humanity except Dickens alone, whose humanity slopped into sentimentality, and scarcely counts more than the others'.

But Dickens even surpassed Mark Twain in characterizing and coloring the speech of his time. We who read Dickens in his heyday not only read him, we talked him, and slavishly reverberated his phrase when we wished to be funny. No one does that to-day, and no one ever did that with Mark Twain. Such a far inferior humorist as Artemus Ward stamped

*Reprinted from *Harper's Monthly*, 126 (January, 1913), 310–12, with the permission of William White Howells.

the utterance of his contemporaries measurably as much as Dickens and much more than Mark Twain, but this did not establish him in the popular consciousness of posterity; it was of no more lasting effect than the grotesqueries of Petroleum V. Nasby, or than the felicities of baseball parlance which Mr. George Ade has so satisfyingly reported. The remembrance of Mark Twain does not depend upon the presence of a like property in his humor, and its absence has little to do with the question which we have been inviting the reader to evade with us.

After all, we are more concerned with a man's past than with his future; and we can more usefully delight in what Cervantes and Molière and Swift and Dickens did and suffered than in vain conjecture of what men will say of them hereafter. Possibly because he is more germane to the American argument than any European or than any other American, we can have more pleasure in the story of Mark Twain than in theirs, but we think we can have a peculiar pleasure in it because it is among the most interesting stories ever lived and one of the most interesting ever told. Mr. Paine's manner of telling it is charming above all for its naive sincerity and manly simplicity. It has its moments of being masterly, and as a whole the book is a masterpiece of portraiture, if by that we mean a work which involuntarily and voluntarily bodies forth the subject with a lifelikeness beyond question. You may say it is not literature, in spite of being sometimes over-literary; but it is better than literature; it is life. Mr. Paine had to tell the story of a man whose experience ranged from the nadir to the zenith of the American sky; from rude poverty to a prosperity that startled the man himself; from the backwoods to a metropolis which the backwoods could never have dreamed of; and he has told it very tenderly, very admiringly, very self-respectfully, and never flatteringly. It could be said that at times he has told it too intimately, and we believe that something like this has been said; but we should be at a loss to choose which detail of intimacy we would have had withheld. We do not believe that there is one which Mark Twain himself would have had withheld; rather he would have had more confided, for though he doubted many things, he never doubted that humanity could be trusted with the entire truth about man. Any one who knew him must believe that he would have liked his story told very much as Mr. Paine has told it, and that he would be lastingly satisfied with having chosen for his biographer a man whose fitness he divined rather than argued.

It would not, indeed, have been easy to spoil the material at Mr. Paine's command, but he has made of it a great biography; though it would be idle to compare it with other great biographies, and it would especially be a pity to talk of him and of Boswell together. The Life of Johnson was the work of a long series of years, the sum of the closest and most constant study recorded in notes of events and traits, and the scrupulous report of conversations invited and led up to with an eye single to the use finally made of them. There is something of this in Mr. Paine's work, but not enough for the comparison, and he has not Boswell's supreme genius for interviewing. Mostly, the story is got together from the words, spoken as well as printed, of Mark Twain himself and from his letters and his friends' letters. His books are instinctively treated as the prime events of the author's life; but as his life was rich far beyond the lives of other literary men in events which his books did not represent, Mr. Paine sets these strongly before the reader, whose own fault it will be if he does not learn to know Clemens as fully from them as his biographer knows him.

It would not be easy for Mark Twain's surviving friends to find the drama of his closing years misrepresented in any important scene or motive. He was, like every one else, a complex nature but a very simple soul, and something responsive to him in his biographer is what has most justified Clemens in his choice of him for the work. The greatest of our humorists, perhaps the greatest humorist who ever lived, is here wonderfully imagined by a writer who is certainly not a great humorist. From first to last it seems to us that Mr. Paine has read Mark Twain aright. He has understood him as a boy in the primitive Southwestern circumstance of his romantic childhood; he has brought a clairvoyant sympathy to the events of the wild youth adventuring in every path inviting or forbidding him; he has truly seen him as he found himself at the beginning of his long climb to an eminence unequaled in the records of literary popularity; and he has followed him filially, affectionately, through the sorrows that darkened round him in his last years. Another biographer more gifted, or less gifted, than this very single-hearted historian might have been tempted to interpret a personality so always adventurous, so always romantic, so always heroic, according to his own limitations; but Mr. Paine has not done this folly. Whether knowingly or not, he has put himself aside, and devotedly adhered to what we should like to call his job. But he has not done this slavishly; he has ventured to have his own quiet opinion of Mark Twain's preposterous advocacy of the Baconian myth, and if he calls his fierce refusal of all the accepted theologies a philosophy, it is apparently without his entire acceptance of the refusal as final and convincing.

Mark Twain, indeed, arrived at the first stage of the scientific denial of the religious hope of mankind; he did not reach that last stage where Science whimsically declares that she denies nothing. He was at times furiously intolerant of others' belief in a divine Fatherhood and a life after death; he believed that he saw and heard all nature and human nature denying it; but when once he had wreaked himself in his bigotry of unbelief, he was ready to listen to such poor reasons as believers could give for the faith that was in them. In his primary mood he might have relaxed them to the secular arm for a death by fire, but in his secondary mood he would have spared them quite unconditionally, and grieved ever after for any harm he meant them. We think the chapters of Mr. Paine's book dealing with this phase are of very marked interest, both as records and as interpretations. He has known how to take it seriously, but not too seriously, to respect it as the cast of a man who thought deeply and felt intensely concerning the contradictions of the mortal scene, yet through his individual conditioning might any moment burst into self-mockery. This witness of his daily thinking, while reverently dissenting from the conclusions which he could not escape, is able the more closely to portray that strange being in whose most tempestuous excess there was the potentiality of the tenderest, the humblest, the sweetest patience.

Every part of his eventful life, every phase of his unique character is fascinating, and as a contribution to the human document which the book embodies is of high importance; but the most important chapters of the book, the most affecting, the most significant, are those which relate to Clemens's life from the death of his eldest daughter and the break of his wonderful prosperity to that ultimate moment in his earthly home when he ceased from the earth with a dignity apparently always at his command. It was as if he had chosen his way of dying, and it is justly to the praise of his historian that he shows an unfailing sense of the greatness which was not unfailing. It was part of Mark Twain's noble humanity that it was perfect only at moments. It was a thing of climaxes, as his literature was, with the faults and crudities marking it almost to the last, but often with a final effect, an ultimate complexion which could not be over-praised in the word sublime. He was essentially an actor—that is, a child—that is, a poet—with no taint of mere histrionism, but always suffering the emotions he expressed. He suffered them rather than expressed them in his later years, when his literature grew less and less and his life more and more. This formed the supreme opportunity of his biographer, and it was not wasted upon him. His record of the long close, with its fitful arrests and its fierce bursts of rebellion against tragic fate is portrayed with constant restraint as well as courageous veracity to an effect of beauty which the critical reader must recognize at the cost of any and every reservation. The death of his eldest daughter left this aging child pitifully bewildered; the loss of his wife and the close of one of the loveliest love-stories that was ever lived realized for him the solitude which such a stroke makes the world for the survivor; and then the sudden passing of his youngest daughter, whom he alone knew in the singular force of her mind, were the events which left him only the hope of dying.

Yet these closing years were irradiated by a splendor of mature success almost unmatched in the history of literature. It seemed as if the world were newly roused to a sense of his preeminence. Wealth flowed in upon him, and adversity was a dream of evil days utterly past; honors crowded upon him; his country and his city thronged him; the path which his old feet trod with yet something of their young vigor was strewn with roses; the last desire of his fame-loving soul was satisfied when the greatest university in the world did his claim to her supreme recognition justice. It was for his biographer to show the gloom of these later years broken and illumined by these glories, and, when their light could not pierce it, to show him, a gray shadow amid the shadows, but walking their dark undauntedly, and sending from it his laugh oftener than his moan. It is his biographer's praise that he has done this so as to make us feel the qualities of the fact; as in the earlier records he makes us feel the enchantment, the joy, the rapture of the man's experience. If we have not yet answered our primary question, how long Mark Twain will last as a humorist, we must content ourselves with the belief that while the stories of men's lives delight, this book will keep him from being forgotten as a man.

The Man Within

H. L. Mencken

I

In *The Curious Republic of Gondour*, a small volume of Mark Twain's early sketches, hitherto unpublished in book-form, there is little that is of much intrinsic value, but nevertheless it is agreeable to see the collection get between covers, for even the slightest of Mark's work has its moments and should be accessible. He wrote these pieces during the year 1870, some of them for the Buffalo *Express*, in which he had lately acquired a proprietary interest, and the others for the New York *Galaxy*, to which he began contributing a monthly department in May, 1870. Some of the other things that he did for the *Galaxy* are well known, for he reprinted them in *Sketches Old and New*. Yet others were done into a book by a Canadian pirate named Backas, and this book was republished in London. I doubt that the present volume has the *imprimatur* of the Clemens executors, or of the Harpers, who control the Mark Twain copyrights. But what if it hasn't? Mark was too vast a figure in the national letters to be edited after death by executors. Whatever he wrote, signed and published during his lifetime should be decently in print today, that readers may judge it for themselves. If, in the exercise of an incomprehensible discretion, his executors venture to suppress this or that, not as of legal right but simply because it offends their susceptibilities, then it seems to me competent for any other publisher to print it as he listeth. In the present case, as I say, no lost masterpiece is revealed, but nevertheless the stuff, in the main, is quite as good as that which got into *Sketches Old and New*. Incidentally, it shows an early flowering of two qualities that marked the great humorist very broadly in his later days, to wit, his curious weakness for the gruesome and his unshakable moral passion—his high indignation at whatever he conceived to be wrong. No one familiar with the Markian canon could possibly fail to recognize the

*Reprinted from *Smart Set*, 60 (October, 1919), 138–43; reprinted under the title used here in *A Mencken Chrestomathy* (New York: Knopf, 1967), pp. 485–89; entitled "Final Estimate," in *H. L. Mencken's "Smart Set" Criticism*, ed. William H. Nolte (Ithaca: Cornell University Press, 1968), pp. 182–89.

authorship of "A Reminiscence of the Back Settlements" and "About Smells." Both the former, with its Rabelaisian sporting with the idea of death, and the latter, with its furious onslaught upon the Presbyterian Pecksniff, T. De Witt Talmage, are absolutely characteristic.

Such a collection, I repeat, has its uses, and it is a pity that it is not more extensive. The official edition of Mark, published by the Harpers, shows serious defects. For one thing, it is incomplete. For another thing, the binding is gaudy and inappropriate (though not, perhaps, so horribly hideous as the Mother Hubbard binding the Harpers put upon poor Dreiser). And for a third thing, most of the illustrations of the first editions are omitted. In a few cases this last is an improvement; the pictures in *Following the Equator*, for example, were unspeakable. But just as certainly there is something lacking in *Huckleberry Finn* when it appears without the capital drawings of Kemble, and something lacking in *A Tramp Abroad* when any of those of Brown are omitted. It would be easy to reproduce all the original illustrations; it would restore to the earlier books something that is essential to their atmosphere. But it is not done. Neither is anything approaching fair progress being made with the publication of the things that Mark left in manuscript, particularly his autobiography. He himself, I believe, desired that parts of it remain unprinted for a long while—he once proposed to the Harpers a contract providing for its publication a century after his death—but certainly there are other parts that might be done forthwith. As for me, I also grew restive waiting for *Three Thousand Years Among the Microbes*, several pages of which are printed by Albert Bigelow Paine in the appendix to his excellent biography, and for the Bessie dialogues, and for *Letters From the Earth*, and for "The War Prayer," and, above all, for "1601." The last-named was once privately printed and contraband copies are still occasionally circulated. Why not a decent edition of it? If the Comstocks are capable of sufficiently throttling their swinishness to permit the open publication and circulation of Walt Whitman's "A Woman Waits For Me," why shouldn't they consent to the printing of "1601"? Must it wait until some extraordinarily literate United States Senator reads it into the *Congressional Record*?

II

The older I grow the more I am convinced that Mark was, by long odds, the largest figure that ever reared itself out of the flat, damp prairie of American literature. He was great absolutely, but one must consider him relatively to get at the measure of his true greatness. Put him beside Emerson, or Whitman, or Hawthorne, or even Poe; he was palpably the superior of all of them. What ailed the whole quartette was a defective contact with their environment, an aloofness from the plain facts of life, a sort of incurable other-worldliness. Emerson was always half lost in the shadows; toward the end of his life they closed upon him completely. The ideas that he spoke for, in the main, were ideas borrowed from men in far lands, and for all his eloquence he never got into them any sense of their pressing importance to the men of his own country. He was the academic theorist *par excellence*. He inhabited a world of mystical abstractions. The very folks who yielded most readily to his soughing phrases were furthest from grasping their exact import; to this day he is chiefly the philosopher, not of men who think clearly and accurately, but of half-educated dolts whose thinking is all a mellow and witless booziness. A man of extraordinary mental equipment and of even more extraordinary nobility of character, he failed both as a great teacher and as a great artist because of his remoteness from the active, exigent life that he was a part of. Set here in the America of the nineteenth century, begirt by politics, railways and commercial enterprise (and no less by revivals, cuspidors and braggadocio), he carried on his inquiries in the manner of a medieval monk, and his conclusions showed all the nebulousness that one associates with the monkish character. To this day his speculations have had no appreciable influence upon American ways of thought. His only professed disciples, in fact, are the votaries of what is called the New Thought, and these idiots libel him quite as absurdly as the Methodists, say, burlesque Christ.

The intellectual foreignness and loneliness of Hawthorne, Whitman and Poe is scarcely less noticeable. They lived in the republic, but were anything but of it. Hawthorne concerned himself with psychological problems that were not only inordinately obscure and labored, but even archaic; his enterprise, in his chief work, might almost be called an attempt to psychoanalyze the dead. It would be ridiculous to say that there was anything in his books that was characteristic of his time and his country. The gusto of a man thoroughly at home in his surroundings was simply not in him, and it is surely not surprising to hear that while he was physically present in America he lived like a hermit, and that his only happiness was found abroad. Whitman was even more solitary. The democracy he dreamed of was simply a figment of his imagination; it had no more relation to the reality sprawling before him than the Sermon on the Mount has to the practical ethic of the average Christian ecclesiastic. His countrymen, recognizing the conflict, regarded him generally as a loafer and a scoundrel, and it was only after foreign enthusiasts began to cry him up that he emerged from the constant threat of going to jail. As for Poe, he was almost the complete antithesis of a great national artist. In the midst of the most sordid civilization ever seen on earth and in the face of a population of utter literalists, he devoted himself grandly to *héliogabalisme*. His countrymen, in the main, were quite unaware of his stature while he lived. They regarded Cooper and Irving as incomparably greater artists, and such eighth-raters as N. P. Willis as far cleverer men. When they went to the works of Poe at all they went to them as, a generation later, they went to Barnum's circus—that is, as to an entertainment fantastic and somehow discreditable—one to be enjoyed now and then, but not too often. The Baptist critic, Rufus W. Griswold, accurately expressed the national view; his judgment was not challenged for years. An American boy of 1848 who had conceived the ambition of becoming a second Poe would have been caned until his very pantaloons took fire.

At the bottom of this isolation of Poe and Whitman and Hawthorne and Emerson there was, of course, the dense ignorance of a nation in a very backward state of culture; a Beethoven or a Mozart or an El Greco, set down amid the same scenes, would have got the same cold shoulder. But the fault, obviously, was not all on one side; the men themselves lacked something. What that something was I have already indicated. It may be described briefly as responsiveness, observation, aliveness, a sense of reality, a joy in life. Around them roared a great show; it was dramatic, thrilling, unprecedented; above all, it was intensely amusing. And yet they were as unconscious of it as so many deaf men at a combat of brass bands. Only Whitman seemed to have the slightest notion that anything was going on—and Whitman mistook the show for a great sacrament, a cheap and gaudy circus for a sort of Second Coming of Christ. Well, such lofty detachment is not the habit of great artists. It was not the habit of Shakespeare, or of Pushkin, or of Thackeray, or of Balzac. More important to our present purpose, it was not the habit of Mark Twain. Mark was the first of our great national artists to be wholeheartedly and enthusiastically American. He was the first to immerse himself willingly and with gusto in the infinitely picturesque and brilliant life of his time and country. He was the first to understand the common man of his race, and to interpret him fairly, honestly and accurately. He was the first to project brilliantly, for the information and entertainment of all the world, the American point of view, the American philosophy of life, the American character, the American soul. He would have been a great artist, I believe, even on the high-flung plane of Emerson or Hawthorne. He would have been *konzertmeister* even among the *umbilicarii*. But being what he was, his greatness was enormously augmented. He stands today at the head of the line. He is the one indubitable glory of American letters.

III

The bitter, of course, goes with the sweet. To be an American is, unquestionably, to be the noblest, the grandest, the proudest mammal that ever hoofed the verdure of God's green footstool. Often, in the black abysm of the night, the thought that I am one awakens me like a blast of trumpets, and I am thrown into a cold sweat by contemplation of the fact. I shall cherish it on the scaffold; it will console me in hell. But, as I have said, there is no perfection under heaven, and so even an American has his small blemishes, his scarcely discernible weaknesses, his minute traces of vice and depravity. Mark, alas, had them: he was as thoroughly American as a Knight of Pythias, a Wheeling stogie or Prohibition. One might almost exhibit his effigy in a museum as the archetype of the *Homo Americanus*. And what were these stigmata that betrayed him? In chief, they were two in number, and both lay at the very foundation of his character. On the one hand, there was his immovable moral certainty, his firm belief that he knew what was right from what was wrong, and that all who differed from him were, in some obscure way, men of an inferior and sinister order. And on the other hand, there was his profound intellectual timorousness, his abiding fear of his own ideas, his incurable cowardice in the face of public disapproval. These two characteristics colored his whole thinking; they showed themselves in his every attitude and gesture. They were the visible signs of his limitation as an Emersonian Man Thinking, and they were the bright symbols of his nationality. He was great in every way that an American could be great, but when he came to the border of his Americanism he came to the end of his greatness.

The true Mark Twain is only partly on view in his actual books—that is, in his printed books. To get the rest of the portrait you must go to Paine's exhaustive and fascinating biography—a work so engrossing as a character study that, despite its three volumes and more than 1,700 pages, I have gone through it three times. The real Mark was not the amiable jester of the white dress suit, the newspaper interviews and the after-dinner speeches. He was not the somewhat heavy-handed satirist of *A Tramp Abroad* and *Tom Sawyer*. He was not even the extraordinarily fine and delicate artist of *Joan of Arc* and *Huckleberry Finn*. Nay, he was a different bird altogether—an intensely serious and even lugubrious man, an iconoclast of the most relentless sort, a man not so much amused by the spectacle of life as appalled by it, a pessimist to the last degree. Nothing could be more unsound than the Mark Legend—the legend of the lighthearted and kindly old clown. Study the volumes of Paine and you will quickly discern its unsoundness. The real Mark was a man haunted to the point of distraction by the endless and meaningless tragedy of existence—a man whose thoughts turned to it constantly, in season and out of season. And to think, with him, was to write; he was, for all his laziness, the most assiduous of scribblers; he piled up notes, sketches of books and articles, even whole books, about it, almost mountain high.

Well, why did these notes, sketches, articles and books get no further? Why do most of them remain unprinted, even today? You will find the answer in a prefatory note that Mark appended to *What Is Man?* published privately in 1905. I quote it in full:

> The studies for these papers were begun twenty-five or twenty-seven years ago. The papers were written seven years ago. I have examined them once or twice per year since and found them satisfactory. I have just examined

them again, and am still satisfied that they speak the truth. Every thought in them has been thought (and accepted as unassailable truth) by millions upon millions of men—and concealed, kept private. Why did they not speak out? Because they dreaded (*and could not bear*) the disapproval of the people around them. Why have I not published? The same reason has restrained me, I think. I can find no other.

Imagine a man writing so honest and excellent a book, imagine him examining it and re-examining it and always finding it good—and yet holding off the printing of it for twenty-five years, and then issuing it timorously and behind the door, in an edition of 250 copies, none of them for sale! Even his death did not quench his fear. His executors, taking it over as part of his goods, withheld the book for five years more—and then printed it very discreetly, with the betraying preface omitted! Surely it would be impossible in the literature of any other civilized country since the Middle Ages to find anything to match that long hesitation. Here was a man of the highest dignity in the national letters, a man universally recognized to be their chief living adornment, and here was a book into which he had put the earnest convictions of his lifetime, a book carefully and deliberately written, a book representing him more accurately than any other, both as artist and as man—and yet it had to wait thirty-five years before it saw the light of day! An astounding affair, in all conscience—but thoroughly American, messieurs, thoroughly American! Mark knew his countrymen. He knew their intense suspicion of ideas, their blind hatred of heterodoxy, their bitter way of dealing with dissenters. He knew how, their pruderies outraged, they would turn upon even the gaudiest hero and roll him in the mud. And knowing, he was afraid. He "dreaded the disapproval of the people around him." And part of that dread, I suspect, was peculiarly internal. In brief, Mark himself was also an American, and he shared the national horror of the unorthodox. His own speculations always half appalled him. He was not only afraid to utter what he believed; he was even a bit timorous about *believing* what he believed.

The weakness takes a good deal from his stature. It leaves him radiating a subtle flavor of the second-rate. With more courage, he would have gone a great deal further, and left a far deeper mark upon the intellectual history of his time. Not, perhaps, intrinsically as artist. He got as far in that direction as it is possible for a man of his training to go. *Huckleberry Finn* is a truly stupendous piece of work—perhaps the greatest novel ever written in English. And it would be difficult to surpass the sheer artistry of such things as *A Connecticut Yankee, Captain Stormfield, Joan of Arc* and parts of *A Tramp Abroad.* But there is more to the making of literature than the mere depiction of human beings at their obscene follies; there is also the play of ideas. Mark had ideas that were clear, that were vigorous, and that had an immediate appositeness. True enough, most of them were not quite original. As Prof. Schoenemann, of

Harvard, has lately demonstrated, he got the notion of "The Mysterious Stranger" from Adolf Wilbrandt's *Der Meister von Palmyra*; much of *What Is Man?* you will find in the forgotten harangues of Ingersoll; in other directions he borrowed right and left. But it is only necessary to read either of the books I have just mentioned to see how thoroughly he recast everything he wrote; how brilliantly it came to be marked by the charm of his own personality; how he got his own peculiar and unmatchable eloquence into the merest statement of it. When, entering these regions of his true faith, he yielded to a puerile timidity—when he sacrificed his conscience and his self-respect to the idiotic popularity that so often more than half dishonored him—then he not only did a cruel disservice to his own permanent fame, but inflicted genuine damage upon the national literature. He was greater than all the others because he was more American, but in this one way, at least, he was less than them for the same reason. . . .

Well, there he stands—a bit concealed, a bit false, but still a colossus. As I said at the start, I am inclined year by year to rate his achievement higher. In such a work as *Huckleberry Finn* there is something that vastly transcends the merit of all ordinary books. It has a merit that is special and extraordinary; it lifts itself above all hollow standards and criteria; it seems greater every time I read it. The books that gave Mark his first celebrity do not hold up so well. "The Jumping Frog" still wrings snickers, but, after all, it is commonplace at bottom; even an Ellis Parker Butler might have conceivably written it. *The Innocents Abroad*, re-read today, is largely tedious. Its humors are artificial; its audacities are stale; its eloquence belongs to the fancy journalism of a past generation. Even *Tom Sawyer* and *A Tramp Abroad* have long stretches of flatness. But in *Huckleberry Finn*, though he didn't know it at the time and never quite realized it, Mark found himself. There, working against the grain, heartily sick of the book before it was done, always putting it off until tomorrow, he hacked out a masterpiece that expands as year chases year. There, if I am not wrong, he produced the greatest work of the imagination that These States have yet seen.

The Tragedy of Mark Twain

Alvin Johnson*

Not many years ago tens of thousands of Americans were working through the volumes of Jean Christophe, hoping, perhaps naively, to come to an understanding of the process by which the forces of natural genius are focussed to the creation of a great artist. But for Americans there was a more relevant inquiry conceivable. Assuming that natural genius is distributed among the peoples, with a fair degree of impartiality, why does the American people fail to produce artists of the first rank? It was incumbent upon some American Rolland to give us our own, though a negative, Jean Christophe, to exhibit the conditions under which natural genius is thwarted and dissipated. That, essentially, is what Van Wyck Brooks has done in his *Ordeal of Mark Twain* (E. P. Dutton & Co.), although I am not certain he was trying to do exactly that. Consider, however, the logical forces inviting a writer deeply interested in the problem of art in America to just such an enterprise. Mark Twain was unquestionably endowed with genius by nature. All through his work are scattered unmistakable proofs of titanic power, and the oral tradition reveals a personality far greater than his work. Yet Mark Twain never attained to artistic ripeness. There is hardly a single specimen of his workmanship in which there is no intrusion of the cheap and grotesque. Is it not a fair working theory that the exuberance of invention and exquisiteness of sympathy so often distinguishing his pages were the true Mark Twain, while the imbecilities and grotesqueries were imposed upon him by his American environment? It is a hypothesis that impresses Van Wyck Brooks with the force of self evidence. If it were established as a scientific verity, we should have at least a partial explanation of the failure of American artists to attain to greatness. We enslave them to our vulgar purposes.

But if our artists are slaves, they must be the first to realize it; and did the godlike Clemens go about chafing under his fetters? He did, argues Van Wyck Brooks. Not only was Mark Twain consciously in revolt against a fate that denied him his birthright of pure artistic creativeness and im-

*Reprinted from *New Republic*, 23 (July 14, 1920), 201–04.

America and her institutions as a tremendous improvement on the rest of the world, just as he accepted the nineteenth century as a great improvement on all the centuries that had gone before. Indeed, one of the most remarkable things about Mark Twain is his naive tendency to proselytize for the American idea. He is continually slipping into the assumption that we do things better than the rest of mankind. He would have liked to Americanize the whole world, not only of today but of the centuries gone by. Did he not in imagination Americanize King Arthur's court and the Garden of Eden?

But was Mark Twain sincere in his panegyrics of his country and his time, or were those panegyrics concessions to the taste of a reading public that would have been impatient of a spirit of criticism? Did Mark Twain sell his approval of America, for popularity and cash? Van Wyck Brooks tries to prove this. But it is a treacherous business for a critic devoid of a sense of humor to hold an incorrigible humorist too strictly to account. One instance of how Van Wyck Brooks has let himself be tricked will suffice. Mark Twain, backed by his father-in-law, had bought a part interest in the *Buffalo Express*, and had made himself associate editor. Thereupon he ran an announcement of which Van Wyck Brooks quotes the following excerpt:

> Being a stranger it would be immodest for me to suddenly and violently assume the associate editorship of the *Buffalo Express* without a single word of comfort or encouragement to the unoffending patrons of this paper, who are about to be exposed to constant attacks of my wisdom and learning. But the word shall be as brief as possible. I only want to assure parties having a friendly interest in the prosperity of the journal that I am not going to hurt the paper deliberately and intentionally at any time. I am not going to introduce any startling reforms, nor in any way attempt to make trouble. Such is my platform. I do not see any use in it, but custom is law and must be obeyed.

To most of the readers of the *Express* that announcement no doubt seemed funny; to some it seemed silly. Mark Twain had reckoned with both of those classes, but certainly not with Van Wyck Brooks. "Never, surely, was a creative will more innocently, more painlessly surrendered than in these words; marriage had been, for Mark Twain's artistic conscience, like the final whiff of chloroform sealing a slumber that many a previous whiff had already induced. With that promise to be 'good,' to refrain from hurting parties having a 'friendly interest in the prosperity' of his paper, the artist in Mark Twain had fallen into a final trance: anybody could manipulate him now." Any well trained medium ought to be able to hear the shade of Mark Twain, reciting between sighs and laughter: "If I had a cast iron dog that could read this criticism and preserve his austerity, I would drive him off the door step."

Mark Twain was not in revolt against American institutions;

therefore he could not have made of himself a satirist according to Van Wyck Brooks's taste. Mark Twain was essentially a pioneer, with his character formed under pioneer discipline or indiscipline. And on the frontier, institutions do not present a front inviting the shafts of satire. Life is a matter of direct fatalistic relations of man with nature, of relations between men based upon personal consent. And out of such an environment the most impressive lessons concern the nature of the human material. In any pioneer community, how prompt is the classification of men as "all right" or "no good." Even among those who are "all right," about every one promptly exhibits some flaw in his material. It is one of the chief functions of pioneer humor to forestall the discovery of flaws by confession, to impose the disclosure of them upon men who refuse to lay all their dog-eared cards on the table. The frontier insisted on the disagreeable truth, but was willing to ease the strain by humor. And there is so much disagreeable truth to be exposed, under the circumstances, that the tone of pioneer life tends to become pessimistic. Mark Twain was not exhibiting any originality in his formula, "There is no hope for the damned race." It was current on the Western prairies thirty-five years ago; you still hear it occasionally.

To "buck up" the individual man, by showing him the truth about himself, was not that what Mark Twain really wanted to do, instead of offering pleasant entertainment for man and beast? The truth that would sear the page, what was it but the truth about himself, as a specimen of the contemptible species, man?

The malady of Mark Twain was no doubt in part a sense of inferior workmanship foisted upon a public that knew no better. But it was more than that. It drew from the general mood of his generation, a generation that pursued remorselessly the end of material success, to find it meaningless when old age tamed the spirit and threw a veil of frost over the illusions, a generation that exhibited, as no other had done, the defective character of the human material bent to purposes for which the ages had not adapted it. Mark Twain, without knowing it, was a tragic figure in an army of tragic figures who, like him, imagined themselves the fortunate ones of the earth, and thereby proved to themselves, that life upon the earth was not worth while.

Mark Twain and the Art of Writing

Brander Matthews*

In an after-dinner speech which Mark Twain made in 1907 in London at the Savage Club, he protested against an interviewer's having made him say that a certain address was "bully," and he asserted that this distressed him, because "I never use slang to an interviewer or anybody else," adding that if he could not describe that address without using slang, he would not describe it at all. "I would close my mouth and keep it closed, much as it would discomfort me."

Possibly a few of those who heard Mark make this assertion, and probably more than a few of those who have read it in the volume in which his speeches are collected, may have been surprised, and perhaps a little inclined to wonder whether Mark was not here indulging in his customary humorous unveracity. Some of them may have recalled the slang which fell unbroken from the lips of Scotty Briggs when he was enlisting the services of the preacher for Buck Fanshawe's funeral.

But in saying that he never used slang to an interviewer or anybody else, Mark was only asserting what must be plain to every careful reader of his works and to every one who has had the delight of hearing him tell a story. In the person of Scotty Briggs, who knew no other way of expressing himself, Mark could disclose his knowledge of the energetic and boldly imaginative speech of the unlettered Westerners:

> Phrases such as camps may teach,
> Saber-cuts of Saxon speech.

In his own person, as Samuel L. Clemens, or in his assumed personality, as Mark Twain, he refrained from this well of English undefiled by pernicketty precisions, tempting as many of its vigorous vocables must have been to him, with his relish for verbal picturesqueness. He knew better than to yield to the easy allurement; and his English is as pure as it is nervous and direct and uncompromising. As he eschews slang, so he does not disfigure his pages with localisms, current only sectionally. He avoids dialectic peculiarities, however picturesque in themselves and however expressive. Of course, he lets his local characters express themselves in their local vernacular, and he took pride in the intimacy of his acquain-

*Reprinted from *Harper's Monthly*, 141 (October, 1920), 635–43.

tance with sectional vagaries of vocabulary. In an explanatory note, prefixed to *Huckleberry Finn*, he tells his readers that he has therein used a number of dialects:

> to wit: the Missouri negro dialect; the extremest form of the backwoods Southwestern dialect; the ordinary "Pike County" dialect; and four modified varieties of this last. The shadings have not been done in a haphazard fashion, or by guesswork; but painstakingly, and with the trustworthy guidance and support of personal familiarity with these several forms of speech.

To a friend who had inquired as to his collaboration with Bret Harte in an unsuccessful and unpublished play, "Ah Sin," he explained that they had talked out the plot and that he had played billiards while Bret wrote the play, adding: "Of course I had to go over it and get the dialect right. Bret never did know anything about dialect."

While Mark never conformed to the British standard, often insular, and sometimes parochial, he disclosed no individual aberrations either in vocabulary or in usage. The Americanisms he employs on occasion are all legitimate, in that they are what may be called American contributions to the language; and he enlists very few even of these.

With his sensitiveness to the form and color of words, he was acutely conscious of the many differences between our habitual speech and that of our kin across the sea. In a chapter, which was crowded out of *A Tramp Abroad* to find refuge later in a volume of his sketches, he tells us of an interview he had with an Englishman who complimented him on his English: "I said I was obliged to him for his compliment—since I knew he meant it for one—but that I was not fairly entitled to it, for I did not speak English at all—I only spoke American." Then he pointed out that he judged that even the educated classes in England had once dropped their h's in *humble* and *heroic* and *historic*, "because your writers still keep up the fashion of putting *an* before those words, instead of *a*. This is what Mr. Darwin might call a rudimentary sign that an *an* was justifiable once and useful. . . . Correct writers of the American language do not put *an* before those words." And he concluded by assuring his chance companion that "if I wanted to, I could pile up differences here until I not only convinced you that English and American are separate languages, but that when I speak my native tongue in its utmost purity an Englishman can't understand it at all!"

This final statement is the extravagant whimsy of a humorist. Yet it is a fact that Mark spoke his native tongue in its utmost purity, which is why every Englishman could understand him. He spoke pure English, as free from obtruded Americanisms as from obsolete Briticisms, the English current on both shores of "the salt, unplumbed, estranging sea," the English of Defoe and Bunyan, of Franklin and Lincoln. He knew that English was his native tongue, a birthright and not a loan or a gift; and he was content with its ample resources, seeking always the exact noun and the inexorable adjective. As Mr. Howells has put it with his delicate felicity, Mark "used English in all its alien derivations as if it were native to his own air, as if it had come up out of American, out of Missourian ground"; and Mr. Howells has also pointed out that Mark had a "single-minded use of words, which he employs as Grant did to express the plain, straight meaning their common acceptance has given them, with no regard to their structural significance or their philological implications. He writes English as if it were a primitive and not a derivative language, without Gothic or Latin or Greek behind it, or German or French beside it." And he adds that the word Mark prefers is "the Abraham Lincolnian word, not the Charles Sumnerian; it is American, Western."

There is a superstition among those who have been educated beyond their intelligence that no man can be master of English who does not possess Latin at least, and perhaps French also. But this absurdity is exploded by the vital vigor of Bunyan and Defoe, not less than by that of Franklin and Lincoln, Grant and Mark Twain. And the vitality of Mark's English was a gainer also by that fact that to him English was always a spoken tongue; he wrote as he talked; but then he was always as careful in his choice of words when he talked as when he wrote. He imparted to the printed page the vivacity of the spoken word, its swiftness and its apparently unpremeditated ease. His sentences never seem labored, no matter how deeply they may have been meditated. In reading them they appear spontaneous; and, whatever the toil they may have cost him, they are not stained with the smoke of the casting or scratched with the mark of the file. Self-taught as he was, no apprentice to the craft of composition ever had a severer teacher. He so mastered the secrets of our stubborn tongue that he was able to write it as he spoke it, with precise accuracy and yet with flowing freedom.

In this Mark, all unwittingly (for he was never interested in the history of critical theories), was only acting on the principle laid down two and a half centuries ago by Vaugelas, the linguistic lawgiver of the French: "The rule is general and without exception, that what one does not say in speaking one ought never to say in writing." And again: "The greatest of all errors in the matter of writing is to think, as many do, that we must not write as we talk." The same point had been made even earlier by the Italian Castiglione, in his once famous book on the *Courtier*: "Writing is nothing but a form of speaking, which continues to exist after man has spoken, and is, as it were, an image of the words he utters. It is consequently reasonable to use greater diligence with a view to making what we write more polished and correct, yet not to do this so that the written words shall differ from the spoken, but only so that the best in spoken use shall be selected for our composition."

This is precisely what Mark trained himself to accomplish. He selected for his composition the best in spoken use. He profited by one of the advantages of writing as we speak, if only we are in the habit of speaking with due respect for the nobility of our tongue, that he did not cumber his pages with dead and gone words. Like every growing language, English has a host of words which have fallen into innocuous desuetude and are no longer understanded of the people. They may run off the pen of the pedantic, but they never fall from the lips of Mark Twain. He was a man of his own time, with no hankering after the archaic. His language is the living speech of those who have English for their mother-tongue, however scattered they may be on all the shores of all the seven seas.

In his *Autobiography*, from which only a few passages were published in his lifetime, Mark has told us that when he made the overland trip to Nevada (which he has described in *Roughing It*) he took with him Webster's Unabridged Dictionary—an early testimony to his desire to spy out the secrets of the mother-tongue. It was a cumbrous impediment, and its carriage was costly, since the stage-coach charged extra baggage by the ounce: "And it wasn't a good dictionary, anyway—didn't have any modern words in it, only had obsolete ones that they used to use when Noah Webster was a child."

It must be noted also that Mark refrained from the employment of the newest words, the linguistic novelties which are on probation, as it were, which may in time win acceptance, but which for the moment are only colloquialisms, uncertain of their ultimate admission into the vocabulary as desirable citizens.

It was Mark's misfortune—in that it long delayed his recognition as a writer to be taken seriously—that he first won the favor of the public, in the United States and also in Great Britain with the *Innocents Abroad*, a book of robust humor, mirth-provoking and often rollicking in its extravagance. His readers thereafter looked into his successive volumes for the fun they were in search of, and, having found it, abundant and sparkling, they sought no further. If they had, they could not have failed to find other things also, not humorous, but grave and even pathetic. Yet even in the *Innocents Abroad*, which compelled their laughter, there are passages which ought to have arrested the attention of those who do not run as they read, passages which proved that Mark was no mere clown, grinning through a horse-collar, and applying mechanically the formulas of John Phoenix and Artemus Ward. There is, for example, the meditation before the Sphinx:

> The great face was so sad, so earnest, so longing, so patient. There was a dignity not of earth on its mien, and in its countenance a benignity such as never anything human wore. It was stone, but it seemed sentient. If ever image of stone thought, it was thinking. It was looking toward the verge of the landscape, yet looking at nothing—nothing but distance and vacancy. It was looking over and beyond everything of the present, and far into the past. It was gazing out over the ocean of Time—over lines of cen-

tury waves which, further and further receding, closed nearer and nearer together, and blended at last into one unbroken tide, away toward the horizon of remote antiquity. It was thinking of the wars of departed ages; of the empires it had seen created and destroyed; of the nations whose birth it had witnessed, whose progress it had watched, whose annihilation it had noted; of the joy and sorrow, life and death, the grandeur and decay, of five thousand slow revolving years. It was the type of an attribute of man—a faculty of his heart and brain. It was Memory—Retrospection—wrought into visible, tangible form. All who know what pathos there is in memories of days that are accomplished and faces that have vanished—albeit only a trifling score of years gone by—will have some appreciation of the pathos that dwells in those grave eyes that look so steadfastly back upon the things they knew before History was born—before Tradition had being—things that were, and forms that moved, in a vague era which even Poetry and Romance scarce know of—and passed one by one away and left the stony dreamer solitary in the midst of a strange new age, and uncomprehended scenes.

This description of a work of man must be companioned by the description of a work of nature, contained in his second book of European travel, *A Tramp Abroad*. It is a vision of the Jungfrau, seen from Interlaken:

> This was the mighty dome of the Jungfrau softly outlined against the sky and faintly silvered by the starlight. There was something subduing in the influence of that silent and solemn and awful presence; one seemed to meet the immutable, the indestructible, the eternal, face to face, and to feel the trivial and fleeting nature of his own existence the more sharply by the contrast. One had the sense of being under the brooding contemplation of a spirit, not an inert mass of rocks and ice—a spirit which had looked down through the slow drift of the ages, upon a million vanished races of men, and judged them; and would judge a million more—and still be there, watching, unchanged and unchangeable, after all life should be gone and the earth have become a vacant desolation.

In the writings of how many of the authors of the nineteenth century could the beauty and the power of these passages be equaled? Could they be surpassed in any of them?

The Innocents Abroad was published in 1869 and *A Tramp Abroad* in 1879, and in the course of the decade which intervened between these books Mark was called up to speak at a dinner of the New England Society in New York. He chose as his topic the subject which forms the staple of our casual conversation, the weather. And never before had the demerits of the New England climate been delineated and denounced with such vigor and such veracity. Never before had Mark displayed more exuberantly the wealth of his whimsy. And then at the very end he made a plea in extenuation for the misdeeds of the culprit he had held up to derision.

But, after all, there is at least one thing about that weather (or, if you please, effects produced by it) which we residents would not like to part with. If we hadn't our bewitching autumn foliage, we should still have to credit the weather with one feature which compensates for all its bullying vagaries—the ice-storm, when a leafless tree is clothed with ice from the bottom to the top—ice that is as bright and clear as crystal; when every bough and twig is strung with ice-beads, frozen dew-drops, and the whole tree sparkles cold and white, like the Shah of Persia's diamond plume. Then the wind waves the branches and the sun comes out and turns all those myriads of beads and drops to prisms that glow and burn and flash with all manner of colored fires, which change and change again with inconceivable rapidity from blue to red, from red to green, and green to gold—the tree becomes a spraying fountain, a very explosion of dazzling jewels; and it stands there the acme, the climax, the supremest possibility in art or nature, of bewildering, intoxicating, intolerable magnificence.

Only by quotation is it possible to indicate the sustaining dignity of Mark's thought, his interpreting imagination, the immeasurable range of his vocabulary, the delicate precision of his choice of words, and the certainty of his construction. To the three passages already chosen for this purpose, it is impossible not to append a fourth, taken from one of the last papers that he penned with his own hand—the account of the death of his youngest daughter, Jean, only four months before he was himself to die. It was written at intervals, after he was awakened on the morning before Christmas by the sudden announcement, "Miss Jean is dead!" and during the days that intervened until she was laid away by the side of her mother, her brother, and her elder sister. He did not write it for publication; it was too intimate for that; but he told his future biographer that if it was thought worthy, it could appear as the final chapter in the *Autobiography*, whenever that should at last be printed. In these broken paragraphs, set down from hour to hour while he was stunned by the blow, he attains to the severest simplicity—the sincere simplicity of the deepest feeling. The selections must be few and brief:

Jean lies yonder, I sit here; we are strangers under our own roof; we kissed hands good-by at this door last night—and it was forever, we never suspecting it. She lies there, and I sit here—writing, busying myself, to keep my heart from breaking. How dazzling the sunshine is flooding the hills around! It is like a mockery.

Seventy-four years twenty-four days ago. Seventy-four years old yesterday. Who can estimate my age to-day?

. . . .

Would I bring her back to life if I could do it? I would not. If a word would do it, I would beg for strength to withhold the word. And I would have the strength; I am sure of it. In her loss I am almost bankrupt, and my life is a bitterness, but I am content: for she has been enriched with the most precious of all gifts—that gift which makes all other gifts mean and poor—death.

It is not a little curious that few of those who have written about Mark Twain have called attention to his mastery of style, and that even fewer have paid any attention to the essays and the letters in which he himself discussed the art of writing. Perhaps this is just as well, since his own work has been judged free from any bias aroused by his criticism of other men's writing. It may have been a disadvantage to Howells and Henry James and Robert Louis Stevenson that they approved themselves as critics as well as novelists, and that they were frank in expressing their opinions and in formulating their theories about the art of fiction and the art of writing; and it may be that the reticence in regard to these matters observed by Hawthorne and Hardy and Kipling is wiser. Mark's ventures into criticism are not many, but they are significant; and they shed light upon his own artistic standards.

There is illumination, for example, in one of the maxims of Pudd'nhead Wilson's Calendar: "As to the Adjective: when in doubt, strike it out." It would be useful to have that stamped in gold on the border of the blotting-pad of many a man of letters. And there are other remarks equally suggestive, scattered through his letters and through his essays on Howells as a master of English, on "Fenimore Cooper's Literary Offences" and "In Defense of Harriet Shelley."

The predisposing condition which led Mark to take up his pen in defense of Shelley's wife was his manly detestation of insinuating insincerity; and the exciting cause was his perusal of Dowden's unfortunate biography of her husband. Mark was moved to wrath, as well he might be, by Dowden's special pleading, by his maneuvers to whiten Shelley by blackening Shelley's wife. Mark begins by a characterization of Dowden's style:

> Our negroes in America have several ways of entertaining themselves which are not found among the whites anywhere. Among these inventions of theirs is one which is particularly popular with them. It is a competition in elegant deportment. . . . A cake is provided as a prize for the winner in the competition. . . . One at a time the contestants enter, clothed regardless of expense in which each considers the perfection of style and taste, and walk down the vacant central space and back again. . . . All that the competitor knows of fine airs and graces he throws into his carriage, all that he knows of seductive expression he throws into his countenance. . . . They call it a cake-walk. The Shelley biography is a literary cake-walk. The ordinary forms of speech are absent from it. All the pages, all the paragraphs walk by sedately, elegantly, not to say mincingly, in their Sunday best, shiny and sleek, perfumed, and with boutonnieres in their buttonholes; it is rare to find even a chance sentence that has forgotten to dress.

From this expressive characterization it is plain that Dowden had a liking for what Kipling has described as "the Bouverie-Byzantine style, with baroque and rococo embellishments," and that Mark Twain did not share this liking. He detested pretense and pretentiousness. Affectation in all its myriad aspects was ever abhorrent to him, and what he most relished in an author was a straightforward concreteness of presentation. We may be sure that he would have approved Brunetière's assertion that "a good writer is simply one who says all he means to say, who says only what he means to say, and who says it exactly as he meant to say it."

It was the false tone and the unfair intent of Dowden's book which compelled Mark to his merciless exposure. In his less carefully controlled essay on "Fenimore Cooper's Literary Offenses," he impales the author of "The Leather Stocking Tales" for the verbal inaccuracies not infrequent in Cooper's pages. Mark declares that the rules for good writing require that "an author shall *say* what he is proposing to say, not merely come near it; use the right word, not its second cousin; eschew surplusage; not omit necessary details; avoid slovenliness of form; use good grammar; and employ a simple and straightforward style." He insists that all seven of these rules, of these precepts for correct composition, "are coldly and persistently violated in *The Deerslayer* tale."

A little later in his searching criticism Mark becomes more specific. He tells us that "Cooper's word-sense was singularly dull. When a person has a poor ear for music he will flat and sharp right along without knowing it. He keeps near the tune, but it is not the tune. When a person has a poor ear for words, the result is a literary flatting and sharping; you perceive what he is intending to say, but you also perceive that he doesn't say it. This is Cooper. He was not a word-musician. His ear was satisfied with the approximate word."

Even an ardent admirer of the broad, bold pictures of life in the green forest and on the blue water painted in *The Last of the Mohicans* and in *The Pilot* cannot but admit that there is not a little justice in Mark's disparaging criticism. Cooper is not a word-musician; he sometimes flats and sharps, and he is often content when he has happened on the approximate term. But the seven rules here cited, while they cast light on Cooper's deficiencies, also illuminate Mark's own standards of style. He was annoyed by Cooper's occasional carelessness in the use of words, as many other readers must have been; but Mark is more annoyed than most of these other readers because his own practice had made him inexorable in precision. He himself was never satisfied with the approximate word; he never flatted or sharped; he had a word-sense that was always both acute and alert.

Although he never prepared a paper on Walter Scott's literary offenses, Mark held that the author of *Guy Mannering* had been guilty of verbal misdemeanors as heinous as those of the author of *The Last of the Mohicans*. And in a letter that he wrote to me in 1903 he asked a series of questions which he obviously held to be unanswerable:

Are there in Sir Walter's novels passages done in good English—English which is neither slovenly nor involved? Are there passages whose English

is not poor and thin and commonplace, but of a quality above that? Did
he know how to write English, and didn't do it because he didn't want to?
Did he use the right word only when he couldn't think of another one, or
did he run so much to wrong because he didn't know the right one when
he saw it?

Here again the loyal lover of *Quentin Durward* and of *The Heart of
Midlothian* cannot deny that there are inaccuracies and inelegancies in
Scott's flowing pages, and quite enough of them to make it a little difficult
to enter a general denial of all these piercing queries. Scott did not take his
fiction over-seriously. He was, as Carlyle put it bluntly, "improvising
novels to buy farms with." His style, like his construction, is sometimes
careless, not to call it reckless. Mark had trained himself to be careful and
to take delight in the dexterities of verbal adjustment, and this had made
him intolerant of the verbal untidiness, so to term it, perhaps not so frequent in Scott as in Cooper, but far too frequent in both of them, even if
their works had major merits which Mark was led to overlook in his
disgust at their minor lapses from rhetorical propriety.

Besides calling attention to these linguistic deficiencies, Mark takes
occasion in the essay on Cooper and in the letter on Scott to express his
dislike for their stories, merely as stories. He holds that Cooper violated
the rules which require that "a tale shall accomplish something and arrive
somewhere"; that "the episodes of a tale shall be necessary parts of the
tale, and shall help to develop it"; that "the personages in a tale shall be
alive, except in the case of corpses, and that always the reader shall be
able to tell the corpses from the others"; and that "the personages in a
tale, both dead and alive, shall exhibit a sufficient excuse for being there."
He asks whether Scott has "personages whose acts and talk correspond
with their characters as described by him?" Whether he has "heroes and
heroines whom the reader admires, admires and knows *why?*" Whether
he has "funny characters that are funny, and humorous passages that are
humorous?" And he asserts that "it is impossible to feel an interest in these
bloodless shams, these milk-and-water humbugs. And, oh, the poverty of
the invention! Not poverty in inventing situations, but poverty in fur-
nishing reasons for them."

Here we come face to face with one of Mark's most obvious limitations as a critic of literature—he is implacable in applying the standards
of to-day to the fiction of yesterday. Despite their occasional slovenliness
of diction and their constant heaping up of adventure upon adventure,
Scott and Cooper could create individual characters, standing upright on
their own feet and dominating the situations in which they are immeshed.
But both of these bold story-tellers did this in their own fashion, in the
fashion of their own time, for they knew no other; and they could not
foresee that their methods would be demoded in fivescore years. Mr.
Howells was right when he declared that the art of fiction is a finer art
now than it was only half a century ago. Of course it is, and so is the art of

the drama and the art of painting also. And equally, of course, this declaration carries with it no implication that the artists of the present are mightier than the masters of the past. There were giants in those days, as we all know, but these giants were not armed and equipped with the weapons of precision now available for men of only ordinary stature. The state of the art—whichever this art may be, fiction or drama or painting—is never stationary; and its processes are continually modified and multiplied.

One explanation for Mark's error of judgment is probably that he is a realist, with all the realist's abiding abhorrence for romanticism, wilful, arbitrary and highflown, for its striving for vivid external effects, and for the departure from veracity which this seeking entails. He so detested the attitude of Scott and Cooper, he was so painfully annoyed by their frequent failure to pierce below the surface that he blinded himself to their major merits, to the outstanding qualities which make them majestic figures in the history of fiction, however old-fashioned their way of telling a story and however blundering their use of language. But this explanation will not serve to elucidate the reason for his hatred of Jane Austen's novels. She was also a realist and a humorist—and her style is not open to the strictures which Scott and Cooper invite by their haste in composition. Yet he once wrote to a friend that he had often wanted to criticize Jane Austen, "but her books madden me so that I can't conceal my frenzy from the reader, and therefore I have to stop every time I begin. Every time I read *Pride and Prejudice* I want to dig her up and beat her over the skull with her own shin-bone!"

There is no denying the vernacular vigor of this whimsical ebullition. Mark knew well enough what he did not like; but why didn't he like Jane Austen? And the answer is far to seek. Perhaps it is that Jane Austen is a miniaturist of exquisite discretion, not a mural painter—because she molds Tanagra figurines and not the Winged Victory, because her little miracles of delicate observation seemed to him only the carving of cherry-stones. Her field is limited and her vision, keen as it is, is restricted, whereas Mark was wont to survey the full spectroscope of American life—that spectroscope which may seem at times to be almost a kaleidoscope. It may be, however, that the explanation lies a little deeper in the difference between the clever spinster of Winchester and the robust humorist of Hannibal, Missouri; it may be that with Mark's ingrained democracy he was outraged by Jane's placid and complacent acceptance of a semi-feudal social organization, stratified like a chocolate layer-cake, with petty human fossils in its lower formations.

It is only fair to note that Mark never wrote a criticism of Jane Austen, although he once went out of his way (in *Following the Equator*) to speak of her disparagingly. He expressed his desire to desecrate her grave only in a letter to an intimate, familiar with his imaginative exaggeration. In the same letter he confessed that he had no right to criticize books, because he could not keep his temper. "I don't do it, except when I hate them." He hated Dowden's biography of Shelley, and for good reason, since it is intellectually dishonest. He persuaded himself that he hated Cooper's *Deerslayer*, and admirers of "The Leather Stocking Tales" must admit that he had a case, even if he does not win a verdict from the jury.

Once, and once only, was he moved to criticism, not by hate, but by love, by a sincere appreciation of the superb craftsmanship of a fellow-practitioner of the art of fiction. His unbroken friendship with Howells is one of the most salient in all the long history of literature, worthy to be set by the side of those of Molière and Boileau, Goethe and Schiller, Emerson and Carlyle. It endured cloudless for twoscore years, and its full significance will not appear until the letters they interchanged are collected and published. Four years before he died Mark wrote a brief essay on Howells. It is a study of style, of Howells's command over the language, of the characteristics which combine to make Howells one of the indisputable masters of our stubborn speech.

> For forty years his English has been to me a continual delight and astonishment. In the sustained exhibition of certain great qualities— clearness, compression, verbal exactness, and unforced and seemingly unconscious felicity of phrasing—he is, in my belief, without his peer in the English-writing world. . . . There are others who exhibit those great qualities as greatly as does he, but only by intervaled distributions of rich moonlight, with stretches of veiled and dimmer landscape between; whereas Howells's moon sails cloudless skies all night and all the nights.

Mark finds in Howells's writing the very virtue which he failed to find in Cooper's (who worked, it must again be pointed out, more than fourscore years earlier).

> In the matter of verbal exactness Mr. Howells has no superior, I suppose. He seems to be almost always able to find that elusive and shifty grain of gold, the right word. Others have to put up with approximations more or less frequently; he has better luck. To me, the others are miners working with the gold-pan—of necessity some of the gold washes over and escapes; whereas, in my fancy, he is quicksilver raiding down a riffle—no grain of the metal stands much chance of eluding him.

And then Mark gives us an explanation certain to be quoted again and again in our future manuals of composition:

> A powerful agent is the right word; it lights the reader's way and makes it plain; a close approximation to it will answer, and much traveling is done in a well-enough fashion by its help, but we do not welcome it and applaud it and rejoice in it as we do when the right one blazes out on us. Whenever we come upon one of those intensely right words in a book or a newspaper the resulting effect is physical as well as spiritual, and electrically prompt; it tingles exquisitely around through the walls of the

mouth and tastes as tart and crisp and good as the autumn-butter that creams the sumac-berry.

These quotations reveal Mark's own standard of style as sharply as they illuminate Howells's practice. And this quotation, the last of all, imposes itself because it exemplifies Mark's own mercurial clutch on the right word:

> As concerns his humor, I will not try to say anything, yet I would try, if I had the words that might approximately reach up to its high place. I do not think anyone else can play with humorous fancies so gracefully and delicately and deliciously as he does, nor has so many to play with, nor can come so near making them look as if they were doing the playing themselves and he was not aware they were at it. For they are unobtrusive and quiet in their ways and well conducted. His is a humor which flows softly all around about and over and through the mesh of the page, pervasive, refreshing, health-giving, and makes no more show and no more noise than does the circulation of the blood.

Did any humorist ever praise another with a more absolute understanding and with a more certain insight into the essence of the best humor?

Mark Twain and Bernard Shaw

Carl Van Doren*

In a note of warning which Mark Twain wrote for his posthumous autobiography, he gave voice to what is in a sense an apology for his whole career. "I am writing," he said, "from the grave. On these terms only can a man be approximately frank. He cannot be straitly and un-qualifiedly frank either in the grave or out of it." To the present age this caution seems unnecessary so far as this particular book is concerned, for it says nothing that there are not now a hundred voices to say quite as em-phatically; but many of Mark Twain's earlier books in the light of such a warning may well be suspected of having said less than was in their author's mind. Certain timidities, or at least certain discretions, re-strained them. *What Is Man?* waited eight years to be privately printed and eleven more to be published in due form. *The Mysterious Stranger* waited eighteen years before it saw type at all. "Captain Stormfield's Visit to Heaven" remained in manuscript just under forty years. After *The Gilded Age* Mark Twain rarely laid his hand upon the contemporary scene. And in most of his work he appears to have considered long before vexing any large body of current prejudice. Uncramped as he might be among his friends, he took pains to put on more formal robes when he came before the world. It may have been mere prudence. It may have been ignorance that any body of human beings existed who were able to look upon his fierier ideas without blinking. It may have been that he lived in a place and in a time which would not tolerate him at his most candid. Whatever his reasons, he trod somewhat stealthily till near the end of his life, and saved his dynamite to be set off by his executors.

Of such prudent devices Bernard Shaw has made but little use. He came bringing the sword of courage, even of foolhardiness. A terrible child of thought, he has stepped upon the toes of almost every respectable opinion cherished in his day. During the recent war, he lifted the voice of a saturnine common sense in the midst of romantic chaos. He has im-pudently challenged and stubbornly wrestled his way from the start, through the preconceptions of the theater, of the economic order, of

*Reprinted from *Century Magazine*, 109 (March, 1925), 705–10.

morality, of statesmanship, of humanitarianism, which he found established. The love of logic has been his only guide, and he has been loyal to it with a tenacity which might have made him a fanatic but for his humor and his high spirits. The doubts which seem occasionally to have assailed Mark Twain show no signs of having assailed Mr. Shaw. In his darkest hours there has been his intelligence, athletic and fierce, sustaining him. That his public has often overlooked the seer in him to laugh with the comedian does not too seriously affect the result. He has spoken his mind, and he has been heard. Like no Briton since Swift, he has shaped an epoch in his country with the knife of satire. Others might stroke or knead; he has cut. It is a tribute to the race that, for all he has been opposed and accused, he has won a substantial victory, with his own weapons, on his own ground. Possibly, the outcome seems to argue, the undeluded intelligence has a better chance in the open field than is ordinarily recognized. The question is raised whether Mark Twain was not more cautious than he had to be. With methods which he avoided, as too likely to raise mortal enemies and so to defeat his purposes, Mr. Shaw has waged his war, and has made, in the long run, innumerable friends.

II

This is not to say that Mr. Shaw has an audacity which Mark Twain lacked, and to say no more. There must also be taken into account a difference in culture and in temper which has made the one of them value pure ideas as the other did not. The American was forever arriving at some discovery or other, and making a stir about it, which to the Irishman would have seemed a truism in the cradle. There was the discovery that Harriet Shelley had been maligned by her husband's biographers, and the accompanying outburst of rage; there was the discovery that Fenimore Cooper could not write the English language or construct a tidy plot; there was the discovery that Mother Eddy was childish in her metaphysics and astute in her economics. While Mark Twain was coming to such conclusions, Mr. Shaw was concerning himself with Ibsen, Nietzsche, and Wagner. Greatness like theirs, to all appearances, Mark Twain never mastered. He had, instead, the romantic notion that astonishing geniuses were tucked away here or there in hidden corners of the world, some day, perhaps, to be turned up by an unconventional explorer with a hazel wand. When the hosts of Captain Stormfield's heaven hear that Edward J. Billings of Tennessee is nearing their gates, they turn out to meet him with a pomp which they assume for no other candidate for eternity. His native village has not known him, but Homer and Shakespeare walk backward before him to honor his hitherto unhonored verse. Such an episode makes clear why Mark Twain's sources of information were so often odd and accidental. He was never really at home, as Mr. Shaw has been, in the world of ideas. Mr. Shaw's disagreement with many things

On the Rating of Mark Twain

Fred Lewis Pattee*

In his biography of Mark Twain, Albert Bigelow Paine speaks of his hero as "our foremost American man of letters, . . . the foremost American-born author, the man most characteristically American in every thought and word and action of his life."

Superlatives put me on my guard: most of them display sentimentalism or prejudice. Here we have a Boswell who lived with his subject and worshipped him. Can we trust him—for instance, when he says that very few of the Boston Brahmins recognized Mark Twain's "mightier heritage"; that it was left to the common people "to exalt and place him on the throne"? Is Mark really "on the throne" of American letters? Is he, indeed, our foremost literary master, "the man most characteristically American"? If so, then is he tremendously worth studying? Let us consider the elements that composed him.

First, he was of English stock, of pioneer origin, from families long in America. His father, a Virginian, had migrated early into the Kentucky hinterland, where he had married Jane Lampton, granddaughter of Indian-fighters and pioneer settlers with Boone. Her grandmother, Jane Montgomery, had worn moccasins, and at sixteen, during a massacre, had saved her life by outrunning an Indian brave. Pioneer stock! All the Lamptons and Caseys and Montgomerys could dance all night and work all day without a dream of weariness. Optimism sat upon their world like a sunrise. Jane Lampton's union with the young Virginian was a mating of like with like. Fabulously rich were both of them—in hope. All of the Clemenses were optimists, dreamers, gamblers with the horizon. Mark Twain has condensed the tribe into a single individual—Colonel Sellers.

And the young couple started out in the American way—they moved. After each failure they moved. But failure was nothing: were they not young and was the horizon not pure gold? Millions were being made in Western lands, and the young attorney for a few cents an acre acquired a veritable province, eleven thousand acres, of virgin Tennessee land. Then, pioneer that he was, he moved on again westward, across the

*Reprinted from *American Mercury*, 14 (June, 1928), 183–91.

Mississippi, into a raw border settlement called Florida, Missouri, a location that he thought would soon become the metropolis of the Southwest, the head of navigation of Salt river. There were millions in it.

But nothing he touched seemed to prosper. Lower and lower sank the family fortunes, and at length, with the four-years-old Samuel, born in Florida, the Clemens tribe—there were seven in the family now—turned backward to the Mississippi and settled down forlornly in the frazzled little river town of Hannibal. It was the last station in the trek to fortune. Frantically the father, a veritable Mark Tapley, fought for affluence, position, fame, leadership, wealth. Always the butterfly was just within his grasp—there was the Tennessee land anyway—but always the butterfly eluded him at the last moment. Golden success was sure tomorrow, but today saw always failure. He was dead at forty-nine of fever caused by exposure while in headlong chase to secure a position that would put his family into the position they deserved, and his last delirious words were, "Cling to the Tennessee land; it will make you all rich." And young Sam, to his huge delight, was taken from school and set to work to learn the printer's trade in a tiny country office. So much for family history.

Until he was eighteen Mark Twain was wholly of the little Pike county hamlet of Hannibal. It explains very much. Consider the Clemens temperament in the boy, the mother's Fundamentalism, which was constantly a shaping influence, and then consider his surroundings: the highly individualized personalities in the little border town—crackers, pikes, rivermen, Negro slaves; the fringe of brutality everywhere present—the boy actually witnessed murders; the atmosphere of slavery; the town itself—a microcosm, where everyone and everything was known with intimacy; and in front of it all and dominating it all the River, the mighty, mile-wide Mississippi, with its mysterious horizons out of which came daily the great steamboats and into which they faded.

That indeed was romance, and it laid hold mightily upon the imagination of the boy. He was only nine when he made his first attempt to escape, stowing himself away on one of the great boats, to be discovered at the last moment and flung back. Until he was eighteen circumstances bound him fast to the little town, but at that break-away age the *Wanderlust* could no longer be subdued. He broke away, became a tramp—a tramp printer. St. Louis he visited, New York, Philadelphia, New York again, Keokuk, Cincinnati. For fifteen months he was foot-loose, a hobo—the rest of his life he was a hobo: where do you find him settled? Over Herndon's book of travels in South America he becomes fired to explore the Amazon and he actually starts. But on the boat down the river a new butterfly crosses him: why not be a pilot like the regal Bixby up there? It had been the ambition of his boyhood.

As a result, during the next four and a half years he was cub pilot and then pilot on the Mississippi, ranging up and down the treacherous, turbid, changing stream—at that time all unlighted, undredged, untamed—

with elemental men in all save the veneer, ruffians, individualists, "half horse, half alligator." It was life keyed to extremes, excitement, high spirits. Everywhere the dramatic,—flourishing entrances into river ports, floods, wrecks, fogs, races with other boats, the surging tide of travelers, most of them pioneers into the new West. Never again after those four epic years could Mark Twain settle into quietness in a corner.

During the next five and one-half years came the second act of the drama. Swiftly the scenery changes and the costumes: soldier, deserter, adventurer across the great Plains, assistant to his brother in Carson City, prospecting ranger of the Nevada mountains, claim-holder, miner, reporter at the Comstock lode in the first wild days of its bonanza boom, reporter of the first territorial Legislature of Nevada, leader of "the third house," newspaper man in California and the Sandwich Islands, writer, pocket-miner, lecturer—it was melodrama in real life, it was vaudeville. Never was a knight of the dusty roads more headlongly restless. After four months in San Francisco he wrote: "We have changed our lodging five times. We are very comfortably fixed where we are now . . . but I need a change and must move again." He was serious. No six months in his after life when he could not have written the same thing. Always there must be newness, extremes, movement. When he writes, it will be in key: *fortissimo, accelerando*, like life at the Comstock, like the river vocabulary.

Five and a half years and then New York City by way of the Isthmus. Never more dramatic entrance: note the picture on the Brooklyn lecture poster, 1869, Mark Twain, "The Wild Humorist of the Pacific Slope," in mid-air astride a jumping frog. Thus he entered the East. Swiftly he was off again. He had planned to girdle the earth, in forty minutes were it possible, but the personally-conducted *Quaker City* tour to Europe and the Holy Land caught his eye and he was off pell-mell into the East just as before he had plunged into the West. The ultimate result of it was the meeting with Olivia Langdon of Elmira, New York, his marriage at the palatial residence of her father, his marriage present of a beautiful home, his acquirement of a newspaper in Buffalo, and his settling down seemingly for good. A most amazing episode surely: for a year he had an office and regular toil, a home, with grace said at meat, daily Bible readings, church on Sunday—a wild horse of the prairies broken to the plow.

II

But by no means was the man settled down: he moved more times than ever his father did. The Buffalo home was only transient. It is useless to try to follow him, or to enumerate the houses he owned or rented or built. Twenty times at least he crossed the Atlantic. No sooner had he succeeded with *Innocents Abroad* than he was off to Europe again. One-third of the rest of his life—thirteen years in all—he spent abroad. He was lionized beyond measure in London, in Paris, in Berlin; his life became a succession of dinners, of receptions, of welcomes, of farewells, of visits—and he loved it. "There never lived a man who took a more childlike delight in genuine appreciation." England went wild over him. "His rooms at the Langdon were like a court." They had found the American they had been for years demanding, and lords with monocles, and social lions, and literary critics, and poets, and all the distinction of the Empire, to put it in Victorian phrase, were "at his feet." Home in America again, it was the same thing: he was "the belle of New York." For years he moved in an atmosphere of perpetual praise and curiosity and excitement.

Leaf through the amazing hodge-podge which Paine in his fourth volume has compiled with the title of "A Chronological List of Mark Twain's Work—Published and Otherwise." Where can you find another such chaos? Everything is in it from mediocrity to genius, from newspaper column humor to Shakespearean criticism, from medieval European history to Biblical exegesis. How shall we approach this colossal salmagundi? How shall we classify even the fraction which appears in his authorized set?

To realize it all we must return to the man himself. First of all, his personality: primarily was he a showman. "The Autobiography of Barnum" was a favorite book. Nature had done much for him. Most remarkable was he in personality: he was irresistible. His peculiar drawl in the old river days had won over even the hard-boiled Bixby, and in later years it never lost its peculiar effectiveness. His mannerisms were as striking as those of Artemus Ward. His hair, auburn at first, and at last a great sheaf of white; his manner of telling a story; his unique vocabulary with its sulphuric river flavor; his endless store of whimsical anecdote and travelogue description—all made him a remarkably good show. He looked his part and he acted his part, unconsciously it may have been, but nevertheless most effectively. Bret Harte had been a failure on the platform. He dressed and acted like a New York aesthete and people were looking for Yuba Bill and Colonel Starbottle. But Mark Twain was Mark Twain to the life. He filled the bill.

To this was allied his second gift from the gods: he was a superb raconteur. Always, says his biographer, "he felt the need of an audience," and once he had it, in proper key, he was at his best. "His evenings after dinner," says George Warner, "were an unending flow of stories." And always he made his point, always he was cheered, even in the British Isles, where American jokes do not always get across. To hear him drawl his adventures with his incongruous gravity at the explosion point of the tale was entertainment unique and incomparable. On and on flowed "the inexhaustible, the fairy, the Arabian Nights story," writes Howells, "which I could never tire of, even when it began to be told over again."

In part this accounts for the amazing miscellany of his writings and for their surprising fragmentariness. Fundamentally, they are raconteur stuff, like the stories poured out to his evening guests. Always is he pell-mell, always is he impatient of revision. He wrote three of his *Life on the Mississippi* instalments in ten days; he dashed off one-hundred thousand words of *Joan of Arc* in six weeks. Like all his work, they are improvisations. In his later years he dictated to a stenographer—his autobiography, for instance, which he poured out in a lawless ramble, insisting that he be not held for chronological sequence, nor even for the truth.

There was an element of the gambler in the man, a legacy doubtless from the Clemenses who had early been inoculated with the spirit of the frontier—riches to be gained without the expenditure of slow accumulating toil. His boyish imagination had been fired early by the legends of the Tennessee lands that were to make them all rich. In his mining days in Nevada he had lived in a veritable fever. It delighted him in later years to tell how again and again he had come within the narrowest margins of being one of the millionaires of America. Read his letters from the mines: tremendously revealing documents. Now it is the Dashaway mine that is to make him a Croesus, now it is the Flyaway, or the Annipolitan, or the Live Yankee. These all failing, still he can write, "I own one-eighth of the new Monitor Ledge Clemens Company, and money cannot buy a foot of it, because I know it contains our fortune." Quickly it was abandoned, but just as quickly was he digging with feverish hopes at another rainbow end.

And not always did he fail. "The Jumping Frog" was a gold pocket richer than any he had ever dreamed of in the Nevada mountains; so was *Innocents Abroad*. And as he began to publish he learned a dangerous secret: for him literature was to be a gambling game with enormous stakes; it was to be associated for him with money, money that came in large checks for small effort, constant streams of money, money. His income first and last from his books and articles and lectures was sensationally large. It well-nigh ruined him not only as an artist, but financially as well. He became a plunger. The type-setting machine and the publishing venture more than stripped him bare, for they took his wife's fortune as well as his own. Had it not been for Henry H. Rogers' skilful management he would have died in poverty.

That all this affected the literary output of the man goes without question. Says Thomas Mason: "He tried to play the business man in place of being a great artist. The reason was, primarily, that he became more or less intoxicated with money." True. He needed money as any gambler needs money, for schemes that would make him suddenly rich so that he could live in mansions with servants and luxuries and entertain with lavishness. And as a result he wrote not as an artist writes, patiently, perfectly, urged on from within, but like an artisan who has contracted to do a job for pay.

His headlong restlessness, too, affected his output. He worked by whims, by spurts, by emotional impulses. At the drop of an idea he was off with a book. After a sojourn in England he was fired to do what Emerson and Hawthorne had done. Hundreds of pages he dashed off of his British experiences—then threw them aside. Count the fragments of volumes in his bibliography. A touch on his emotions and he exploded into an article, as, for instance, the defense of Mrs. Shelley or the damnation of Leopold or Fenimore Cooper.

His emotions: temperament was an inheritance; sensitiveness with him was almost a disease. Orion summed him up in a phrase: "Sam, whose organization is such as to feel to the utmost extreme of every feeling." It made him a reformer, perpetually indignant, perpetually pouring out sarcasm and damnation on what to him seemed unjust or cruel or inconsistent. When editor of the Buffalo *Express* his editorials were either "savage assaults upon some human abuse, or fierce espousals of the weak. They were fearless, scathing, terrific." "In later years," says his biographer, "he used to say that he had always felt it was his mission to teach, to carry the banner of moral instruction."

It was partly inherited, especially from his mother, the tenderest of sentimentalists. It was nurtured by his small-town rearing: democracy is bred in provincial areas where the world is small. The fierce individualism of the border breeds intolerance of oppression. The country boy is likely to think that all men are as fundamentally honest as those in his own home and that the under dog deserves help. A large area of Mark Twain's writings, the most arid of all, was written in the crusader spirit, with the suppressed premise always that it was still possible to make the world over. *A Connecticut Yankee at King Arthur's Court*, he declared, "was not written for America; it was written for England, . . . to pry up the English nation to a little higher level of manhood."

Disillusion comes inevitably. The extreme optimism of the Clemenses was bound to have a reflex as extreme. The sky-larking high spirits of the man's youth—everything in *fortissimo*—, and his amazing success with the whole world bowing in adulation, were bound to end in reaction. "He travelled always," says his biographer, "a broad and brilliant highway with plumes flying and crowds following after." By and by the adulation became boresome. He had got everything, and *what* had he got? And then came family griefs, the death of children and dearest friends. His whole life had been an awakening from the dreams of his youth and young manhood. The first glimmerings of disillusion we find in *Innocents Abroad*. He had gone in all innocence to see the glories of Europe and the Holy Land, and everywhere he had been forced to reduce the picture his imagination had painted. He had expected gold and he had found gilding. He awoke soon to the realization that America too, was gilded. And like all the creative Americans before him, he would change it, he would write his Utopia, "The Curious Republic of Gondour," detailing what he would have it to be. All in vain! He was living in the Gilded Age, the age of the Tweed Ring, and universal greed, and the exploiting of the weak by the strong, and so he wrote at last *What is Man?* A curious anticlimax it makes: our leading humorist become our most caustic pessimist! Everywhere you touch the man there is anti-climax: fundamentally he is a romancer, yet he will demolish with fury King Arthur's Court, and Fenimore Cooper enrages him like a red rag. Fiercely he demands reality, but all his own tales and pictures are laid in a land that is like the setting of the Thousand and One Nights.

That his marriage and his New England circle of friends were the Delilah shears that robbed him of the full of his native powers is the veriest nonsense. Without this saving element he would have been merely another Joaquin Miller. His wife turned him constantly to the areas where he was the strongest; she vetoed positively such inanities as "The Autobiography of a Damn Fool," begun with vast enthusiasm: "Livy wouldn't have it, so I gave it up." She struggled with his natural tendencies to drifting and ease, and urged him constantly to make use to the full of his splendid powers. "Mrs. Clemens," he wrote, "has diligently persecuted me day by day with urgings to go to work and do that something." His own promptings led him always into grotesque fields below the levels of his best powers: hoaxes, imaginary reviews, burlesque autobiographies, local applications of "The House That Jack Built," fanciful adventures in the African diamond mines, "Shem's Diary," and the like. It was his literary group of friends in the East who pointed out to him where his real distinction lay, and who held him, so far as they could do it, in the areas he could best cultivate. It was Joe Goodman who kept him at work on what ultimately became *Roughing It*; it was Charles Dudley Warner who made possible *The Gilded Age*, some parts of which are at the height of his powers; it was Joseph Twichell who suggested *Life on the Mississippi*, and outlined what it should contain; and it was Howells who, at the critical moment of his career, gave him help that was nothing short of priceless.

To say that Mark was hamstrung by the East and that as a result of his marriage he lived his later years a thwarted genius is to argue that ignorance which has in it a touch of genius should be quarantined from all contact with art and culture lest its originality be vitiated.

III

That he *was* a thwarted genius is evident, but his environment and his times were the elements that undid him. Fate had dropped him into the Gilded Age and at the one moment when his peculiar combination of powers could receive full recognition. It is impossible to understand Mark Twain unless one views him in the setting of the seventies. As his biographer has expressed it, "He was always exactly in his setting."

The eighteen seventies were a period unique, the unnatural, the inflated, the excited period following the Civil War. It was the time of the rapidly expanding West, of government lands squandered by Congress with a gambler's abandon, of the Tweed ring and the Crédit Mobilier, of the slaughter of the buffalo herds, of Jay Gould and Vanderbilt and Jim Fisk, of the Pacific Railroad, of the swift rise of industrialism and the concentration of money power. Everything was in superlatives, keyed to the utmost pitch. Vast fortunes had been made during the war and the newly-rich were building rococo palaces and endowing college halls that are today the nightmares of city and campus reconstructors. And into the centre of it all suddenly jumped Mark Twain, on the back of a frog.

For a writer in the inflated seventies to begin his career with an extreme of uncouth humor, based on exaggeration and inflated high spirits and burlesque, was to enjoy a certain moment of vaudeville glory. Witness the fate of such other returned California humorists as Orpheus C. Kerr or Charles Henry Webb. Literary permanence in any field of endeavor could be won only by a genius who had balance and patience and ability to bide his time. None of these qualities was in the makeup of Mark Twain.

He gave his age what it delighted in: local color laid on with lavish profusion—local color not to be examined too closely,—and he gave it what seemed to be a new American evolution: the humor of the great midland rivers and plains and of the Western mining camps pictured by Bret Harte. In the twenty years following 1865 there was worked out that variety of humor which we call distinctively American. It was the work of a school of humorists which in a way stands unique. Derby and Artemus Ward had been the pioneers, and now in the seventies were flourishing Nasby and Bill Arp and Josh Billings, the Danbury *News* Man and Bob Burdette, and scores of others. At the proper instant came Mark Twain, vaulting into New York on his frog. His world was ready for him. The regions from which he came had been tremendously advertised, and the great tide of migration into the new lands beyond the Mississippi was filling the word West with romance. Here was the very West itself. At last, *American* humor!

Humor has fashions that change often; it is something that has not only national but also provincial limitations. Always it seems at its best in the presence of the living humorist. Mark Twain brought his humor *viva voce*. The chief pungency and the effervescing surprise of it came from the man himself. Placed on the printed page some little of the drawl still lingered and some of the surprising whimsicality of the man's mannerisms and his personality, but the leakage was great.

Peculiarly was he fitted for the platform, and when he arrived in the East the platform was peculiarly fitted for him. It was the golden era of the peripatetic professional humorist. The lecture lyceum which in the mid-years of the century, with Emerson and Wendell Phillips and the Brahmins, had been such an educating force, had become decadent, and now it was laughing itself to death over the vaudeville antics of the new

humorists. Mark Twain was first of all a lecturer; his other powers followed this one supreme gift. Never was he better than when he faced a
happy audience, greeting every joke with roars. Always he spoke to full
houses. And all at once money began to pour down upon him in a golden
shower. He had found his place.

The humor he gave purported to be the humor of the vast newness of
the utter West, of the steamboats, and the Roaring Camps of California.
It satisfied its day. The seventies were not realistic; embroidery did not of-
fend them. To them Mark Twain was holding up a mirror to the vanished
West. To them it was reality, as to them Dickens and Bret Harte were
reality. We know today that it was nothing of the kind: it was romance,
the whole of it. All our so-called American humor is in reality romance. It
received its shaping touches on the lecture platforms of the moribund lecture lyceum of the seventies.

IV

The elements that most contributed to the phenomenal contemporary fame of Mark Twain for the most part have vanished. His inimitable presence we no longer can feel. The world for which he wrote
has passed utterly. The circle of friends who knew him and loved him and
sustained him is growing small. To the majority of readers today he is but
a set of books. The real ordeal of Mark Twain is at hand now. Is he to endure at the old valuations? It is time to put away sentiment and
superlatives and face the facts.

At certain points we can be dogmatic. First of all, a surprising mass
of his work must be thrown overboard at the start: it is journalism, it is
ephemeral, it has served its day. Many of his early extravagances he
weeded himself from his final edition. His friendly critics would throw
out more of them, would cease, indeed, to emphasise his humor at all,
and place him among the serious writers—"our foremost man of letters."
It means that his humor is no longer keyed to the times, that Mark Twain
as humorist is on the decline. The fact is significant.

It must not be forgotten that the man during the whole of his creative
period, the decade of the seventies, looked upon himself primarily as a
humorist of the California variety. He had awakened to literature in a
Southwestern country printing office; his early standards one might learn
from his "Josh" letters if they were extant—the illiterate outpourings of an
assumed country bumpkin. His Nevada journalizings, his contacts with
Artemus Ward, his comic lectures, his "Jumping Frog" extravaganza and
its reception held him to the conviction that literature for him meant rolling along with the prevailing tide of humor. To the men of the seventies
he was classed with Josh Billings and Artemus Ward and Nasby. They
bought his writings of book agents who assured them that nothing could
be funnier. He was engaged at once by the *Galaxy* to let himself go

monthly in his most killing vein. His literary plans, all of them at the start, involved the creation of humor, as witness "Shem's Diary," "The Autobiography of a Damned Fool," and the rest. The fact determined his future; it handicapped him almost beyond remedy. When he wished to turn the corner into seriousness he found it all but impossible. His readers insisted upon humor. To make his first reputation as a joker has ruined many a genius.

Then, again, literary success came to him too early, with too little effort. His contemporary, Bret Harte, was forced to spend seventeen years of patient apprenticeship before he could produce "The Luck of Roaring Camp." For Mark Twain bookmaking was from the very first a success of bonanza proportions. It turned his head: he must have quick and sensational rewards. He got them. It bred the habit of easy writing—journalism, copiously poured out. He began without plan and rambled on and on. The book grew by accretions. Often it ended in a sprawl like *Life on the Mississippi*.

Always is it anecdotal, always desultory. The author as he writes has an imaginary audience before him; moreover, every evening he must hasten to his family to read what he has written. It is raconteur work, stories, descriptions, gargoyle characterizations, pictures—pell-mell it comes, like the hodge-podge of a humorous lecture of the seventies. Everywhere overstrain, everywhere extremes, dramatizations with stage scenery colossal: the Mississippi, the Rocky Mountains, the South Seas. One thinks of Hazlitt's dictum of years before. The American mind, he observed, is deficient in "natural imagination. It must be excited by overstraining, by pulleys and levers."

And yet it was in this period of the seventies that Mark did the only parts of his work that promise to endure. To all that he wrote after the opening of the eighties—the *Connecticut Yankee, The Prince and the Pauper, Joan of Arc* and the rest—time is already applying the chloroform. *Life on the Mississippi, The Gilded Age* (his part of it), *Roughing It, Tom Sawyer* and *Huckleberry Finn*, with bits perhaps from *Pudd'nhead Wilson,*—these volumes have promise for the years to come.

Pure romanticism they are. The romance of the fading days of the old regime on the Mississippi and the sunset glories of the dying great days of the Plains and of California is in them, but the ruling flavor in them all is undiluted Mark Twain—the Mark Twain of the Sandwich Islands lecture and the "Jumping Frog" fragment. Episodes and pictures, pages of graphic impressionism, flashlights, stories, sometimes whole chapters there are which are worthy of even Paine's superlatives. There are areas intense, like the steamboat explosion scene in *The Gilded Age*, there are paintings of marvellous beauty, there are characterizations on the highest levels of mastery.

And right here is the tragedy of Mark Twain. Constantly we find ourselves saying: Oh, the pity of it! Oh, that all of his work might have reached the heights that a fraction of it attained! Oh, that there might have been the added touch of discipline, of restraint, of the architectonic, of the rounded, the finished! All too often he was concerned only with the surface, with mere incongruities of manners, oddities, grotesqueries, extremes. In all his work of the seventies, the period of his genius, his point of view is adolescent. Mrs. Clemens, who knew him as no one else knew him, gave him the pet name of Youth.

A turning point there was after there had passed over him the first great tidal wave of success. He awoke to the fact that humor such as the seventies demanded had small hope in it of permanence. But his attempt to escape to more substantial literary foundations was based on totally mistaken estimates of his powers. Like Cooper, he turned his back upon American romance and began to work in foreign materials. Just as Cooper wrote *The Bravo* with a sigh of relief to get away from the thinness and baldness of subjects American, so Mark Twain wrote his *Joan of Arc*.

More and more now he sought to penetrate below the surfaces of life,—a surprisingly large area of his later work deals with the moral and the religious—but always he was temperamental, always he was extreme. Whatever Mark Twain may have been, he was not a scientist or a scholar or an unprejudiced seeker of the truth. Would that he could have dropped his European themes, his sentimental fightings for inconsequential underdogs, his layman homiletics, and given us that in which he was supreme—that he could have reproduced in full the wonder world he knew, the epic West at its golden moment, the supreme romance of America!

The pity of it! He who alone of his generation, or of all generations, had the materials and the power to make this master epic, used his days in tinkering at medieval romance or satirizing the legends of King Arthur to reform the unreformable British! It was like Shelley's pamphlet to do away with Catholicism in Ireland. *Joan of Arc*, tremendously advertised, enjoyed its little day. The critics and the professors are still praising it, but to the American people who loved the man it was not Mark Twain. They demanded Mark Twain stuff, but he misunderstood them. Money he must have, a deluge of money, and he gave them "Adam's Diary," "Eve's Diary," and the other inanities of his decline period. There are few more pathetic spectacles in literary history than that of Mark Twain with such glorious possibilities within him, dancing in cap and bells for money.

To rate him with our greatest American literary masters, Emerson or Thoreau or Hawthorne, is poor criticism. To place his work, with its fragmentariness, its exaggerations, its burlesquery and extravagance, alongside the great serious classics of our literature is to realize its deficiencies. Mark Twain must be rated as a thwarted creator like Melville, one ham-strung by his times and his temperament. He must go down to posterity as a collection of glorious fragments, as an enrichment to anthologies rather than as a maker of rounded masterpieces. He will endure long: he was a pioneer humorist, he had a compelling personality which to a small degree is alive in some of his writings, and he has become one of our national legends like Washington even and Lincoln, but to make of him a literary classic, to place him among the great masters of our American literature—that is indeed a paradox of truest Mark Twain texture.

Mark Twain: 1835–1935

Newton Arvin*

In a little book on American literature which makes the history of writing in this country sound like a long good-natured lunch-hour, Mr. Carl Van Doren observes that Mark Twain was "one of the 'powerful uneducated persons' Whitman had asked America to produce and value." As a matter of fact, Whitman himself once expressed an opinion of the younger writer which Mr. Van Doren's remark makes it interesting to recall. "I think he mainly misses fire," he said to Traubel one day: "I think his life misses fire: he might have been something: but he never arrives." This was at the end of the eighties, to be sure, and possibly Whitman would have judged Mark Twain differently at a later hour; but one's guess is that he would have put the point still more emphatically. In any case, the old man's comment is of the richest interest partly because it is so true that Mark Twain *was* a powerful uneducated person, that he *was* potentially the kind of Answerer Whitman had asked America to produce, and that he *was* the embodiment, or began by being, of so many of Whitman's ideas of the democratic personality. But the older writer had the acuteness of a stethoscope in such matters, and it told him that a great promise had not been fulfilled. Mr. Van Doren cheerfully assumes that it had been, but not everyone will find it so easy to ignore Whitman's lead.

From one point of view, it seems absurd to speak of Mark Twain as missing fire. Twenty-five years after his death, there appears to be plenty of evidence that he hit one bull's-eye with sensational accuracy. According to an article published last year in the *American Mercury* by Charles H. Compton, a St. Louis librarian, Mark Twain is far and away the most widely read and best loved of American authors. Library shelves, it is said, tell a conclusive story. And not only in Mark Twain's Middle West. The Boston Public Library owns 1,479 copies of his various works, as compared with 272 copies of Henry James, and this proportion is representative. Zane Greys come and go; *Anthony Adverses* roll up their hundreds of thousands for a few months; but *Huckleberry Finn* and *The*

*Reprinted from *New Republic*, 83 (June 12, 1935), 125–27.

Innocents Abroad are the books that Americans continue to read from year to year as they read no others.

Beyond this fact, however, lies the more interesting question, Why; and by writing to a large, well distributed number of Mark Twain readers, Mr. Compton collected some of the evidence for an answer. In the letters he received, he says, the "desire for an escape was repeatedly brought out." Not only so, but it appears that the largest single class of devotees is made up of students, high-school students chiefly, and the impression this makes is confirmed by a passage from a letter written to Mr. Compton not by a student but by a presumably mature chemical engineer: "As to the favorites," he says, "I still cling to my first loves of Tom and Huck. As to why, probably my childish mentality. . . ."

The engineer's modesty is of course disarming. But how can one fail to make out the signals in the picture that takes shape out of these researches? The best loved of American writers is read chiefly by adolescents; he is read also, however, by adults who apologize for the immaturity of their tastes and confess to a desire to "escape." One may agree with Kenneth Burke's dissolution of the cliché, "escape"; may concede the honor there is in being read eagerly by children, and still feel that these facts are indicative. I do not mean that they say everything, but so far as they go they say that Mark Twain's appeal is chiefly to the very young and to the "eternally youthful," and that he is read not because he makes experience more intelligible or enriches the imagination with the possibilities of new experience, but because he cooperates with the desire to play hooky.

He certainly does more than that, but his centenary seems a natural occasion for attempting again to focus his work as a whole, and the attempt itself is enough to suggest that his very popularity with that great host of public-library readers is an omen of the decline that seems so likely to be his fate, just as a writer, among the tremendous changes of the future. In a socialist culture in which adulthood will prevailingly be more than a matter of numbered years, how much of Mark Twain can possibly preserve its charm or its interest? A good many pages, one guesses; but how little in proportion to the whole! There was a jinni at Mark Twain's service such as few poets of his time could command, and when he rubbed the lamp the right way the result was the first half of *Life on the Mississippi*, or the beginning of *Huckleberry Finn*, or Chapters 11 and 28 of *The Gilded Age*, or Jim Baker's blue-jay story, or "To the Person Sitting in Darkness." It is hard to imagine such writing losing its spell in many years. But the jinni in question was exacting, and the price of invoking him successfully was a self-discipline that Mark Twain was not willing to undergo. The consequence is a spectacle of monotonously repeated flashes in the pan such as literary history rarely sees.

The children who read him in such numbers will not complain, but the adult reader who has learned to expect in literature the effect of culmination, the triumph of the whole over parts, the long and steady flight, is bound to feel constantly let down. Hardly a breath intervenes between rich foolery and mere silliness in *The Innocents Abroad*. The gold of a masculine romanticism lies side by side with the slag of buffoonery and fake sentiment even in *Life on the Mississippi* and *Roughing It*. The fat and the lean of *The Gilded Age* are compounded of a wild dionysiac humor and the narrative effects of Nick Carter. The lovely opening chapters of *Huckleberry Finn* are succeeded by the puerile humors of the King and the Duke and the dreary elaboration of Tom Sawyer's rescue of Jim. Even *A Connecticut Yankee*, which in spite of Mr. DeVoto is exceptionally sustained, lapses far too often into tired nonsense and irritable argumentation.

If his best books are abortive in these ways, so too was Mark Twain's artistic career as a whole. Instead of growing clearer and firmer, his sense of reality grew dimmer and more flaccid with every decade; his inventiveness sagged to the plane of the newspaper culture about him; and the intensely romantic strain in his imagination, which might have been toughened and disciplined up to the level of Gogol or Melville, dribbled away in school-girl medievalism and drug-store melodramatics. The inanities of *The American Claimant* are the sequel to the Hogarthian high spots of *The Gilded Age*, and the candy of *Joan of Arc* to the gusto of *Roughing It*. Nor did the misanthropy which grew sourer as his sentiment thickened and stiffened enhance in any way the vitality or the truthfulness of Mark Twain's fictions. "The Man That Corrupted Hadleyburg" and *The Mysterious Stranger*, fierce and real as their Timonism is, are as phoney in their rendering of human behavior as *The American Claimant* and *Joan of Arc*.

The reasons for all this were of course partly personal and partly a matter of history, and with the aid of Van Wyck Brooks's insight it becomes easier and easier to see these reasons in perspective. As American culture deteriorated with the shift of social power from the farmer and the merchant to the industrial capitalist, Mark Twain's problem both as man and as artist was either to cling to and enrich the individualism he inherited from the Lamptons and the Clemenses, or to think his way ahead, as his friend Howells did, to a broader philosophy. He should have remained true to the best traditions of his family and his class, or have gone beyond them. He did neither. Abandoning the self-trust in which Emerson had said all the duties of the Scholar could be comprised, abandoning Whitman's "boundless impatience of restraint," he adopted not a revolutionary philosophy of comradeship—to which he certainly had inclinations—but a self-contemptuous system of cynical acquiescence. If a man would prosper, he says in "Corn-Pone Opinions," "he must train with the majority; in matters of large moment, like politics and religion, he must think and feel with the bulk of his neighbors, or suffer damage in his social standing and in his business prosperities . . . Self-approval," he continued, as if to magnify fantastically the distance he had come from Emerson and Whitman, "is acquired mainly from the approval of other people. The result is conformity."

The result, too, in Mark Twain's case, was stultification at the hands of a class that demanded of its writers what Mr. Compton's investigations reveal. But the stultification was never complete, and something of his original freedom of spirit remained alive to the end. In his heart, as many commentators have observed more or less perfunctorily, Mark Twain loathed cruelty and despised pretense. The social world about him was on many sides both cruel and pretentious, and neither early nor late could he wholly conceal his disgust with it. The fate of *The Gilded Age*, which Mr. Compton finds to be the least read of all his books, no doubt taught him a lesson, but there it stands none the less as an expression for other potential readers of Mark Twain's instinctive attitude toward the morality of business. As time went on, he took to venting his fury through perhaps unconscious symbols, and flayed the dead lions of feudal injustice in such books as *The Prince and the Pauper*; or he let himself go flamingly in letters that are now more valuable than most of his fiction; or he broke out with his real feeling in apparently innocent contexts, as when in "The Esquimau Maiden's Romance" he made a character say: "In my heart of hearts I hate all the ways of millionaires!" Nor, though the practice has been to ignore them utterly, can it be forgotten that Mark Twain in his old age wrote those blistering onslaughts upon American imperialism, race persecution, foreign missions and militarism—"To the Person Sitting in Darkness," "The War Prayer" and "The United States of Lyncherdom."

Through such things as these, and despite the vast wastage of his career, Mark Twain may well survive as a writer in the affections of later generations and of a class to which he did not directly address himself. Survive one feels certain he will, but surely far less as a writer, at the best, than as a figure, a folk hero, a grand half-legendary personality. That, as a matter of fact, in a sense in which it is not true of most writers, is the role he really played in his own time. The people of his class, despite their self-hypnosis, could not seriously venerate the canny iron-masters, the swindling monopolists or the dull and paltry politicians who prevailed in the public life of the country; and they turned with a deep human instinct to a man whom they did not properly value but whose essential largeness and sweetness they rightly idolized. They helped to defeat him as a writer, but it is perhaps the highest tribute that can be paid to their arid culture that it *was* a writer whom they spontaneously elected as their Cid, their Robin Hood, their Barbarossa. He bewitched the popular imagination as those other worthies had done, and it is not hard to see why. Nor is it hard to conceive the glamor of his personality outliving the society that produced and thwarted him. One almost suspects the existence among the people of a tradition that Mark Twain is not dead after all but sitting fast asleep in some Kyffhauser cavern from which in the vague future he will again emerge and renew his leadership, though not until the obscene ravens have stopped their flapping and screeching about the mountain peak.

A Century of Mark Twain

Mark Van Doren*

The quarter of a century since Mark Twain's death has done as much as any equivalent period to give us the author we now possess. The first twenty-five years of his life gave him, of course, his best subject matter—the Mississippi River, the Valley frontier. The next twenty-five years brought him to the point of understanding this material and embodying it in his two masterpieces, *Life on the Mississippi* and *Huckleberry Finn*. Another twenty-five years and he had become the white figure of the legend—eccentric, funny, and upon occasion fierce. But it is only since 1910 that criticism has been busy with him in a serious way, establishing him as an artist and considering him in perspective. Albert Bigelow Paine's massive and fascinating biography, following as soon as possible after its hero's death, prepared the ground for many particular studies; and the finest of these, Van Wyck Brooks's *The Ordeal of Mark Twain*, is still a center about which opinion and interpretation can whirl. The contemporaries of Mark Twain were content for the most part merely to enjoy him. Already, however, he has grown into an object of thought, a stimulus to abstraction. For better or for worse he has become the author he never quite dared to hope he would have to be.

For better, because no writer perhaps can survive very long without the aid of an articulate criticism which isolates, describes, and keeps on talking about his special quality. For worse, because the special quality of Mark Twain is unusually difficult to describe without destroying, unusually delicate under the threat of analysis. It is delicate because it is not his alone. It is the quality of a people also—his people, the American people—and if it is notorious that we bungle when we dissect the heart of a nation it should be still more obvious that we have little reason to hope for success in the business of cutting the cord between a popular writer and his race. Mark Twain was almost indissolubly attached to America, and America to him; and this is still the case. He still can be read, and is read, merely for enjoyment. So distinctly and happily so, in fact, that it is a question whether there is any better way to read him, and whether most

*Reprinted from *Nation*, 141 (October 23, 1935), 472–74, with the permission of Mrs. Dorothy Van Doren.

of the criticism has not been worse than irrelevant. To say as much is not of necessity to take literally his words to Andrew Lang: "I have never tried in even one single instance to help cultivate the cultivated classes. . . . I always hunted for bigger game—the masses. I have seldom deliberately tried to instruct them, but have done my best to entertain them. To simply amuse them would have satisfied my dearest ambition at any time." Nor is it to suppose that he was thinking of himself when he dictated the following paragraph to Paine, pretending that it was what an Albany bookseller had said to Robert Louis Stevenson about the works of a hack named Davis:

> Nobody has heard of Davis; you may ask all round and you will see. You never see his name mentioned in print, not even in advertisements; these things are of no use to Davis, not any more than they are to the wind and the sea. You never see one of Davis's books floating on top of the United States, but put on your diving armor and get yourself lowered away down and down till you strike the dense region, the sunless region of eternal drudgery and starvation wages—there you will find them by the million. The man that gets that market, his fortune is made, his bread and butter are safe, for those people will never go back on him. An author may have a reputation which is confined to the surface, and lose it and become pitied, then despised, then forgotten, entirely forgotten—the frequent steps in a surface reputation. A surface reputation, however great, is always mortal, and always killable if you go at it right—with pins and needles, and quiet slow poison, not with the club and the tomahawk. But it is a different matter with the submerged reputation—down in the deep water; once a favorite there, always a favorite; once beloved, always beloved; once respected, always respected, honored, and believed in. For what the reviewer says never finds its way down into those placid deeps, nor the newspaper sneers, nor any breath of the winds of slander blowing above. Down there they never hear of these things. Their idol may be painted clay, up there at the surface, and fade and waste and crumple and blow away, there being much weather there; but down below he is gold and adamant and indestructible.

Yet both passages have their pertinence, and the second one has the additional value of perfectly illustrating what has just been said. An American is talking there, and no other kind of man. No American but would talk that way if he could—if he had, that is, the genius. Mark Twain had the genius. And the American people were first to recognize the fact. The critics were second, but it is essential to Mark Twain's reputation that millions of persons should continue capable of feeling the glory of such prose—feeling it immediately, without reflection and without recourse to the idiom of analysis.

Such prose has form, a thing Mark Twain is customarily accused of lacking. His books, as books, do lack it; they trail off, they ravel out, they are heaps of fragments. And in the long run this will doubtless work against him, since a book which does not hold together is doomed to a particularly hard battle with oblivion, there being much wind and weather there. Yet the very looseness of his structure has a certain advantage, for it means that if the good parts are indeed good they will be all the freer to separate themselves from the bad. The mortal parts will blow away in time, leaving the gold and the adamant all the more inviolable. And what are the immortal parts? They are the passages in which Mark Twain has done what he did in the dithyramb to Davis; in which he has exaggerated according to the laws of his own language and of his own people.

It is not enough to say of him that his humor consisted in exaggeration. His whole art consisted in that, and his only art. There was nothing else that he knew how to do with an absolute perfection. He did not think far, even if he thought clearly; he was often deficient in taste; he could be outrageously sentimental; he was in many respects an ignorant man, and could be in turn too proud and too apologetic about this ignorance. But whenever, as frequently happened, he got going about something, it was more than likely that he would develop the speed and the beauty and the form by which we have learned to recognize him at his height. At such moments and in such passages he was possessed by that ancient and noble thing, poetic rage. It possessed him at the same time that he controlled it for the purposes of his peculiar art. He mounted through his theme with an incredible celerity, riding the fieriest steeds known to rhetoric, and the broadest-winged—iteration, reiteration, and multiplied example. He mounted with gigantic ease and a vast naturalness, reaching the top of his subject at last and breathing the great air there with happy lungs; then suddenly descended to the ground and jogged along to the next inspiration. Or, to change the metaphor, he blew a bag up till it almost burst; at his best he did not let it burst, but tossed it lightly away and left it floating. Or, to change the metaphor once more, his prose was a river which regularly widened its banks, swelling and accelerating until there was danger that it should cease to look like a river; then it subsided and narrowed again, pulling us onward to new bays.

The story of the three matches in *Roughing It*, or of Slade, or of the lost claim; the picture of Hannibal's indolence in *Life on the Mississippi*, or of its animation when a steamboat lands at the wharf, or of the river itself as fearfully studied from a pilot house; the first description of Huck's father; the parody of Mrs. Eddy; the whole of "My Watch"; many an unmailed letter—any of these and a hundred other passages will serve as an illustration of what is meant. Such passages place Mark Twain against that portion of the American background where he belongs. It is not, incidentally, the portion which produces at least once each generation an Artemus Ward, a Mr. Dooley, a Will Rogers. Mark Twain could do what they do, but he never did it better than Artemus Ward, if indeed he did it as well. He was not a cracker-box philosopher, a homespun wit with the gift of sly, dry talk out of the corner of his mouth. Their forte is under-statement. His was overstatement, and the tradition which supported him was the tradition of the tall tale, the mighty mendacity. Their pride is in the truths which they insinuate; his pride was in the boldness and grandeur with which he could lie. This is the finer tradition; or at any rate by doing what he did with it he has made it seem so. What he did with it was to realize all its possibilities and to prove that they were beautiful. They had seldom been actually beautiful; we can be sure that a majority of the Sellerses, both then and now, have been tiresome men who did not know when to stop or how as they went on to improve the quality of their utterance. Yet there is a deep instinct in any American which tells him that one liar may be better than another and which en-courages him to listen for the perfect note. He heard it in Mark Twain and recognized a master—one who began where he did and who followed all the rules, but who somehow soared and sang; and who, furthermore, lied in a precise, a disciplined language which was so far from being ignorant of irony as almost to use that instrument as its grammar. One more ex-ample, a little-known one, must suffice. It is the letter, signed Samuel Langhorne, sent in 1871 to the *New York Tribune* proposing that a substitute be hanged in place of one Ruloff, a condemned murderer whose learning was being set forth in the press as remarkable. The contemporary fame of this letter is not wholly to be explained on the ground of its nov-elty; papers must have copied it across the country because it got going so well on the theme—not of Ruloff's learning merely, but of learning in general as the mass of men understand it:

> I am not sorry that Ruloff is to be hanged, but I am sincerely sorry that he himself has made it necessary that his vast capabilities for usefulness should be lost to the world. In this, mine and the public's is a common regret. For it is plain that in the person of Ruloff one of the most marvelous of intellects that any age has produced is about to be sacrificed, and that, too, while half of the mystery of its strange powers is yet a secret. Here is a man who has never entered the doors of a college or a university, and yet by the sheer might of his innate gifts has made himself such a colossus in abstruse learning that the ablest of our scholars are but pigmies in his presence. By the evidence of Professor Mather, Mr. Sur-bridge, Mr. Richmond, and other men qualified to testify, this man is as familiar with the broad domain of philology as common men are with the passing events of the day. His memory has such a limitless grasp that he is able to quote sentence after sentence, paragraph after paragraph, chapter after chapter, from a gnarled and knotty ancient literature that ordinary scholars are capable of achieving little more than a bowing acquaintance with. But his memory is the least of his great endowments. By the testimony of the gentlemen above referred to he is able to *critically analyze* the works of the old masters of literature, and while pointing out the beauties of the originals with a pure and discriminating taste is as quick to detect the defects of the accepted translations; and in the latter

case, if exceptions be taken to his judgment, he straightway opens up the quarries of his exhaustless knowledge, and builds a very Chinese wall of evidence around his position. Every learned man who enters Ruloff's presence leaves it amazed and confounded by his prodigious capabilities and attainments. One scholar said he did not believe that in matters of subtle analysis, vast knowledge in his peculiar field of research, comprehensive grasp of subjects, and serene kingship over its limitless and bewildering details, any land or any era of modern times had given birth to Ruloff's intellectual equal. What miracles this murderer might have wrought, and what luster he might have shed upon his country, if he had not put a forfeit upon his life so foolishly!

The words "serene kingship" mark the high point here, but there has been a steady climb to them, and as always the end comes shortly after, with an abruptness both expected and prescribed.

Of course there is more to Mark Twain than this. He had a heart and a brain, and he stood in a very interesting relation to the America of his time, a relation which has been stated quite differently by Van Wyck Brooks and by Bernard DeVoto. But in the long run it may appear that his sheer literary energy, surpassed in amount by no American writer except perhaps Melville, may tell the tale most truly. Whatever the merits of our controversies about his "significance" and about what he reflected or represented, he still stands in a relation to us which will be valuable and delightful as long as we remain capable of responding to great language—the tall tale, the swelling theme. Much of him has ceased to mean what it meant fifty years ago, and his personality no longer dominates the land; nor is the same land here that he observed with such an all-seeing eye. Yet enough of it lingers—in ears born waiting for the magnificent word whenever and by whomever it may be spoken—to suggest that his reputation will be permanent. It is in this respect that he was a great writer, and it is in this sign that he will continue to conquer.

In Homage to Mark Twain

Owen Wister*

Don Pedro: Out of question, you were born in a merry hour.
Beatrice: No, sure, my lord, my mother cried; but then there was a star
  danced, and under that was I born.
  —*Much Ado About Nothing*, Act II, Sc. I.

By November 30, 1935, Samuel Langhorne Clemens would have been a hundred years old. Listen, before we expatiate, to these two anecdotes. I have one at first hand and was present at the telling of the other.

In the days before he was a bishop the Rev. William Doane went one Sunday to preach in Hartford, and Mark Twain was in the church. After the service he lingered to meet the clergyman and say with what interest and pleasure he had heard him, adding that, most strangely, every word of the sermon was in a book he had at home. The Reverend Mr. Doane was appalled. They spoke of unconscious plagiarism and looked at the coincidence from various angles. On taking his leave Mark Twain offered to send the book around to Mr. Doane's hotel, which offer was eagerly accepted. The parcel arrived and on being untied out came the dictionary. That must have been during the seventies. Mark Twain was rising forty, and married.

During the nineties he let me come to see him. His gallant lecture journey round the world was over, his heavy load of debt paid off by the sole exertion of his genius; he was a world figure and sixty years old. His hair, like the foaming crest of a breaker, was going to be snow white before long, but his eyes were hot and bright and young. Who could forget them? Blue fire under bushy brows, steady when he fixed them on you, inquiring, penetrating, fierce, and genial at the same time. He was living in New York, but he referred to Hartford in a little while. Had I been writing anything new? he asked.

I had just finished a story, "Sharon's Choice," suggested by certain real events. The citizens of Sharon had voted the prize for school elocution

*Reprinted from *Harper's Monthly*, 171 (November, 1935), 547–56; at the time, appeared also in *The Family Mark Twain*, ed. A. B. Paine (New York: Harper, 1935), and (in part) *Scholastic*, 27 (November 23, 1935); "reprinted frequently," according to Thomas A. Tenney, *Mark Twain: A Reference Guide* (Boston: G. K. Hall, 1977).

to a small boy in spite of his speaking like nothing at all—voted it tumultuously over the heads of the appointed judges, upsetting their decision, because the small boy's father had recently left town with a voluptuous Mexican and the family cash; still more recently his mother had turned out to be a dope fiend; his aunt, who had taken him to raise, had the personality of a decayed tooth; and only two days before the prize speaking the boy had experimented with the couplings of a freight train and parted with three of his fingers. "And do you know," I said to Mark Twain, "when my informant piled those fingers on top of that load of calamity, my overcharged sympathy exploded and I just roared."

To this Mark Twain had listened with piercing attention. He now sprang up and shot out his arm at me. "I know what you mean," he exclaimed. "Just what you mean!" And with that he was striding back and forth, talking in a stream more and more impetuously. "It was on a Sunday up at Hartford some years ago," he began. And this was what he told me:

A missionary preached that morning. His voice was beautiful. He told of the sufferings of the natives, he pleaded for help with such moving simplicity that Mark Twain mentally doubled the fifty cents he had intended to put in the plate. As the address proceeded, describing so pitifully the misery of the savages, the dollar in his mind gradually rose to five. A little farther along, the missionary had him crying. He felt that all the cash he carried about him would be insufficient and decided to write a large check.

"And then that preacher went on," said Mark Twain, suddenly whirling on me and coming to a standstill, and falling into a drawl, "went on about the dreadful state of those natives. I abandoned the idea of the check. And he went on. And I got back to five dollars, four, two, one. But he went on. And when the plate came round—I took ten cents out of it."

Later in that visit Mark Twain was striding up and down again, whirling on me once in a while, scowling fiercely at me, his blue eyes burning beneath the scowl, and the mound of hair all of a piece with the electric total of the man. But this time Zola was the subject, he was wholly serious, very concentrated; and I shall come back to it.

In any case, I should have told you these anecdotes; but my chief point is not that I think them worth telling; I believe if they had been told without names to any American boy or man forty years ago, and the boy or man had been asked to guess who it was, he would have guessed right. There was a twist, a tang, a something the community had come to recognize as being particularly Mark Twain's. Already the *Jumping Frog* had leaped round the world, the *Innocents Abroad* had followed it, Bemis and his buffalo were known to everyone who had read *Roughing It*. At school we repeated with zest that whimsical passage about Horace Greeley's having to make a speech at Placerville, and the stage driver, Hank Monk, who said he would get Horace there in time—why, I remember how we enjoyed it then! I read it over the other day and enjoyed it at seventy-four as much as I did at fifteen. There was nobody like Mark Twain. We said it in the seventies, we say it now; and, as an eminent painter observed to me, one of his outstanding qualities is that he interests you as much when you are grown up as he did when you were a boy.

But is there nobody like Mark Twain? And was there nobody? Will Rogers makes me think of him. A certain essence which I will call the true American essence, flavors his remarks—precisely the same which flavors Mark Twain's complaint that "Everybody is talking about the weather, but nobody seems to do anything about it," or his reply to a friend who asked where was he going for the summer: to Europe on five hundred dollars the plumber didn't know he had. This essence lurked in him to the end. Professors have defined it. I doubt if I shall try; but a great number of Americans have possessed it—Lincoln, for instance—as well as unknown thousands who never wrote anything or spoke a recorded word, but who emotionally vibrated to it, and made a nation-wide audience for those whose public utterance it inspired. It wasn't only what they had to say, *but also the way they said it.*

II

The mood of an epoch sets its stamp on men's faces and upon what they create in art and in letters. Have you never noticed a resemblance between Dr. Johnson and John Adams? Many other faces of that type stare at you in picture galleries. The style of hair and dress counts in the resemblance, but that is not all. A broad, solid molding of countenance and an expression at once weighty and serene, as of men who dined well, drank port, and signed important documents prevail in dozens of those physiognomies. It is the 18th century type. You could walk and walk all day long in New York without seeing a single face that looked like that; and you could read and read all the latest books and never meet a paragraph which suggested the style of *Tom Jones*. Whereas you could cut passages of full-blooded prose from Fielding, Smollett, Sterne, even Addison, and others less eminent, shuffle them, and deal them round, and I doubt whether the authors themselves could identify their own child at sight.

Can you tell me who wrote this bit of dialogue?

> Eumenides. Why, she caused you to be pinched with fairies.
> Corsites. Ay, but her fairness hath pinched my heart more deeply.

Not many of the one-half-of-one per cent of our population on speaking terms with English literature could name the author. I couldn't if I didn't happen to know. But any of our devoted little minority could recognize the Elizabethan *expression* in those sentences, just as plain as it is in Walter Raleigh's face. Many of those dramatists might have written it. And several of them look as if they were some sort of cousins to one another, and to Sir Walter Raleigh, as well as to a dozen more belonging to that era. Again, it is not merely the hair and costume; they share an expression imparted by the prevailing mood of their time—a mood produced chiefly by the Renaissance and England's victory over the Spanish Armada. The island was all exultant patriotism and intellectual excitement.

Abraham Lincoln was born in 1809 and died in 1865. He did not look like John Adams. Few of that type remained. But a new type had appeared, and Lincoln is an example of it—the lean, keen, agile product of roughing it; the man on the lookout for Indians as he walked beside his west-bound wagon, cracking his black-snake whip, or hewed logs for his cabin, or cleared a patch for his corn and his still. Pioneers, O Pioneers! as Walt Whitman sang. An outdoor face. The face of many, many soldiers on both sides in our Civil War. The face we see generalized in Uncle Sam. He's with us still, is Uncle Sam; but how many of him would you see if you walked and walked in New York all day long? Commercialism and Ellis Island have driven him into the quiet and rustic hills. And we have a new type of the epoch—the face of the fat apple. An indoor face.

That epoch, that Lincoln era, as you might call it, since it pretty nearly began with Lincoln's life and ended with it, was the era of our jubilant adolescence. Bonaparte had sold Louisiana to Jefferson six years before Lincoln's birth. Lewis and Clark next had explored the red man's continent that the white man was to take. Next, Jackson won the battle of New Orleans. And what did the exulting American spirit do? Did it think? Not at all. It didn't have to. That has been its snare throughout. It proceeded to cut pigeon-wings. Westward the star of Empire took its way, at times very much like a fire-cracker; and the new epoch began to write with a pen of its own, often a quill from a pigeon-wing.

Let no one confront me with Edgar Allan Poe, and inquire if I discover pigeon-wings and the battle of New Orleans to be latent in his prose and verse. Poe is not the only figure outside that picture as well as outside the New England group. These exceptions perform their proverbial office. "Now and then on the stream of time," says Mark Twain, "small gobs of that thing which we call genius drift down, and a few of those lodge at some particular point, and others collect about them and make a sort of intellectual island—a towhead as we say on the river—such an accumulation we call a group, or school, and name it."

Yes, indeed. And the particular point at which these towheads have often lodged is the moment of some sweeping national emotion. Thousands of hearts beat as one. You will easily recall other towheads beside that in which Shakespeare overtops the rest so far that he dwarfs every one of his fellow-dramatists.

The whole nineteen were born after 1550 and before 1600, all felt the

elation of the Renaissance and the thrill of the Armada. This rings
through the most superb outburst of passion for one's native soil that I
know in any literature—Lancaster's speech in *Richard II*:

> This royal throne of kings, this sceptr'd isle,
> This earth of majesty, this seat of Mars,
> This other Eden, demi-paradise;
> This fortress built by nature for herself
> Against infection and the hand of war;
> This happy breed of men, this little world,
> This precious stone set in the silver sea . . .
> This blessed plot, this earth, this realm, this England—

Oh, who has ever equalled that? But who else has ever been Shakespeare?
And Mark Twain could suppose that Bacon wrote that! It's another point
I shall come back to.

All our native group, to which Mark Twain stands as Shakespeare
stood to Marlowe and the rest (I am not making a comparison but sug-
gesting an analogy), were born in the middle of the Lincoln era. The
earliest, John Phoenix (I use the names they wrote or lectured under) in
1823; Petroleum V. Nasby ten years later; Artemus Ward in 1834; Bret
Harte in 1839. Not one of these came from the West; they were born in
Massachusetts, Maine, New York; but how little any of them resembles
Emerson, Hawthorne, Longfellow, Whittier, Lowell, Holmes!—that
other group, also native, but regional, rather than nationwide in its
scope. You must add Josh Billings, Bill Nye, Ambrose Bierce, Eugene
Field, James Whitcomb Riley, and John Hay to the Mark Twain group;
H. C. Bunner, Frank Stockton, and O. Henry were postscripts.

Much that each of them wrote or spoke differed individually from
the work of others; yet certain fragments could belong to any of them,
came from the pen of the epoch, were spiced with the same Lincolnian
essence which flavored brains and veins from the Atlantic to the Pacific.
When Mark Twain cabled from Europe that the report of his death was
grossly exaggerated, you have it triple distilled.

In his San Francisco days Mark Twain might have written John
Phoenix's anecdote of the dentist, Dr. Tushmaker, published almost ten
years before *The Jumping Frog of Calaveras*. A man came to have a tooth
out. When Dr. Tushmaker pulled, it didn't come; but the patient's right
leg went up. "Why do you do that?" asked the dentist. "Because I cannot
help it," replied the man. "Come back in a week and I will attend to
you." During the week the doctor invented an instrument combining the
properties of the lever, the screw, the wedge, the hammer, and the
inclined plane. One turn of the crank, and out came the tooth. Its roots
were hooked under the patient's right big-toe, his whole skeleton was extracted with the tooth, and he had to be sent home in a pillow-case.

Artemus Ward said that Harvard College was pleasantly situated in the Parker House, School Street, Boston. In the darkest hours of the Civil War, Lincoln would read Artemus Ward aloud to his Cabinet and laugh. Lincoln said it was bad to swap horses while crossing a stream. The essence, the mental consanguinity of the epoch, was in both of them. Bret Harte wrote the "Heathen Chinee." Again the essence; and don't you remember his parody of Victor Hugo in *Condensed Novels?* And this?

> Then Abner Dean of Angel's raised a point of order, when
> A chunk of old red sandstone took him in the abdomen,
> And he smiled a kind of sickly smile, and curled up on the floor,
> And the subsequent proceedings interested him no more.

No need to labor the point. The writings of the others will easily disclose you many specimens which in spirit match one another, and do not match anything else. "Prattle," the column contributed once by Ambrose Bierce to the *San Francisco Examiner*, is full of this spirit, more corrosive; it is present in some of his sulphuric stories. Just two instances more.

Bob Burdette wrote of an election bet paid him in a box of cigars. "They were the awfullest cigars," he says, and gives an impression of them, ending by his lighting one, pointing it at a dog, and the dog turns to stone. This theme of the bad cigar is treated less fantastically by Mark Twain—but then, he is dictating his reminiscences; fact is present, it is only as he goes on that fancy cuts a pigeon-wing.

"George brought the box . . . and began to pass them around. The conversation had been brilliantly animated up to that moment—but now a frost fell upon the company. That is to say, not all of a sudden, but the frost fell upon each man as he took up a cigar and held it poised in the air—and there, in the middle, his sentence broke off. And that kind of thing went all around the table, until, when George had completed his crime the whole place was full of a thick solemnity and silence." Then he tells how, one by one, each guest after a few puffs rises and explains that he has an important engagement and leaves the house. And then, next morning, George brings him his cup of coffee, and asks: "Mr. Clemens, how far is it from the front door to the upper gate?" I said, "It is one hundred and twenty-five steps."

He said, "Mr. Clemens, you know, you can start at the front door and you can go plumb to the upper gate and tread on one of them cigars every time."

III

You will notice how vivid he makes that scene of the smokers; whatever he describes, you can't help seeing it instantly. His eye unerringly registers details, his selective sense picks out the right ones, the image starts to life; his inveterate humor does not distort the picture, merely intensifies it. In *A Tramp Abroad* he has been scolding Harris, his private agent, for larding an account of the Furka Pass with foreign words. The criticism, fantastically conveyed, is the soundest common sense; and then he describes the effect of the scolding upon Harris: "When the musing spider steps upon the red-hot shovel, he first exhibits a wild surprise, then he shrivels up. . . . I can be dreadfully rough on a person when the mood takes me." Even when his fancy is executing its loftiest pigeon-wings the realism somehow is not disturbed; you hear and see the actual thing. In the same *Tramp Abroad* he places some observations about blue jays in the mouth of an old California miner. "There's more *to* a blue jay than any other creature. He has got more moods, and more different kinds of feelings than other creatures; and, mind you, whatever a blue jay feels, he can put into language. . . . And another thing: I've noticed a good deal, and there's no bird, or cow, or anything that uses as good grammar as a blue jay. You may say a cat uses good grammar. Well, a cat does—but you let a cat get excited once; you let a cat get pulling fur with another cat on a shed, nights, and you'll hear grammar that will give you the lock-jaw. Ignorant people think it's the *noise* which fighting cats make that is so aggravating, but it ain't so; it's the sickening grammar they use. . . . Now on top of all this there's another thing; a jay can outswear any gentleman in the mines. You think a cat can swear. Well, a cat can; but you give a blue jay a subject that calls for reserve powers, and where is your cat?"

That laughter was expected, and for a long while laughter only, from whatever Mark Twain wrote, is quite natural when you remember that he made his first appearance with *The Jumping Frog*. There ran a very different thread beneath, destined to be uppermost in after years. Plenty of seriousness can be found in *The Innocents Abroad*; but it was such passages as his finding the tomb of Adam at Jerusalem which caught the appreciation of his readers. "The tomb of Adam! How touching it was, here in a land of strangers, far away from home, and friends, and all who cared for me, thus to discover the grave of a blood relation. . . . I leaned upon a pillar and burst into tears. . . . Noble old man—he did not live to see me. . . ."

Habit dies hard. *Roughing It* and *Tom Sawyer* were not at first perceived to be better portraits of their period than any history has been. I remember (and this was during the nineties) telling a dear old clergyman who had taught me Greek, Latin, and English twenty years before, that Mark Twain was a great writer and a master of style. He was utterly astonished. I sent him *Life on the Mississippi*. It converted him. He was precisely the cultivated, delicate, civilized American of college tradition and gentle background whom the spirit of *Innocents Abroad* shocked. That class of Americans bowed down too low to Europe and all her works; with them whatever was European was right.

Innocents Abroad was a sort of Declaration of Independence in matters aesthetic, and in several other matters too; the comment of a strong, original, raw, voraciously inquiring mind suddenly confronted with the civilized, complicated Past. Now and then it got his back up. In consequence he was too sweeping, and remained so. Do you remember his furious outburst against *Lohengrin*? A remark about the composer of that opera, made by Bill Nye, delighted him. "I am told that Wagner's music is better than it sounds." Well, that is certainly delightful: Nye and Clemens were chips of the same American block. Do you remember what Mark Twain says about St. Mark's of Venice? Or his wholesale scorn and rejection of the Old Masters? Do you remember his remarks about the "divine Hair Trunk of Bassano"? He will take no man's valuation but his own for Titian, Tintoretto, Giotto—anybody. Indeed, he seldom takes it for anything, till in middle life he adopts W. D. Howells as his literary mentor. Beneath his genius, realistic and humorous, lies changeless independence of judgment. I think it is the foundation of his nature, the root of his upstanding moral and intellectual integrity. But it doesn't seem to have struck him that other people may have been occasionally right. Very American, this, of its epoch! We flourished ourselves and our institutions in the Old World's face, and defied it to show us anything there as good as everything here.

Mark Twain never lived on close terms with either art or letters. At sixty-eight Walter Scott becomes known to him, and he is amazed that such artificial trash should be admired until he reads and likes *Quentin Durward*. He speaks of paintings by their area and the number of figures in them. Of that folk melody, the "Lorelei," he says: "I could not endure it at first, but by and by it began to take hold of me, and now there is no tune that I like so well." No wonder that Wagner had small chance with him. What would he have had to say about the *B-minor Mass*? Later in life, he owned a music machine whose sounds were agreeable to him; certain operas gave him pleasure; but I find no record of his attendance at symphony concerts. And although he came to examine and sometimes to read and to write about various books, I think that it was generally because they aroused the didactic or reforming or protesting element in his character, his hostility to sham, his passion for justice. The pretensions of Christian Science, Dowden's too indulgent *Life of Shelley*—these stirred up his militant spirit, and both his satire and his humor were poured out on them. You must keep in mind his partially New England blood and the dismal prayers he was taught. But—he believed and said that Bacon wrote Shakespeare. If he ever read the works of either, to the quality of both he was stone blind. It is *utterly impossible* to know these two authors and suppose them identical. As sensible as to say that Darwin wrote *Vanity Fair*. I don't believe Shakespeare interested him in the least. He doesn't refer to him with any intimacy; when he sees *King Lear* played in German all that he speaks of is the thunder and lightning.

Susan, his daughter, felt that he would have been better for "advantages" in his youth. Advantages, to be sure, do not hurt everybody.

why? What underlies this pilgrim's progress from the sunshine dawn of *The Jumping Frog*, through the noon splendor of *Huckleberry Finn*, to the sinister dusk of *The Man Who Corrupted Hadleyburg*, with its grim, disillusioned lesson? Most of us die saddened, but not embittered.

Yet Mark Twain when declining an invitation to attend a celebration in California writes:

> If I were a few years younger I would accept it. . . . I would let somebody else do the oration. . . . I would talk—just talk. I would renew my youth; and talk—and talk—and talk—and have the time of my life! I would march the unforgotten and unforgettable antiques by, and name their names, and give them reverent hail and farewell as they passed . . . and then the desperadoes, who made life a joy . . . Six-fingered Jake, Jack Williams, and the rest of the crimson discipleship. . . .
>
> Those were the days!—those old ones. They will come no more; youth will come no more; they were so full to the brim with the wine of life . . . it chokes me to think of them. Would you like me to come out there and cry? It would not beseem my white head.
>
> Good-by—I drink to you all. Have a good time—and take an old man's blessing.

And so you see, like all of us, he could be inconsistent. That warm, affectionate, nostalgic message was written in the heart of his pessimistic eclipse. Then how to account for this?

Doubtless one can shake loose from a creed; but the seed planted in us during childhood lurks and bides its hour. Soon or late, it will sprout in some fashion. Shall we suppose that monstrous, inhuman Calvinism has something to do with what happened to Mark Twain's gay, electric, adventurous spirit; that his New England blood and the vengeful God he had said his childish prayers to, fermented? We know that in the article in which his conscience takes shape outside him and he chases and vainly tries to catch it, he tells it that if he could he would give it to a yellow dog. Is that an indication? We know that he saw straight, thought straight, spoke out; that when an ugly truth stared him in the face he didn't shut his eyes—a rare thing with Americans. How could he witness the death of the rough, heroic Lincoln era, the birth of our many-headed greed, the quality of our congressmen of whom he never speaks without contempt, and not feel that at this point in our growth we were like certain apples which rot while they are still green? Moreover, he came late to his knowledge *and realization* of history—empire after empire fallen, faith after faith turned to mythology. This realization can tear a man's illusions up by the roots; not every nature is able to withstand the shock; Mark Twain's *The Mysterious Stranger* is a tale by one in the bottomless pit of pessimism. We know also that he had been mortally wounded by grief; and perhaps illness played a part. I think these several reasons combined are more likely to have evoked in him his hostile gloom than the single explanation advanced by Mr. Van Wyck Brooks. Well, Mark Twain and his literary kin were the direct product of a buoyant epoch, just as the rout of the Persians at Salamis produced the age of Pericles. I believe that what set in after our Civil War accounts for the change in this glowing spirit. . . .

Read again, if you will, as I have, that chapter in Mr. Albert Bigelow Paine's admirable biography, where Clemens at sixty-seven returns to Hannibal and goes over all the old playgrounds and swimming places with the old men, the playmates who in the days of the Lincoln era had been Tom Sawyer and Huckleberry Finn. You will be deeply moved, I think; and you will see how alive were warmth and affection in that emotional spirit; and you will wish that no cup of bitterness had ever touched his lips. For among all our writers he is not only the most interesting figure, but also the best beloved.

ing how much better Mark Twain would have written had he not been Mark Twain at all, had he not come under the baleful influence of Mrs. Clemens, and the still more barren influences of Hannibal, Mo., and the Mississippi river, the Nevada mining camps and San Francisco journalism. I do not know what kind of monstrosity he might have been had he been born into the world Mr. Van Wyck Brooks would have prepared for him, but I know he would not have been Mark Twain, the most deeply American spirit, as millions have recognized him to be. That sort of criticism, born of European nostalgia and a spurious psychology, fails to realize the strength of "limitations." Mrs. Clemens disapproved of her husband's profanity and his rawer conversation, but Mark Twain idolized her and idolized in her just these standards which judged him—and that was one important trait of his Americanism, of his tradition: respect for and idolization of womanhood, a romantic trait. Another naive characteristic of that tradition was respect for accomplishment in whatever field: witness Twain's close friendship and admiration for H. H. Rogers, the Standard Oil magnate. His patriotism—his admiration for Grant, with all Grant's mistakes. Even more typically American was Mark Twain's many personal efforts to make a fortune, usually by way of some very risky speculations; he had a trunk full of mining shares; there was his investment in a typesetting machine (and turning down an offer of Bell telephone!) and his publishing Grant's memoirs. To make money, honestly—and pay back your debts when unfortunate enough to lose was in the sound American tradition that Mark Twain so richly exemplified.

Indeed, instead of suffering from a barren and inhibiting environment I should say that Mark Twain had had the richest soil a creative genius could be born into, and the most saturatedly American. He was born of poor, but pure stock, never submitted to the sordid penury of our industrial civilization, never indurated in inferiority, living always where he could get at the sun and the soil, close to his equals and to nature. He was trained in three great popular schools: the printing office, the Mississippi river, and the newspaper. He saw, he was part of, the last great pioneer trek across the Rockies and lived in the West when it was indeed another country from the States! and among men who felt all the freedoms possible to men in a state of nature to feel and express.

By divine good fortune he escaped almost every imprint of the Civil War. He was born close enough to slavery to have a just reprobation of it and at the same time a just sympathy with those unconscious victims of its system—slave owners. His America was still the land of immense promise, not merely to its own children, but to those brave enterprising spirits who took their fortunes in their hands and left Europe in the middle of the last century. Men of ability and character who were free to adventure wherever chance and the spirit within them suggested. It still seemed true in the U.S.A. that "All men are born equal," at least equal in opportunity to test themselves, to make venture for fortune or disaster—and it is a world of such free, individual, independent human beings that Mark Twain presents in his tales, sketches, more ambitious works. It is from the vantage point of such a youth that he observes and reacts to the old European world, to humanity.

And among all the privileges of his youth I should not place least or last the unconscious, natural road into literature through the daily newspaper. All his early work was anonymously contributed to crude little sheets, not self-consciously prepared for literary fame. His critics were his fellow workmen; his success was the appeal he made to the men and women he met on the street. Much of the most authentic literature America has produced has happened that way, not through magazines literary and less literary, not ordered in advance and paid for like attar of rose at so much per word, but poured out carelessly onto the reporter's pad with the greedy presses waiting for their meat. Think of Bret Harte, George Ade, Peter Dunne, Will Rogers and many others.

Mark Twain was over thirty when having served his apprenticeship, having achieved rather more than local fame and acquired the tools of his trade—his command of language—he turned back to the East and confronted Europe, the seat of the other tradition. Quite half of Mark Twain's literary work is concerned, oddly enough, in one way or another, with Europe and the European tradition. It may not be the better half, the more significant half, although some rank his *Connecticut Yankee*, his *Joan of Arc*, very highly, and hardly anything he wrote has been so steadily popular as *Innocents Abroad*. Personally I prefer the other half of his work, books whose material and themes were drawn from his own vivid past, from the Mississippi and its half-southern towns, from Nevada, from boyhood acquaintances. Few writers have been more autobiographical than Mark Twain. He used every experience.

But his preoccupation with Europe all his later life is very important. As a people we Americans have always been great wanderers, not necessarily because we are so much bored at home, but because we have curiosity. There are as many different ways in which Americans take Europe, as there are Americans; as a sensuous riot; in abject adoration and reverent imitation; or with scorn and a flaunted superiority. I have seen specimens of all these manners and many more. Mark Twain himself includes all of them and more. He did not take Europe at its face value by any means. (See his description of a French duel.) The English found it hard to forgive him for his ridicule of some sacred shrines in the *Yankee*, and he was at times not above the banality of saying in the presence of great art which he did not comprehend, "Well, I know what I like!" (as if it made any difference what the ignorant and ill-informed happened to like!). But if one reads over his European based books one is struck by the amount of very real knowledge and culture this wandering American journalist had acquired of Europe and European art, letters, and history. But what interests me more than that is Mark Twain's independence of mind towards what he saw, his staunch maintenance of his American standards of common sense and humanity. His reaction to the European tradition might be easily summed up—hatred of cant, of pretense, either social or religious or cultural; hatred of all arbitrary authority (*Prince and Pauper, Joan, Yankee*); belief in the limitless possibilities of the individual regardless of origin or environment. Are these not the foundation stones of the older American tradition? Mark Twain walked among the sacred places of Europe, not irreverently, not flippantly, but with a native keenness of vision and a desire to appreciate honestly, at a correct value, at *his own* value, the traditional estimates of European ways and expressions. Europe always attracted him vastly, but never humbugged him. And Europe in return, especially the English part of it, did him the highest honors, even to the "academic" ones. He did not sit beneath the salt in Oxford!

Mark Twain was a humorist, by classification, but as has been the case with all great humorists from Cervantes to the present was primarily moralist and philosopher: his humor was a form, often a cloak for his deep earnestness. (As with Peter Dunne and Will Rogers.) The sternness within his soul deepened with age—see "The Man Who Corrupted Hadleyburg"! His burlesque, his buffoon manner lessened, his irony deepened. *The Yankee in King Arthur's Court* has much buffoonery; his *Prince and Pauper*, almost none, and *Joan of Arc* none at all. Contemporaries who knew him intimately have said that Twain's private talk was very serious and the best of him. His joking manner covered lightly a passionate sincerity about life, a scorching, withering denunciation of evil, of selfishness, hypocrisy.

There is no doubt that his estimate of humanity became more caustic, more condemnatory with age. A poor branch of the anthropoid ape family would be his final verdict on humanity—yet withal lovable, individually.

The essence of that older American tradition that Mark Twain so richly exemplified was a passionate individualism, a love of freedom, of self-expression, a religious faith in the power of individuality to conquer, to triumph, to achieve. Hence our worship of success, our defiance often of law, always of tradition. Also there was in it a great generosity of purpose. Ours is the only great nation in history that ever entered upon a bloody war with such slight selfish reason as ours was in the World War, with so little preoccupation with personal gain, with so much to lose, so little to win. (And we lost!) Whatever may have been in the minds of Washington and Wall Street, in the hearts of Americans there was largely a disinterested passion for freedom and justice, a hatred of the old world political order and the will to put it right. Maybe an illusion, nevertheless strongly operative among the American people.

What is there left in the American spirit today of the older tradition? What would Mark Twain feel akin to today were he to come back to the present American scene? For one thing, thus far, we have as a people resisted the voices that proclaim the defeat of democracy: we are as a people neither fascist nor communist at heart. If we can hold out against all the new forces let loose since the end of the great war we may be the one people of the earth to discover a middle way between autocracy and chaos, between the tyranny of regimentation and the disintegration of the mob instinct. We may preserve the ideal of individual liberty and prove that men in the mass can be taught to govern themselves, not revert to some form of slavery or barbarism. We as a people abhor war, do not believe war to be an inescapable condition of human life. We may—if we are wise and strong enough—endure as a people without resort to the insanity of war or to the suicidal mania of revolution, in spite of all the powerful examples and influences pressing the rest of the world on into the dark gulf of chaos. We, having benefited most from the machine, may yet save ourselves from the degradations of industrialism, neither rejecting the machine nor permitting it to throttle the human lives it was designed to free. We, who today are suffering most from the errors and excesses of the past, may be the people first to discover the way into the new life, the new conceptions of evolving personality now necessary for our very survival.

It is a good sign that such a great American individualist as Mark Twain was, whose Homeric laughter exploded so many of our weaknesses, whose blasting irony revealed so many of our secret sins, should be today the most widely read of all our American masters by the mass of American readers. For he believed in the ultimate saving virtue of the mass: he trusted them for all their follies rather than Kings, or Dictators, or Oligarchs. He believed in the spirit of Democracy, as I do, in spite of its every failure.

Mark Twain's Views on Education

Robert T. Oliver*

Mark Twain, America's greatest humorist, was also an educational philosopher with remarkable insight. Although he had only a few months of formal schooling, and almost no acquaintance with the "moderns" who were revising the educational theories of his youth, his common sense and observation led him to many liberal conclusions.

So constant was his concern with educational problems that his comments on them are found in almost every volume he wrote. However, the basic principles of his "system of education" may be found in a representative selection of his writings, namely: *The Connecticut Yankee in King Arthur's Court, Pudd'nhead Wilson, What Is Man?, The American Claimant, Following the Equator*, his *Letters*, and in the official biography by Albert Bigelow Paine.

In this article Twain's views are set forth so far as is possible in his own words. Almost all of the quotations are from the works that have been named. The remainder of his writings have all been examined, and from them could be drawn many more comments to be set down beside the ones which follow. But, if used, they would only elaborate (and perhaps obscure)—but would not change to any important degree—the summary of Twain's educational theory.

Twain's faith in the power of education would seem at times to be almost boundless. "My land, the power of training! of influence! of education!" cried the Connecticut Yankee. "It can bring a body up to believe anything. I had to put myself in Sandy's place to realize that she was not a lunatic. Yes, and put her in mine, to demonstrate how easy it is to seem a lunatic to a person who has not been taught as you have been taught." Pudd'nhead Wilson, in his laconic calendar, remarked, "Training is everything. The peach was once a bitter almond; cauliflower is nothing but cabbage with a college education." It would be hard to find a more emphatic testimony of the value of training.

"When we set about accounting for a Napoleon," Twain explained, "or a Shakespeare or a Raphael or a Wagner or an Edison or other ex-

*Reprinted from *Education*, 61 (October, 1940), 112–15.

traordinary person, we understand that the measure of his talent will not explain the whole result, nor even the largest part of it; no, it is the atmosphere in which the talent was cradled that explains; it is the training that it received while it grew, the nurture it got from reading, study, example, the encouragement it gathered from self-recognition and recognition from the outside at each stage of its development: when we know all these details, then we know why the man was ready when his opportunity came."

Amidst all his pessimism regarding what he called "the damned human race," he still nourished the hope that education might lift man to higher levels. "Inestimably valuable is training, influence, education, in right directions—training one's self-approbation to elevate its ideals," he said in the midst of the stark pessimism of *What Is Man?* "*Training* is potent. Training toward higher and higher, and even higher ideals is worth any man's thought and labor and diligence." Then he explains the broad meaning he gives to the term. "Study, instruction, lectures, sermons? That is a part of it—but not a large part. I mean *all* the outside influences. There are a million of them. From the cradle to the grave, during all his waking hours, the human being is under training. In the very first rank of his trainers stands *association*. It is his human environment which influences his mind and his feelings, furnishes him his ideals, and sets him on his road and keeps him in it. If he leave that road he will find himself shunned by the people whom he most loves and esteems, and whose approval he most values. He is a chameleon; by the law of his nature he takes the color of his place of resort. The influences about him create his preferences, his aversions, his politics, his tastes, his morals, his religion. He creates none of these things for himself. He *thinks* he does, but that is because he has not examined into the matter."

As the foregoing extract hints, Twain's faith in training did not extend to approval of the formal education then offered in the schools, and certainly not to the methods then in vogue with the schoolmasters. He deplored the undue emphasis placed on "the artificial culture of books, which adorns but doesn't really educate." He was before Dewey in urging that the students be made partners in the educational enterprise. He urged that the teachers should eschew dry rules, explain the nature and significance of the facts as they are studied, and help the students to learn, so far as possible, by doing.

For example, "History," he reminded the school masters, "requires a world of time and bitter hard work when your 'education' is no further advanced than the cat's; when you are merely stuffing yourself with a mixed-up mess of empty names and random incidents and elusive dates, which no one teaches you how to interpret, and which, uninterpreted, pay you not a farthing's value for your waste of time." History was one of his own favorite studies. He invented a method of teaching English history to his children—by driving a row of pegs in the lawn, each peg representing an English king, and each foot of space between the pegs representing one year of their reigns. By this method, supplemented with absurd drawings of the kings and wild tales of their times, history took on glamor and life. One of the reasons why he over-estimated the relative value among his works of *The Prince and the Pauper* was its service in making history real to children. When this book was dramatized and presented on the stage of various children's theatres, he wrote:

> The children's theatre is the only teacher of morals and conduct and high ideals that never bores the pupil, but always leaves him sorry when the lesson is over. And as for history, no other teacher is for a moment comparable to it: no other can make the dead heroes of the world rise up and shake the dust of the ages from their bones and live and move and breathe and speak and be real to the looker and listener: no other can make the study of the lives and times of the illustrious dead a delight, a splendid interest, a passion; and no other can paint a history lesson in colors that will stay, and stay, and never fade.

He deplored the tendency to direct all education toward the professions, when it was self-evident that not all students being educated could be received into professional ranks. "At home," he declared, during his world tour, "I once made a speech deploring the injuries inflicted by the high school in making handicrafts distasteful to boys who would have been willing to make a living at trades and agriculture if they had but had the good luck to stop with the common school. But I made no converts. Not one, in a community overrun with educated idlers who were above following their fathers' mechanical trades, yet could find no market for their book knowledge." Philip and Henry, in his satirical novel *The Gilded Age*, are fair samples of intelligent young men of this type; Berkeley in *The American Claimant* is another.

Twain dwelt in an age of remarkable scientific and mechanical advancement; he was himself vastly interested in these fields, and in his books foretold not only the use of finger-prints to identify criminals, but the development of television as well. He was among the very first users of the telephone and the typewriter. He lost a fortune in promoting the development of a linotype machine, and he himself patented a number of inventions. Hence it was but natural that he should speculate upon the cause of the mechanical advance. Significantly, he did not ascribe it to the work of the schools in gathering and disseminating information. It seemed to him to be due, rather, to a new spirit of open-mindedness, of inquiry; a turning from tradition to experiment. "If I were required to guess offhand, and without collusion with higher minds, what is the bottom cause of the amazing material and intellectual advancement of the last fifty years," he said, "I should guess that it was the modern-born and previously non-existent disposition on the part of men to believe that a new idea can have value."

Twain himself had singularly little of the formal schooling which he deplores. And he came to regret that fact in after years. His biographer, Albert Bigelow Paine, with questionable judgment, found comfort in Twain's lack of training. "How fortunate Mark Twain was in his schooling," Paine declared, "to be kept away from institutional training, to be placed in one after another of those universities of life where the sole curriculum is the study of the native inclinations and activities of mankind! Sometimes, in after-years, he used to regret the lack of systematic training. Well for him—and for us—that he escaped that blight." It is good to know that Twain himself rejected such an idea.

If Paine were by chance right, it would be best to exclude all promising young lads of talent from the blighting effects of education—and then the schools might as well be closed, since, as Twain pointed out, those without talent need mechanical rather than scholastic training. No academic critic, naturally, would agree with Paine, and one of them, Edward Wagenknecht, found fault with Paine's conclusion for the following reasons: "This kind of thinking [the spontaneous kind, without formal training] has its drawbacks: one generalizes from insufficient data; one is often carried away by emotion; one fails sometimes to look up the necessary information and consequently must retrace one's steps." This judgment represents Twain's own views more nearly than does the opposite conclusion of Paine.

In sum, we find Twain over-emphasizing the role of environment, and, thence, strongly stressing the value of education. He disliked the "stuffing" and rote-memory methods of the schoolmasters of his day, and advocated instead learning by association, learning by doing, learning for pleasurable motives rather than from fear of punishment, and learning for a practical adjustment to a changing world, rather than merely plodding through a traditional curriculum.

The Two Mark Twains

Robert M. Gay*

Mark Twain left an autobiography of some 400,000 words, of which Albert Bigelow Paine published about half in 1924. Now Bernard DeVoto publishes half of the other half, and assures us that there is nothing in the remaining quarter of supreme interest. The new book, *Mark Twain in Eruption*, contains many passages heretofore not only unpublished but suppressed, either by the author's direction or by the decision of the estate. They do not prove to be soul-shaking revelations.

I approached the book half expecting to find it a kind of chamber of horrors. In it, I suspected, we should at last get to the bottom of Mark Twain's tragic mystery which we have heard so much about. What I found is extremely interesting and characteristic, sometimes distressing and sometimes laughable, but not different in essence from what was already known. There are records of black moods, but we were already aware that Mark Twain had such moods, in which he looked upon the race as worms, democracy as decaying if not already as good as dead, human conduct as merely a mechanism, as the behaviorists have found it since. But I should not say that these pages reflect the mind of an unhappy old man or of one who thought he had failed.

The darkest impression one gets from the "eruptions" is that Mark Twain was puzzled or baffled by phenomena too complex for him to comprehend. The very violence and irrationality of his tirades are those of a feeling rather than a thinking man. He has set down his dislikes of certain persons with vigor and sometimes with violence, and they help us to round out our picture of him. But his notes on minstrel shows, mesmerism, his early memories, his own methods of writing and speaking, make grand reading. I would not give one of them for all his sombre musings or petulant tirades upon his times and the men and women he despised. Mr. DeVoto's Introduction, besides compressing much useful information in small space, arrives at what seem sound conclusions regarding Mark Twain's inability to express the mental confusion I have mentioned.

*Reprinted from *Atlantic Monthly*, 166 (December, 1940), 724–26. Copyright 1940, 1968, by the Atlantic Monthly Company, Boston, Massachusetts, and reprinted with permission.

We now probably have everything anybody is likely to want from the unpublished manuscripts, and, with the publication of *Mark Twain's Travels with Mr. Brown* (edited with an introduction by Franklin Walker and G. Ezra Dane), everything from the earliest hitherto unreprinted works. This book is a collection of letters written in 1866–1867 to the *Alta California*, about Mark Twain's travels, between the Sandwich Islands voyage and the European tour. All of these sketches were preliminary practice for *Innocents Abroad* and *Roughing It*, and are therefore valuable to the scholar as well as amusing to the general reader. The present book has the freshness, good-humored impudence, straight-faced hyperbole, and shrewd observation of the young journalist feeling his oats. Much of it is also very good writing of its kind.

Neither this book nor *Mark Twain in Eruption* contains much of that which made him magical and inimitable. But the latest work, like the earliest, illustrates his power as a raconteur; and really no one could tell a story better. If the fault of the early writing is uncertainty of taste, that of the late is wordiness, though this may be the result of dictation. But both prove once more his artistry even in telling the most trifling anecdote: the sense of timing and climax, of the very tones of a speaking voice, of the values of over- and under-statement, of the effect of surprise. He is always best when most spontaneous, and yet one can never be certain that his apparent spontaneity is not the result of shrewd planning. But much of this writing is really the result of rhetoric delicately applied. It is when he forgets rhetoric and effect and relies on his intuitions and especially on his memories of his boyhood that he becomes charming.

The history of Mark Twain's reputation is a curious one, and in some ways exasperating to his lovers. A perverse fate has pursued it. Ever since his greater works appeared, opinion about him has flown off at tangents, until it seemed as if he never would receive a sober appraisal. At one time it was his morality that was questioned; at another, his taste; at a third, his spiritual honesty. He was accepted by the great public as a mere jester, and by the critics was used as an example to illustrate critical theories. Thousands of pages were covered in showing what he was not, but hardly ever did anyone try to show what he really was. The reason was partly that there were two Mark Twains: one, the man I have called the rhetorician; the other, one whom we may call the poet. The former was showy, obvious, and delightful, but hardly competent to win a position as a great writer. The latter was often hidden behind the jester and showman, and was sometimes, even in his best work, in abeyance.

Perhaps the showman was diffident about the poet, afraid of his tenderness, wistfulness, and human sympathy. Strength is always afraid that sentiment is effeminate, and the realist in Mark Twain was never quite at ease with the dreamer. When he relied on his intuitions he was nearly always right and true, and instinctively he was a lover of his kind.

But he hardly ever expressed this love without self-consciousness except when he was viewing the world through the somewhat nostalgic atmosphere that surrounded his boyhood memories. In *Mark Twain in Eruption* it is a little pathetic to see how, the moment his mind goes back far enough, his style kindles, his smartness disappears, charm suffuses the most trivial incident.

I wonder whether his later critics have not mistaken what was really the matter with him in his old age. They have assumed that he became cynical and pessimistic. But he always was so. His mind always told him that life was bad. But his feelings told him that it was good, and as long as his feelings had fuel to burn, as long as they were engaged with affections formed before he became a thinking being, he could safely let them be. All his life he had a good and a bad angel at his two shoulders; there is nothing new in the melancholy of the *Autobiography*—only, the time came when he had used all the memories about which his good angel could sing and was left only with later impressions about which his bad angel could prose or snarl.

In this he is really not different from other men. The Greeks made poetry the daughter of Memory; and perhaps the myth suggests the reason why so many great novelists have written their masterpiece about the memories of their youth.

If I can trust my own memory, the popular view of Mark Twain before the turn of the century was that he was a writer of excruciatingly funny stories and of books for children. Of the latter, two—*The Prince and the Pauper* and *Joan of Arc*—were quite safe reading for children, but two others—*Tom Sawyer* and *Huckleberry Finn*—though no doubt very amusing, were far too rowdy for nice little boys and girls. It is hard for me to believe that *Tom Sawyer* was published before I was born and *Huckleberry Finn* when I was five years old, because I certainly never read them until I had grown up. In our provincial neighborhood Mark Twain was a familiar name all through my boyhood, because many of his sketches—no doubt his worst—were favorites with parlor elocutionists; but my own lack of acquaintance with his masterpieces suggests that they were carefully kept out of my reach.

My elders no doubt thought they were protecting my taste and morals, and I cannot believe that they were unique or even unusual in this. Van Wyck Brooks records that the books were excluded from the public libraries of my home town. I certainly remember that some of my playmates were reading *Huckleberry Finn* secretly in the attic.

It is possible that the general public ran true to form in liking the worst books best; but this hardly accounts for the slowness of the professional critics and literary historians to recognize that *Tom Sawyer*, *Life on the Mississippi*, and *Huckleberry Finn* were national masterpieces. Reasons can be assigned, the main one being critical inertia and timidity.

Gradually, nevertheless, the realization came that Mark Twain was one of our great writers, whom it was not extravagant to compare with Dickens, Molière, Dumas, and Cervantes. These comparisons really were made, though somewhat casually, before he attained, in the nineteen-twenties, a vogue among the intellectuals.

In that peculiar decade he became the centre of a controversy which tended further to postpone a final estimate of his quality. Everyone remembers it, I suppose, and it has not even yet entirely subsided. It began when the cult of the frontier or Middle West found in him a handy example of a product strictly made-in-America. It was only a step to the conclusion that his history presented a parable of the distressful condition of the artist in America. This theory found an eloquent advocate in Van Wyck Brooks and a pugnacious opponent in Bernard DeVoto. The fallacy in the theory was perhaps natural to intellectuals: it treated Mark Twain as if he were an intellectual. But if there was ever an intuitionalist it was he. He was so creative that whenever he attempted philosophic thought he seemed like a great, solemn, lovable baby. His at times astonishing insight and wisdom were the fruit, not of philosophy, but of human sympathy. His illuminations came through his feelings.

Has not the time come to continue the work laid out by DeVoto in *Mark Twain's America*? To reexamine the works, not for what they lack, but for what they have? Concerning his greatest work, nearly everybody is now agreed that it has exuberance of vitality. Like all great fiction, it has a positively therapeutic power, not only because it contains the great cure-all, laughter, but because it is so completely sane. This sanity, which shows as a balance of laughter and tears, of observation and imagination, of thought and feeling, is found only in a few writers, and these of the greatest.

America's Voice Is Mark Twain's

Herman Wouk*

To begin with, American literature is not a thing in itself.

It is the offspring of an aristocratic and somewhat aging father, European literature. It is like a burly son of 20 or so—still very much in the wild oats stage, still kicking at parental rules, still more inclined to tear the house apart than to conserve it.

There is good and bad in such a son. Some of the good things are a fresh outlook, bouncing vigor, an almost drunken love of life, and a rude frankness that now and then cuts to the bone of truth as politeness never can.

Some of the bad things are hasty judgment, cocksure pessimism (nobody can be more gloomy than the 20-year-old with the world at his feet) and—too often—young ignorance mistaking itself for new insight.

The work of Mark Twain, the commanding figure in our literature, has all these traits. American writing ranges far beyond Twain, of course. Elementary entertainers of the Mickey Spillane variety, subtle poets like Jeffers and MacLeish, critics as profound as Mencken and Wilson, historians with the sweep and brilliance of Sandburg and Catton, novelists as different as the dark Gothic Faulkner and the panoramic Dreiser—all these, and many more, are part of American literature.

I shall treat Mark Twain as an archetype of United States writers, indicating as well as I can my reasons for so doing. A discussion as brief as this can become a mere roster of great names, unless a focal point is taken at the start.

Mark Twain burst on the world with *Innocents Abroad*, a scathingly funny attack on European culture. Later, when he came to know Europe better, and to live it, he modified some of his cracker-barrel judgments. But his assault on the genteel fakery which is often a curse of civilized European life remains quite sound. We can laugh at it today, returning from a trip abroad.

It was no accident that Twain's wife called him "Youth" all his life

*Reprinted from *San Francisco Chronicle*, August 5, 1956, "This World," p. 20; the item was credited to the Associated Press.

long. His work breathed youth to the end. In this he was deeply and characteristically American.

Twain had a cold sharp eye for fact, and a passion for exactly observed detail, in his writing. Yet his novels are all extravagant romances; for he was also a restless dreamer, a man who spent his life pursuing phantom millions in alluring schemes.

This paradox in the American character often strikes thoughtful Europeans. Churchill writes in his history of World War II that he was amazed, during his first encounters with the United States Chiefs of Staff, at the way the Americans combined a merciless grasp of facts with plans that seemed wildly visionary.

It was Twain's great inspiration that he wrote his masterpiece in the words of an ignorant river boy, looking at life with fresh uncivilized eyes. He thus established at a stroke the colloquial style which has swept American literature, and indeed spilled over into world literature.

We do have noble writers in the European tradition. Irving, Hawthorne, Melville, Poe, Emerson, Henry James owe nothing to Twain. But after him comes the march of the moderns.

The names alone would fill the rest of this article. Jack London, O. Henry, Sherwood Anderson, Dreiser, Fitzgerald, Lewis, Mencken, Tarkington, Hemingway, Runyon, Thurber, Steinbeck, Marquand, Lardner, Faulkner—all of these, with their disciples and imitators, are hardly conceivable except coming after Twain, as well as many other major writers who have not generated trains of followers.

Huckleberry Finn's unwelcome companions on his immortal voyage are a phony King and Duke, actually a pair of leech-like tramps; and the last part of the book is an insanely comic parody of the traditions of British Chivalry. Twain never stopped rebelling against Europe. However, like most rebellious sons, he loved what he was fighting against.

He seems to have known Scott, Defoe, and Swift almost by heart; he read widely in European history; he returned to Europe over and over. He was no mere bad boy from the wrong side of the tracks, heaving bricks through the windows of the aristocrats. He was a teller of the truth; and he had some new truths to tell.

Huckleberry Finn is a jerky, uneven, patchwork tale, as jerry-built as a pioneer's hut on the prairies, or a real estate development on Long Island. By the classic standards of European fiction it is one long barbarous mistake. Yet it is the crown of our literature.

With its unquenchable sense of romance in common life, its never-ending movement down a wide turbid river, its jazzy spurts of action, its feeling of the open air, its savage mockery of outworn forms and phony ideas, its smell of green leaves in the wild, its surface pessimism and deep-running optimism, its strong colors and sounds, its crazy scrapes and crazier escapes, above all its picture of the dignity of human nature shorn bare of any social distinctions—for the guttersnipe Huck and the black slave Jim have a natural dignity not surpassed by Shakespeare's kings—*Huckleberry Finn*, with these qualities, first gave America its voice in world culture.

It is a novelist's weakness to think of novels when writing an appreciation of our literature. A poet doing this job would perhaps place his focus in Whitman; a literary historian, in Emerson or possibly Lincoln; a philosopher, in John Dewey or William James. But I wonder whether anyone would in the end deny Twain a central place.

America's literature, young as it is, stands as our patent of civilization; and it is a patent that will defy attack. The picture painted of our land by anti-Americans—a brainless Carthage, brutally money-mad, obsessed with luxury and power, dead to the spirit—is a lie. Our literature proves that it is a lie.

We cannot match the great Pantheons of British and French classic authors—not yet! But judging only by Twentieth-Century output, I think most critics would say that American literature has at least equaled that of any other nation; a sure sign that our culture is a live and growing one.

Humor in a Tough Age

Was Mark Twain a schizophrenic? Van Wyck Brooks established his own critical reputation with a book proving that he was. T. S. Eliot, who has provided two generations of professors with their slim stock of ideas, said he was. It has often been remarked that he was a *laveur*, at least as far as clothes were concerned. Dressing only in white suits laundered every day, he must have been awful guilty of something awful. From the point of view of a small office in a provincial English Department, with rows of Henry James and Sören Kierkegaard on the shelves and hapless coeds slipping exercises in Creative Writing under the door—from this elevated point of view, Mark Twain certainly looks very *queer*.

I think this is all balderdash. Too few critics of his own kind have written about Mark Twain. What he suffers from in the midst of this twentieth and American century is a lack of peers. He needs somebody like Walter Bagehot or even H. L. Mencken or James Gibbons Huneker. He was a man of the world. He was a man of the nineteenth-century American world where presidents chewed tobacco and billionaires couldn't spell and vast audiences flocked to hear Bob Ingersoll (whom Twain in this book calls "the silver tongued infidel") and the labor movement was dominated by another silver tongued cornball named Terence Powderly, who could do nothing but orate, and "Thanatopsis" was considered the most philosophical utterance in the English language, and a small gang of merciless and ignorant brigands put through America's Five Year Plans, and finally "overtook and surpassed" Europe. He was a man of that world that Henry James fled in uncomprehending horror. We have only to look abroad to understand exactly the kind of world it was. It was a world of driving expansion and brutal hard work that brooked no interference or dissent. A world of "primitive accumulation."

It was the official culture which was schizophrenic, not Mark Twain. The whole meaning of Mark Twain is that he "saw life steadily and saw it whole." T. S. Eliot thought his billiard room jokes childish.

*Reprinted from *Nation*, 188 (March 7, 1959), 211–13; a review of *The Autobiography of Mark Twain*, ed. Charles Neider (New York: Harper, 1959).

They are pretty bad, but are they as bad a joke as Eliot's essay on Crashaw? Mark Twain's low humor was a technique of adjustment to the broadest possible areas of society. It made him a public figure, it gave him the confidence of presidents of the United States and of the principal corporations of the United States. And it gave him entrance to the American Home, back in the days before Mom had emasculated that institution. All sorts of people, practically everybody, thought he was very, very funny. T. S. Eliot's essay on Crashaw is a snickering little joke on a very small clique of people who were viable themselves only within a scarcely less minute clique—the few High Church members of the now long dead Bloomsbury circle. Furthermore, it owes its character as humor entirely to its incongruous treatment of the standard undergraduate course in Jacobean and Caroline literature—in other words it is *College Humor* in spats and bowler. In his autobiography, Mark Twain tells the story of his absurd brother Orion, who used to cool his brain by kneeling in the full bathtub and immersing his head for two minutes at a time. Once the chambermaid opened the unlocked door and ran screaming, "Mr. Orion is drownded!" and his wife said, "How did you know it was Mr. Orion?" Who is childish, Mr. Eliot or Mark Twain?

Like Jack London, Mark Twain says he went into writing because it was the easiest work he could find, so easy that at the end of his life he could say he hadn't worked a lick in fifty years—it had all been play. This is the remark of a man thoroughly at home in literature. Anything less like Henry James's ridiculous prefaces would be hard to imagine. Writers like Mallarmé and James and Flaubert, who are always squawking about how artistic they are and how much it hurts, really accept the judgment of bourgeois society that they are loafers. They are ashamed of being writers and endlessly try to justify themselves. The amateur psychoanalysts of Mark Twain are the guilty ones, straddling their double standards. They can't understand this man who was hail fellow well met with cowboys and duchesses, who told the Kaiser that his cook baked potatoes just like a pocket miner he'd known during the Gold Rush. Since they are terrified even at a cocktail party given by another Literary Personage and have no social presence whatsoever and go into rages when their very freshmen can't see the relevance of the *Summa Theologica* to *Deerslayer*, they think Mark Twain must be a fraud and crazy to boot.

Mark Twain was just a very wise nineteenth-century man. He knew his way around socially in the age of the Robber Barons. He knew how to keep his head above water in the Period of Primitive Accumulation. Corny humor, broad anecdotes, after-dinner oratory, primitive vaudeville roles—the Missouri hayseed abroad, a Connecticut Yankee at King Arthur's Court—these may be protective coloration, but they are not selling out. If it weren't Mark Twain but somebody several centuries previous—or Charlie Chaplin—the high-brows would call it the adaptation of folk forms to serious literature. Because those guffawing, tobacco-spitting travel books that made Mark Twain's reputation in the first place and that gave Van Wyck Brooks fainting spells are fundamentally right. Always Mark Twain points out the human meaning of St. Peter's or the pyramids or the Pantheon. What was the social price paid for the Sistine Chapel when it was painted? What is the social price being paid today? It is true that he sweetened the pills, but the word for this is "mastering the terms of the folk culture." Who objects to it in Charlie Chaplin or Little Abner, or, for that matter, Count Basie? That he had to do this is shown by Charles Neider's preface to this very book. At the most, Mark Twain was a mild agnostic, usually he seems to have been an amused Deist. Yet, at this late date his own daughter has refused to allow his comments on religion to be published.

What is there to say about this book? It is a more coherent collection of Mark Twain's random reminiscences than the Paine or DeVoto volumes, but it omits some of the political and social criticism that DeVoto printed and that is certainly important to an understanding of Mark Twain. It is, of course, a book of Mark Twain in his bedroom slippers. Everybody who has read much of Mark Twain is familiar with this aspect of him because he went around that way most of the time. He was never ashamed to be seen in the maximum state of personal dishevelment. Only people who find it impossible to deal with other human beings unless they have on their social masks find this embarrassing. It is very corny, very male, very smoking car and billiard room. But it is all very normal too. Mark Twain remembered his childhood, and loved his wife and daughters and mourned their deaths just as your own relatives back home in Elkhart, Indiana, did those things in 1906. He didn't do any of those things the way the folks do that you meet drinking Pernods in the Deux Magots. Those people in the Deux Magots find him very square— "straight" is the term in the *milieu*. They think he didn't really mean it, that something was going on behind the scenes. He meant it. This is not Mark Twain's public mask. It is him. He didn't have a public mask. Like all adults, his contradictions and contraries were simply part of him, like his right and left hand.

If Baudelaire was the greatest poet of the capitalist epoch—and he was a mild schizophrenic, a sexual freak and a syphilitic—Mark Twain wrote its saga, its prose *Iliad* and *Odyssey*. And he wrote it because he knew how to survive to write it. He survived because he was an eminently normal man. No wonder it is the favorite prose fiction of the Russians. It is the archetypal epic of precisely the historical period they are now in themselves. Unfortunately, so far, nobody has known how to survive to write that epic in Russian.

Twain: A Yearning for Yesterday

Leslie Hanscom*

"Even popularity," Mark Twain wrote in *Pudd'nhead Wilson*, "can be overdone. In Rome, along at first, you are full of regrets that Michelangelo died, but by and by you are only sorry that you didn't see him do it."

This year the most beloved of American writers will be paraded before the public to an extent which defies his own warning. Wherever producers, publishers, and editors gather there is no problem more epidemic than how to wring another profitable idea out of Twain's spectacular personality or out of his writings. If the old master were alive today he might comment on all this with the same words he gave the Dauphin in the *Adventures of Huckleberry Finn*. "Hain't we got all the fools in town on our side? And ain't that a big enough majority. . . ?" Unlike his giant contemporaries, Henry James and Herman Melville, who slipped into neglect, Twain has always been a popular author. His high stature as an artist has long been accepted. ("All modern American literature," said Ernest Hemingway, "comes from one book . . . called *Huckleberry Finn*.") But even his most ardent admirers were unprepared for the adulation of the last few years.

The first small sign of this was the enthusiastic reaction of the critics when Charles Neider published a complete collection of Twain's short stories in 1957. Then last year came the stunning success of Hal Holbrook, a young actor who catapulted to fame on Broadway and elsewhere by impersonating Mark Twain, lion of the lecture platform, in an evening's entertainment. From this moment on, Twainophilia was unrestrained, and it reaches a crescendo this month.

On May 2, Franchot Tone will wear the wig and snap the galluses in a show based on Twain's lecture tours of 1895–1905. On May 10, Ernie Ford will clamp his shins in armor and let on that he is *A Connecticut Yankee at King Arthur's Court* in a "Ford Startime Special." Three nights later, James Daly will again sport the Twain mane and white flannels in a

*Reprinted from *Newsweek*, 55 (May 2, 1960), 51–53. Copyright 1983 by Newsweek Inc. All rights reserved. Reprinted by permission.

dramatization of *Roughing It*. Both shows follow closely upon last week's NBC presentation of "Mark Twain's America," a superb hour of still photographs with music and narrative. This telescreening was largely aimed at feeding the nostalgia for the American past which is one root of the Twain vogue. But it was also notable for letting the discerning eye catch a glimpse here and there of the dark places in our history which haunted Twain even at the height of his fame. And the hour ended unforgettably with a close-up of the old man's face, wearing that look of his last days which seemed to say, "What do you do when you're too old to cry?"

In this same year that Twain is shaping up as a hot property in television, he is attracting more than the usual amount of heed from the scholar-critic and the serious reader. Four books on Twain from academic sources have already appeared—notably *The Mark Twain-Howells Letters* (edited by Henry Nash Smith and William M. Gibson). This scholarly bonanza in two volumes marks the first publication of Twain's complete correspondence with his bosom friend, William Dean Howells, the novelist who, in their day, towered above him in the world's regard—and in Twain's.

It was Howells who prophetically recognized his friend as "the Lincoln of our literature," and the years have deepened this likeness. Like Lincoln, Twain haunts the folk consciousness of the American people as a sort of visually stylized embodiment of the American integrities. To Hal Holbrook, the old boy also inhabits the collective psyche as a national grandfather image. Interviewed the other day in New York's Hospital for Joint Diseases where he lay propped up in a framework of weights and pulleys to correct a slipped disk, Holbrook dilated on this theme. "The trouble is," the actor said, "that none of us really have any families any more—no old folks in our lives to give us that wonderful feeling of having come from some place. And we miss them. Seeing Twain on the stage—an especially virile old son-of-a-gun at the age of 70—seems to be good for our feelings of insecurity."

Holbrook—who probably deserves more individual credit for the Twain boom than anybody except Twain—admits that he has learned not to challenge the good feeling of his audiences by delivering any of Twain's more controversial utterances. Twain's dim view of religion ("Faith is believing what you know ain't so") still has the power to antagonize even when it is funny. But he is proud that his reading from *Huckleberry Finn*—the episode in which Huck strives with his conscience over his seeming duty to turn in a runaway slave—found one of its warmest receptions just outside Little Rock only a couple of weeks after the school-integration crisis. In fact, said Holbrook, the Huck Finn bit usually goes better in the South than in the North, where audiences have a tendency to stiffen into a dutiful attitude of here comes the message.

It was always Twain's genius to transcend the barriers which people build between each other. In his lifetime, he was so widely loved abroad that his biographer, Albert Bigelow Paine (*Mark Twain: A Biography*), tells of the British stevedores greeting Twain with cheers when he walked down the gangplank in England. In our own time, the Prime Minister of Ceylon (S.W.R.D. Bandaranaike in 1956) has been quoted as saying, "How could I feel hostile to a country that produced Mark Twain?"

Twain's popularity in the U.S.S.R. is a commonplace of the headlines. Two years ago when the Russians placed on sale a twelve-volume subscription edition of his collected works, the whole thing sold out in a single day. Tom Sawyer is a familiar figure in the Soviet theater repertory. And Moscow's *Literary Gazette* has added its mite to the recent swell of interest in Twain among his own countrymen by quarreling with Charles Neider—who edited a recent version of the great man's helter-skelter autobiography—over the question of who understands Twain better, the Russians or we.

To the Russians, Twain is the consummate social critic on two grounds. Of the Czarist regime he wrote: "It seems to me that a crusade to make a bonfire of the Russian throne and fry the Czar in it would have some sense." And when it came to his own country, he gibed mercilessly at its excesses and vulgarities as it grew to maturity. ("I think I can say and say with pride," he commented, "that we have legislatures that bring higher prices than any in the world.") It pleases the rulers of the Soviet Union to keep this picture of the United States alive. "Who," commented the *Literary Gazette* critic, "does not know Twain's famous pronouncements about American 'democracy,' his indignant notes about the predatory wars which the U.S. carried on half a century ago, his satirical sketches . . . of the oil king Rockefeller, of Senator Clark, General Wood, President Theodore Roosevelt, and other knights and henchmen of American expansionism."

It was the Gilded Age, as Twain named it—a time of mammoth corruption, double-dealing ruthlessness in business, and sickly Sunday-school piety which served as a screen to cover an ugly multitude of wrongs. One memorable manifestation of the religious spirit of the time, which exercised Twain's ire, was the act of the Rev. T. De Witt Talmage of Brooklyn, in closing his church to working people because their smell offended his better-heeled parishioners. Twain gave him the roasting in print that he had coming. It would be a shame, he said, in a heaven full of who knows what kind of people to miss the company of Dr. Talmage who could give the place more tone than "any other contribution Brooklyn could offer."

It is an irony of the current Twain revival that it is partly based upon nostalgia for the very world that he castigated with vigor for 40 years. Even dreamy Hannibal, Mo. (the place now has everything from a Becky Thatcher Bookstore to statues of Huck Finn and Tom Sawyer), will not bear a really level look across the years. It was here that Twain, during the brief years of his childhood, was actual witness to no fewer than four murders. As for the Wild West, which still feeds the American male's fantasies of personal freedom, it meant something less gratifying to Twain. Van Wyck Brooks asserts that, in Twain's days as a gold hunter in Nevada and California, this was a region in which any show of individuality was viewed almost as outright crime. When he tried to remain alone to write, Twain was persecuted by his fellow miners with loutishly violent practical jokes. Twain's feeling that writing was no work for a man, Brooks believes, stemmed partly from this ordeal.

Authorship was a trade which he turned to after the Civil War ended the steamboat era and—with it—Twain's proud career as a river pilot, the joyous episode which he later made into the book *Life on the Mississippi*. At 13, he had learned the printer's craft in Hannibal "when none but the pure in heart were in that business." As with Walt Whitman and so many others of the early Republic's men of letters, it was a trade which led to eager reading and then writing. Out West ("when I was a young man studying for the gallows"), he plunged briefly into the silver craze, then, with considerably more success, into journalism. Fame came in a rush when he spun a yarn which seemed to him nothing but a "villainous backwoods sketch" and sent it to a New York newspaper. It was "The Celebrated Jumping Frog of Calaveras County," and it was the beginning of a reputation which would make "Mark Twain"—a riverboat cry meaning 2 fathoms or "safe water"—the greatest nom de plume of all time. (Probably the all-time favorite piece of erudition among those who have little is the awareness that Twain's real name was Samuel Langhorne Clemens.)

"Pleasure, Love, Fame, Riches," he wrote, "they are but temporary disguises for lasting realities—Pain, Grief, Shame, Poverty." This can be read as a capsule autobiography. By 1885, the author of *The Adventures of Tom Sawyer* and *Huckleberry Finn* was the most widely read of living authors. Money from books, articles, and lectures poured upon him in a tide which delighted and alarmed him. ("I'm opposed to millionaires," he said, "but it would be dangerous to offer me the position.") He was publicly loved and privately adored by his family of womenfolk—his wife, Olivia ("No man . . . really knows what perfect love is until [he has] been married a quarter of a century"), and his three daughters. But the money melted away in a series of wild business ventures (one of his get-rich schemes was a spiral hatpin), and the womenfolk—all but one—went before him to the grave. In the end, Mark hated life and the human race, which he said consisted of "the damned and the ought-to-be damned. I am full of malice," he wrote eight months before his death, "saturated with malignity."

As Van Wyck Brooks analyzed it 40 years ago in his critical bombshell, *The Ordeal of Mark Twain*, Twain's pessimism and eventual misanthropy grew because he betrayed his destiny as a born artist and went over to the camp of the Philistines. Although he hated the Gilded Age, he bowed to its standards of success, so Brooks felt, turning himself into a clown on the lecture platform and allowing his over-genteel wife and his friend Howells to tame his talent. Brooks used him as a dire warning to the American writer to "put away childish things and walk the stage as poets do." It was a thesis which made debate all through the '20s, and was mercilessly attacked in the next decade by the critic Bernard DeVoto, Twain's literary executor, who insisted that Twain, just as he was, made so towering a figure that the question of what he might have been was of no account. Twain's great achievement, said DeVoto, was in giving poetic voice to all that part of American life which Brooks believed had balked his genius.

Today, however, the ghost of Twain seems to be going through a new "ordeal." Harmlessly enthroned on a cracker barrel, he has been turned into the perfect period piece, full of mellow wisdom and snappy sayings. As dispensed by the mass media, he seems to be a bit of Americana rather than an artist. But the one ordeal he will certainly not suffer in the near future is neglect. A new movie version of *Huckleberry Finn* will be released this summer by M-G-M. On June 5, a Mark Twain Memorial Shrine—a somewhat fearsomely modernistic building erected over the cabin of his birth—will be dedicated at Florida, Mo. Throughout the year, his prominence in the public eye can be anticipated with "the serene confidence which a Christian feels in four aces." The reports of his death, in short, have—in the words of the hoariest Twainism—been greatly exaggerated.

Mark Twain's Use of the Comic Pose

John C. Gerber*

Mark Twain's range in point of view is readily apparent in those works in which he uses fictional narrators. To reassure oneself on this point it is necessary only to recall some of his more famous narrators: Thomas Jefferson Snodgrass, Huckleberry Finn, Hank Morgan, Sieur Louis de Conte, King Leopold, and Captain Ben Stormfield, not to mention Adam, Eve, a horse, and a dog. What is not so readily apparent, however, is that an analogous range in point of view exists in those works narrated not by personae but by "Mark Twain"—such works as the travel letters and books, "Old Times on the Mississippi," "The Private History of a Campaign That Failed," and the bulk of the short newspaper and magazine sketches.[1] In some of these Twain played it straight; that is, he employed in them a point of view that was essentially his own. In others he assumed a pose, a point of view other than his own. And in still others, especially in the longer works, he alternated between real and assumed points of view.[2] My concern in this essay is with the nature and range of these assumed points of view.

Fundamentally, there are two ways to confront life falsely. Either one can pretend that life is more agreeable to the spirit and more amenable to the will than it really is, or one can pretend that it is less so. One can exaggerate his superiority to human affairs or his inferiority to them. As the narrator "Mark Twain," Twain did both. He pretended undue superiority, for example, in posing as the Gentleman, the Sentimentalist, the Instructor, and the Moralist; he assumed undue inferiority in posing as the Sufferer, the Simpleton, and the Tenderfoot. On examination, each of these poses proves to have identifiable characteristics and quite discernible effects on style.

The discussion that follows has three parts: a description of some of the more common comic poses of superiority, a description of some of the more common comic poses of inferiority, and certain general reflections upon Twain's use of the comic pose.

*Reprinted from *PMLA*, 77 (June, 1962), 297–304, with the permission of the author.

I

Among the poses of superiority, that of the Gentleman most clearly identifies Twain with the Southwestern humorists who preceded him. Like A. B. Longstreet, Johnson J. Hooper. T. B. Thorpe, and Joseph G. Baldwin, Twain endowed his Gentleman with social elevation, an air of condescension, and a language notable primarily for its formal elegance. Appropriately, this was the chief pose that Twain assumed in the first piece known to be signed "Mark Twain," a letter from Carson City that appeared in the Virginia City *Territorial Enterprise* in February of 1863. In this letter he pretends to view Clement T. Rice, a reporter for the rival *Daily Union*, with lofty disdain. Referring to Rice as "The Unreliable," Twain brings him on the scene in this way: "About nine o'clock the Unreliable came and asked Gov. Johnson to let him stand on the porch. That creature has got more impudence than any person I ever saw in my life. Well, he stood and flattened his nose against the parlor window, and looked hungry and vicious—he always looks that way—until Col. Musser arrived with some ladies, when he actually fell in their wake and came swaggering in, looking as if he thought he had been anxiously expected."[3] In this and in later *Enterprise* letters Twain as the Gentleman sniffs at the way Rice eats, drinks, sings, borrows money and clothes, carries on at concerts, and reports events in the *Union*. Once, when the Unreliable falls ill, the Gentleman as the true patron of the needy sends him a coffin.

When he left Virginia City in May 1864, Twain carried the pose of the Gentleman along with him as an important part of his arsenal of comic devices. In the San Francisco years just following, he used it most successfully in the piece that not only boosted his reputation in the West but started it in the East, "The Notorious Jumping Frog of Calaveras County." The patronizing attitude and the formal narrative style of the Gentleman narrator in "The Jumping Frog" are almost too familiar to need repetition: "I have a lurking suspicion that *Leonidas W.* Smiley is a myth; that my friend never knew such a personage; and that he only conjectured that if I asked old Wheeler about him, it would remind him of his infamous *Jim* Smiley, and he would go to work and bore me to death with some exasperating reminiscence of him as long and as tedious as it should be useless to me."[4]

In subsequent travel letters to the Sacramento *Union* from Hawaii, and to the *Alta California* from Nicaragua, New York, Europe, and the Holy Land, Twain made the role even sillier. Possibly in imitation of currently popular English as well as American travel-burlesques, he posed in these letters as the Gentleman chiefly when reporting his altercations with Mr. Brown, his fictional companion.[5] Having made Brown a thorough vulgarian, Twain extracted as much comic contrast as he could from the scenes with Brown by making himself a thorough stuffed shirt. In one letter from Hawaii, for instance, Brown suggests a change in what "Mark

Twain" is writing and is rebuked thus: "Brown, that is the first charitable sentiment I have ever heard you utter. At a proper moment I will confer upon you a fitting reward for it. But for the present, good-night, son. Go, now. Go to your innocent slumbers. And wash your feet, Brown—or perhaps it is your teeth—at any rate you are unusually offensive this evening. Remedy the matter. Never mind explaining—good-night."[6] In other letters Twain as the Gentleman patronizes Brown for his inability to stay on a donkey, for becoming seasick, for substituting "pheasant" for "peasant," and for mistaking water-closet signs for signs designating the names of French railway stations. When Twain dropped Brown in revising the *Alta* letters for *Innocents Abroad*, he dropped the pose of the Gentleman, and seldom used it thereafter. It was the kind of pose that lent itself to buffoonery but not to more subtle comic effects.

Another pose of superiority confined largely to the early work was that of the Sentimentalist. In this pose Twain pretended to a sensitivity, often an elation, denied to more cloddish mortals. As the Sentimentalist he viewed life as a sequence of such exquisitely moving experience that it could be communicated only in the most rhapsodical terms. The comic possibilities of acting in such fashion seem to have occurred to Twain most forcefully after he created Mr. Brown, for it was not until he did so that he began to exploit the role extensively. Usually he assumed the pose in order to give Brown a chance to demolish it. Thus when Twain as Sentimentalist grows lyrical about the sights and sounds of Honolulu, Brown reminds him of its scorpions and "santipedes" and mosquitoes.[7] When in a fine poetic frenzy he reads his own version of "Polonius' Advice to His Son," Brown vomits.[8] And when he waxes ecstatic over Nicaraguan girls ("such liquid, languishing eyes! such pouting lips! such glossy, luxuriant hair! such ravishing, incendiary expression!") Brown brings him to earth with, "But you just prospect one of them heifers with a fine-tooth"—[9]

Interestingly, the exclusion of Brown from *Innocents Abroad* did not eliminate the pose of the Sentimentalist as it did the pose of the Gentleman. On the contrary, there is more of the Sentimentalist in the book than in the original letters. The most frequently quoted example, possibly, occurs where Twain adopts the pose of the Sentimentalist to lampoon the mawkish treatment of the Holy Land to be found in other travel books. At the tomb of Adam his filial affection is "stirred to its profoundest depths." He leans upon an altar and bursts into tears. "I deem it no shame to have wept over the grave of my poor dead relative. Let him who would sneer at my emotion close this volume here, for he will find little to his taste in my journeyings through Holy Land. Noble old man—he did not live to see me—he did not live to see his child. And I—I—alas, I did not live to see *him*" (*Works*, II, 307). Toned down somewhat, the pose of the Sentimentalist is observable in *Roughing It* where Twain's eyes secrete "generous moisture" for Mormon women, and in later works such as "A Burlesque Biography" and "A Wonderful Pair of

Slippers." But in these the sentimentality is not pushed so close to lunacy. It was only during the eighteen-sixties that Twain substantially exploited the giddier possibilities of the role.

A pose of superiority that Twain never completely discarded was that of the Instructor, the experienced person anxious to be of help to his less knowing readers. The motive of the Instructor Twain himself sets forth at the beginning of his little essay on "Curing a Cold":

> It is a good thing, perhaps, to write for the amusement of the public, but it is a far higher and nobler thing to write for their instruction, their profit, their actual and tangible benefit. The latter is the sole object of this article. If it prove the means of restoring to health one solitary sufferer among my race, of lighting up once more the fire of hope and joy in his faded eyes, or bringing back to his dead heart again the quick, generous impulses of other days, I shall be amply rewarded for my labor; my soul will be permeated with the sacred delight a Christian feels when he has done a good, unselfish deed. (*Works*, VII, 363)

With similar high resolve Twain informed his readers about the habits of the Siamese twins (aged fifty-one and fifty-three), provided them with hints about the raising of poultry, and showed them (with illustrations) how through practicing from three to seven hours a day any one of them could become as fine an artist as he. Twain soon discovered that the Instructor was a "natural" for his travel accounts with the result that no travel book is without several instances of the pose. Sometimes the explanation of the Instructor appears as a setpiece, such as the retelling of a European legend or the disquisition at the end of *A Tramp Abroad* on "The Awful German Language." More frequently it is simply a paragraph or two slipped without warning into the middle of a passage of straight travel reporting. The lead-in may be perfectly sensible: "It may interest the reader to know how they 'put horses to' on the continent" (*Works*, X, 19). But the explanations themselves show a wild over-eagerness to be helpful. The details become absurd, the time sequence confused, and the language vague or inappropriate. Later humorists like Benchley and Perelman may have exploited the role of the Instructor more fully than Twain, but none of them has extracted from it such boisterous idiocy.

Of all of Twain's poses of superiority, that of the Moralist is the most common—and the most complicated. Twain's pose of moralism may be distinguished from his sincere expression of moral indignation by the contrived details, the exaggeration or falsification of feeling, the inappropriateness of tone. What is especially interesting about this pose, however, is that Twain uses it for such variant purposes and with such diverse effects. Sometimes, for instance, he adopts the pose simply to appear coy; he pretends to be shocked when he is not really shocked at all. There is little reason to suppose that he did not enjoy girlie shows as much as the bulk of his male readers did. Yet in his letters to the Sacramento *Union* and to the *Alta* he pretends like a prim Victorian to be repelled by such goings-on as the Hawaiian hula and the lavish New York production of "The Black Crook." In *Innocents Abroad* he reports that at a performance of the can-can in the Paris suburb of Asnières he placed his hands before his eyes "for very shame." But then, giving the game away, he adds that he looked through his fingers (*Works*, I, 130). In somewhat more serious vein he uses the pose of the Moralist to make fun of such things as moralism itself. The very titles indicate this intent in "Advice to Little Girls" and "Some Learned Fables, For Good Old Boys and Girls" (*Works*, XXIV, 305–306; VII, 137–167). Loftily in "Aurelia's Unfortunate Young Man" he advises Aurelia Maria to marry her intended, even though the lad has successively lost his smooth complexion, one leg, both arms, an eye, the other leg, and his scalp. "We must," Twain abjures her, "do the best we can under the circumstances" (*Works*, VII, 309). Much more seriously—and somewhat more grotesquely—he uses the silly pose of the Moralist to mount an attack on such serious evils as the treatment of the Chinese in San Francisco, the insanity plea in murder charges, and the lynching of Negroes in the South. In "The United States of Lyncherdom," for example, with shock tactics worthy of Swift he implores the American missionaries to come home and go to work in the South, asking them whether they have anything so appetizing in China as a Texas lynching. "O kind missionary," he pleads, "O compassionate missionary, leave China! come home and convert these Christians!" (*Works*, XXIX, 249). In such a passage Twain uses the pose to mask outrage instead of delight, and the pose becomes the instrument of satire instead of farce. But it is the pose of the Moralist nonetheless, and the style of writing exhibits the same exclamatory and histrionic quality it possesses in the description of the can-can.

II

Although there are humor and variety in Twain's poses of superiority he never manages to achieve with them the sharply conceived characterizations he creates with his poses of inferiority. Like so many humorists, he is at his best when portraying himself as the butt, the person of inexperience in an alien and malevolent world. As the butt, his three most common poses are those of the Sufferer, the Simpleton, and the Tenderfoot. Of these, the pose of the Sufferer is easily the most farcical.

Unlike Benchley and Thurber in their roles of the little man in an alien world, Twain as Sufferer endures travail that is more the result of the machinations of others than of his own confusion or ineptness. Then, too, his woes are more physical than psychological. Most of the situations he gets into are the hackneyed ones: riding a bony mule, bathing without soap, eating nauseating native food, being cheated by clever merchants, falling over chairs in the dark, having to listen to amateur musicians, being victimized by heartless chambermaids. Some of the situations, however, are more novel. At Steamboat Springs, Nevada, Twain is given a "Wake-up Jake" which has him retching and bleeding at the nose for forty-eight hours; at Niagara he is thrown over the Falls by a band of resentful Irish Indians and almost drowns because the only person in a position to rescue him is unhappily the local coroner on the prowl for business; in Tennessee as a new writer for the *Morning Glory and Johnson County War Whoop* he is stoned, shot, cow-hided, thrown out of the window, and scalped.[10]

When set upon, Twain's Sufferer usually reacts in one of two dramatically different ways. Either he becomes paranoid or he becomes unbelievably stoical. When paranoid, he is sure that he is being deliberately tortured or swindled. The torturers become "imposters" or "villains" or "assassins," and the Sufferer longs to get even. Sometimes he does, too, as in the instance of the seventh incompetent watchmaker to whom Twain in "My Watch" takes his timepiece for repairs. This one, a former steamboat engineer, advises Twain that his watch "makes too much steam—you want to hang the monkey-wrench on the safety-valve!" This is too much for the Sufferer. He brains the watchmaker on the spot, and has him buried at his own expense (*Works*, VII, 5). On other occasions, however, the Sufferer reacts with almost formal dignity. In *Innocents Abroad*, for instance, he remains calm and composed even while being vilely "polished" by the attendant in a Turkish bath. "I soon saw that he was reducing my size. He bore hard on his mitten, and from under it rolled little cylinders, like macaroni. It could not be dirt, for it was too white. He pared me down in this way for a long time. Finally I said: 'It is a tedious process. It will take hours to trim me to the size you want me; I will wait; go and borrow a jack-plane' " (*Works*, II, 90–91).

The Sufferer is easily the most farcical of Twain's comic roles. The results of the pose can be seen in the ludicrous situations, the wildly exaggerated imagery, the disproportionate reactions of the narrator, the tone of grossly injured innocence, and the gaudily pictorial style. In no other role did Twain so fully exploit the Western penchant for exaggeration. It is not surprising, therefore, to discover that he employed the pose most frequently during his Western years and the decade and a half just following. In all its pristine rowdiness the Sufferer appeared as late as 1879 in *A Tramp Abroad*. Thereafter, however, Twain turned to the role less and less frequently though he never finally rejected it.

In the Simpleton Twain created a role in which his main trouble was mental rather than physical. As Simpleton he pretends to believe the impossible—or at least the outrageously improbable. What is more, he pretends to be anxious that his readers believe it too. The result is an earnest and solemn style quite in conflict with the silly evidence and the absurd logic. Probably the most famous example of Twain as Simpleton is in *Innocents Abroad* where he tells about visiting the tomb of Adam and the column there marking the center of the earth. It *is* the center of the earth, the Simpleton solemnly assures us, because among other reasons it was from under this very column that the dust was taken from which Adam was made. "This can surely be regarded in the light of a settler. It is not likely that the original first man would have been made from an inferior quality of earth when it was entirely convenient to get first quality from the world's center. This will strike any reflecting mind forcibly. That Adam was formed of dirt procured in this very spot is amply proven by the fact that in six thousand years no man has ever been able to prove that the dirt was *not* procured here whereof he was made" (*Works*, II, 306). In the same straight-faced fashion the Simpleton in *Roughing It* passes along various whoppers about Brigham Young, such as the one that for reason of economy he had to sell seventy-two bedsteads for his wives at a loss and substitute a communal contraption seven feet long and ninety-six feet wide. At other points in the book he tells of a Mr. Harris riding by "with a polite nod, homeward bound, with a bullet through one of his lungs, and several through his hips"; of Washoe winds that blow the hair off of the heads of Carson residents while they are looking skyward for their hats; of a former high chief of Honaunau who was fourteen or fifteen feet tall and who carried a coffin-shaped stone weighing several thousand pounds a considerable distance because he wanted to use it for a lounge.[11]

Despite the appealing idiocy of the Simpleton, it was with the Tenderfoot that Twain created his most effective and most memorable comic pose. The Simpleton is a manufacture: an adult imbecile created for the purpose of comedy and satire. The Tenderfoot comes more out of real experience. As Twain develops the point of view, it is that of the greenest of greenhorns, a youth certainly more stupid than Twain actually was, and probably more lovable. Eventually, of course, the pose of the Tenderfoot is the one that gets transmuted into the greatest of his narrative personae, Huck Finn. But as a pose its most interesting treatments can be found in *Roughing It*, the cub pilot chapters in *Life on the Mississippi*, and in "A Private History of a Campaign That Failed."

In the travel letters and in *Innocents Abroad*, the Tenderfoot, like his other poses, is a pretense Twain adopts for the single incident and then quickly discards for his real viewpoint or another pose. In the first half of *Roughing It*, however, Twain uses the Tenderfoot pose consistently enough to make it a controlling element in the movement of the story. Although the pose is never a firm one, since it frequently slides off into another pose or into the point of view of the thirty-five year old author, it is nevertheless sustained well enough in the early parts of the book that, as Henry Nash Smith has already pointed out, a basic movement is perceptible from the point of view of the Tenderfoot to that of a knowing old-timer. "The narrative is not everywhere controlled by this theme, but the pattern of initiation is sufficiently clear in the first half of the book, to constitute an expressive structure."[12] Unfortunately for the total unity of *Roughing It*, this pattern disappears in the second half of the book, where in rewriting the Sandwich Island letters Twain once more becomes the quick-change artist, playing a whole repertoire of roles.

It is in "Old Times on the Mississippi" that Twain manipulates and sustains the role of the Tenderfoot successfully enough to make it a consistent and appealing characterization. Even here, though, the pose is not a firmly held one. Typically, what Twain does is to introduce each incident from his own viewpoint as an adult of about forty, then slide into the pose of the Tenderfoot in narrating an incident, and finally return to the viewpoint of the adult for comment on the incident. The pose, therefore, is not maintained throughout the work but is assumed and discarded so adroitly that one is hardly conscious of the change. Furthermore, its effects are not dissipated by resort to other and more raucous roles. As a matter of record, Twain was almost twenty-two when he apprenticed himself to Horace Bixby to learn the river from St. Louis to New Orleans, and he undoubtedly knew as much about the river as most beginning pilots. But he pretends in "Old Times" that he was not more than sixteen and that he was so green he did not know he had to stand a regular watch or memorize landmarks. From the beginning it is obvious that the pretense is one that Twain found congenial. When writing as the Tenderfoot he is at great pains to see his material as the greenhorn might. The results appear especially in the sharply pictorial detailing, the colorful rendering of river talk, and the combination of wonderment and anxiety—sometimes fear—in the Tenderfoot's attitude toward the river. Except for Huck Finn, no other point of view excites his sensibilities so richly.

> I even got to "setting" her and letting the wheel go entirely, while I vaingloriously turned my back and inspected the stern marks and hummed a tune, a sort of easy indifference which I had prodigiously admired in Bixby and other great pilots. Once I inspected rather long, and when I faced to the front again my heart flew into my mouth so suddenly that if I hadn't clapped my teeth together I should have lost it. One of those frightful bluff reefs was stretching its deadly length right across our bows! My head was gone in a moment; I did not know which end I stood on; I gasped and could not get my breath; I spun the wheel down with such rapidity that it wove itself together like a spider's web; the boat answered and turned square away from the reef, but the reef followed her! I fled, but still it followed, still it kept—right across my bows! I never looked to see where I was going, I only fled. The awful crash was imminent. Why didn't that villain come? If I committed the crime of ringing a bell I might get thrown overboard. But better that than kill the boat. So in blind desperation, I started such a rattling "shivaree" down below as never had astounded an engineer in this world before, I fancy. Amidst the frenzy of the bells the engines began to back and fill in a curious way, and my reason forsook its throne—we were about to crash into the woods on the other side of the river. Just then Mr. Bixby stepped calmly into view on

the hurricane-deck. My soul went out to him in gratitude. My distress vanished; I would have felt safe on the brink of Niagara with Mr. Bixby on the hurricane-deck.[13]

Whereas Twain adopted the pose of the Tenderfoot in these cub pilot sketches primarily for comic effect, it seems clear that something deeper motivated its use in "The Private History of a Campaign That Failed." Twain could hardly have been unaware of the criticism levelled at him by fellow Missourians for his failure to fight for the Confederacy. Certainly he could not have been unaware of it in the winter of 1884–85 when he visited St. Louis, Hannibal, and Keokuk, Iowa, on a lecture tour with George Washington Cable. Indeed an anonymous account of his war "experience" appeared in the Keokuk *Gate City* either while he was in Keokuk, or just after. Published in the *Century Magazine* of December 1885 "The Private History" therefore may properly be considered a reply to his critics and something of an apology. Ultimately his defense rests on the contention that he was young, green, and, in short, a Tenderfoot.

For his purposes, Twain's strategy in "The Private History" was extraordinarily astute. He could not have fully submitted to the pose of the Tenderfoot without making the sketch a farce; on the other hand, he could not have used only his adult point of view and gain the sympathy for his actions that he coveted. So he wisely combined the two points of view. On the surface, the "Private History" is the reminiscence of a fifty-year old man who is looking back upon experiences he had when he was presumably about sixteen (he was actually twenty-five). He calls himself and his companions in the Marion Rangers "boys" and he recalls indulgently how they played games, showed off, and scrapped among themselves. Yet as he maintains this adult point of view on the surface, he adds to it the point of view of the Tenderfoot by confronting the important material as the boy might. The sense of excitement is the Tenderfoot's; so are the resentment at the discipline, the increasing discouragement, and finally the panic when it becomes known that Union troops are approaching. Almost irresistibly, as Twain merges his mature point of view with that of the innocent Tenderfoot, the reader does so too—and finds himself empathizing with the boy and excusing him for all that he does. His antics become the buffoonery of a youngster rather than the irresponsibility of a grown man. The major struggle becomes not one of the Confederacy and the Union, but of boys pitted against men. When Twain as the Tenderfoot kills a stranger supposed to be a Union soldier (a piece of pure fiction) and subsequently retires from soldiership to save his self-respect, the "retirement" seems somehow admirable. A sensitive and idealistic boy is simply pulling out of a malignant conflict in which he does not belong. Huck Finn is once more "lighting out."

The Tenderfoot of "The Private History" is, in short, one of Twain's most subtle poses. He adopts it while seeming not to do so; he employs it for serious purpose while seeming to extract from it only the usual comedy. Without doubt, it is one of the best demonstrations of his dexterity in handling point of view.

III

Even so brief a sampling of Twain's poses suggests several conclusions. The first is that the pose offered him the kind of psychic support that he wanted and needed. Since he slips into a pose at least once in almost every "Mark Twain" work, it is clear that the pose was a device that Twain found agreeable. If it did nothing else, it gave him a chance to extend into his writing his penchant for acting. One suspects, however, that he found the pose agreeable for more profound reasons. Ridden by anxieties, Twain undoubtedly welcomed the pose because its restricted point of view simplified life and made it more tolerable. From the maze of conflicting ways of seeing and judging experience the pose isolated one. Even when he did not fully submit to its demands, the mask still tended to effect a point of view less complicated than his own. Furthermore, it pushed life to a distance and made it less disturbing. Without the pose, Twain had to confront the human scene immediately and directly. And being the kind of man he was, his emotions almost inevitably became excessively engaged. What he found to his liking he sentimentalized about; what frustrated him he raged at. With the pose inserted between himself and the human scene, however, Twain could be more equable, for in effect his position became that of a spectator rather than that of a participant. In addition, since his poses were chiefly comic ones, the scene itself became not only more distant but less ominous. How profoundly the pose served Twain as a psychic prop is, of course, a matter of speculation. But one cannot help observing that for a person of Twain's temperament, it seemed to offer the ideal therapy: simplification, detachment, minimization.

Whatever question there may be about the pose's psychic aid to Twain, there can be little or none about its aesthetic usefulness. While tending to set bounds for the operation of his imagination, the pose stimulated its operation within those bounds. It is the nature of the pose to break up old habits of perception by introducing fresh or at least different ones. What results is not a new vision but a dual vision. In effect, two consciousnesses are at work, that of the pose and that of the author. The pose consciousness disciplines the imagination; the interplay between the pose consciousness and the author consciousness energizes it. When Twain contemplated Mississippi valley life simply as the adult author, as he did in much of the latter part of *Life on the Mississippi*, he wrote in what can only be called a pedestrian fashion. But when he imposed upon this adult point of view the consciousness of a sixteen-year-old boy, as he did in writing the cub pilot chapters, the perceptions became more acute, the situations more ingeniously contrived, and the style more richly dramatic. One is tempted to go further, especially with the travel accounts, and assert as a general truth that Twain's "posed" writing, taken as a whole, shows greater ingenuity and often greater sensibility than his straight writing.

The principal effects of the pose on Twain's humor are apparent in the humor's variety, continuousness, and economy. The variety is self-evident. When added to his narrative personae like Huck Finn and Hank Morgan, his repertoire of poses gives him a range in comic viewpoint that few other humorists—if any—have enjoyed. In the individual work, the pose, so long as he was willing to hold it, enabled him to sustain his humor by providing a second self-consistent system of thought continuously juxtaposed and at odds with the normal. So long as Twain poses as the Simpleton, for example, the thought processes and values of the Simpleton are in continuing though implicit conflict with the more sophisticated processes and values of Twain himself—and of the reader. Instead of the final and all-destroying flash that comes with the capper on a joke, the pose results in a persisting sense of incongruity. The joke, so to speak, never ends so long as the pose is retained. Furthermore, since the pose creates this conflict in thought processes and values implicitly, it encourages economy in statement. By the rules of the game, the pose barred Twain—or at least discouraged him—from injecting the personal interpretation and fulmination that so often made his "unposed" writing tedious. Instead, he was encouraged by the pose to concentrate upon his narrative. One of the reasons why "The Jumping Frog" is a superior work is that, controlled by the pose, Twain forgot himself and focused steadily upon the comic possibilities of his material. Every statement is a rendering of one of these possibilities. There is no waste, no gratuitous authorial underlining.

Similarly, the pose encouraged Twain to make his satire implicit and hence more economical in statement. Confronting his targets directly, Twain tended to belabor them unnecessarily, often resorting to a heated sarcasm that called more attention to itself than its subject. But with the pose he could point up the foibles and evils that offended him simply by observing them through the eyes of one of his comic constructs. As reported by the gullible Simpleton, for example, the cupidity of those in charge of the Church of the Holy Sepulchre becomes humorously and yet depressingly apparent in *Innocents Abroad* without any editorial comment from Twain.

Yet for all that Twain achieved with the comic pose, it cannot be said that he substantially exploited its finest aesthetic possibilities. For one thing, he did not consistently take advantage of its capacity, just described, for sustaining the humor or satire and for achieving economy of statement. Too often his adoption of a pose was so casual and so brief that it exerted almost no control over the narration. For another thing,

Mark Twain and Charlie Chaplin as Heroes of Popular Culture

Glauco Cambon*

If Mark Twain had survived by just a few years the reappearance of Halley's comet, he would have seen the beginnings of Charlie Chaplin's comet-like career through the American galaxy of Hollywood; and it is easy to conjecture that the author of *A Tramp Abroad, Tom Sawyer* and *The Gilded Age* would have cheered the antics of Chaplin's *Pilgrim*. At the risk of incurring imaginary biography, that nasty temptation of biographers, I will say that I cannot conceive of a Samuel Langhorne Clemens who, given a new lease of life, had proved unresponsive to films like *Gold Rush, The Kid, City Lights.* . . . And since, metaphorically speaking, the news of his death remains "greatly exaggerated", my anachronistic fancy has no great chance of being resented by serious scholars. Historically conscious but not time-bound, the curious mind keeps arranging improbable parties where, for example, Charlie Chaplin can finally meet Twain or listen to one of his lectures with the delight that our great-grandparents knew and for which Hal Holbrook has given us posthumous generations the best available substitute. I haven't done any research into this particular matter, but it seems safe to guess that Chaplin knows and likes his Twain.

Should this ever prove untrue, it wouldn't make the slightest difference to me, for my purpose in bringing the two artists into the same context is to show certain fundamental affinities between them as popular mythmakers. Both reached the largest audience an artist can hope to get, without sacrificing their standards. Leslie Fiedler has sociologically defined Faulkner "the highbrow's lowbrow", but of our two chosen worthies it can be said that they are "the lowbrow's highbrows" as well. Twain's popularity was not of the meretricious kind, and popularity failed to corrupt Chaplin, who in his pig-headed way (whatever the merits of the case) preferred ostracism to obeisance. A distinction must be drawn between the former's closeness to agrarian folklore (Southern, Negro and Western) and the latter's use of a commercial mass-medium like the movies to dramatize the hopeless anonymity of modern city-man; though that distinction itself will have to be qualified when we realize

*Reprinted from *Minnesota Review*, 3 (Fall, 1962), 77–82, with the permission of the author.

how the practice of journalism, that king of the mass-media, concurred with folk-speech to shape Twain's art, while Chaplin, in focusing his camera-eye on the uprooted masses of the industrial age, discovered whatever "folklore" they could be said to harbor at the potential or residual stage. He could do that because, stark realist as he was and is, he never suppressed his sense of fable, something to which the disinherited will always respond. Russian critics, anthologized by Sergei Eisenstein in what is perhaps the most impressive tribute to Chaplin's genius, predictably emphasized the social criticism that operates in his screen-fables, but they did so without pedantry, and they brought out the Shakespearian affinities of our new-fangled clown. And there is no need to point out how warmly received Mark Twain is in Soviet Russia. I doubt this can be reduced to a matter of propaganda distortion. Whatever the dogmatic interpretations to which the American writer and the London-born moviemaker may be amenable, it is their secret commerce with Queen Mab that endears them both to so many people across so many boundaries.

Her whispered counsels have certainly inspired Chaplin to become a redeemer of vulgarity rather than artistically succumb to "mass culture." That mass culture need not be kitsch has become increasingly hard to believe since the era of the dime novels, of the slick movies and of doctored advertising; Chaplin has made that belief possible with his single-handed accomplishment as actor, scenarist, director and producer. Other users of the mass media for entertainment purposes have evaded the clichés of mass culture to shroud their artistic purity in sophistication; he instead faced them from the start and reconverted them into artistic assets. One readily thinks of Poe's, Dostoevsky's or Chesterton's use of the detective story, and, to be sure, of Twain's reliance on certain dime-novel narrative devices.

The main point of comparison between him and the screen actor who has indelibly colored the Twenties in the filmy perspective of nostalgia is their successful dramatization of the Tramp as mythical figure. As such, "Charlot" acquired a life of his own beyond the limits of each plot, to dominate a screen saga that did an awful lot to keep the imagination alive in the urban masses all over the globe, so much so that we must count it as one of the humanizing forces at work in our Brave New World. Charlot, the popular mask, became more real than Chaplin himself, and when Chaplin dropped this mask for other impersonations in his postwar movies, it came as a shock of historical recognition: the times had changed indeed! Something of the kind happened to Mark Twain, who kept up his public *persona* of the "tramp abroad," with a touch of Tom Sawyer and Huck Finn, as a world-acclaimed lecturer. And certainly, both Twain's and Chaplin's late productions are attempts to get behind their respective mythical masks, to converse with them, to explain or transform them . . . whatever the results. There is no doubt, anyway, that Charlot's pantomime and Huck's fluvial monologue reflect the unfailing theatrical instinct of their creators.

In pointing out the kinship between these two signal embodiments of the Tramp myth I do not lose sight of their differences; but the latter can be taken for granted once we admit the artistic individuality of each creation. Achieved uniqueness—the success of art—still leaves room for significant comparison. Charlot is an adult moving around in a crowded urban world, while Huck is a frontier boy ranging the exhilarating spaces of the Mississippi and surrounding area; but Huck's brushes with the shore settlements' folks clearly anticipate Charlot's pathetic entanglements with his city milieu, and Charlot had his fling with the American romance of the promising wilderness in *Gold Rush*. Moreover, Charlot is a very childlike adult, and Huck is a child who has to shift for himself, the only adult he can trust and accept being Nigger Jim—the member of a primitive race that seeks emancipation. Jim and Huck have become one of the archetypal pairs of world literature (for broader reasons than Leslie Fiedler seems to admit) much in the same way as Charlie Chaplin and Jackie Coogan came to establish their linked images in the popular mind, through a more ephemeral medium.

Both pairs, in fact, represent homeless innocence in a brutal or at best stuffy world. Their intuitively grasped paradox is that, fleeing away from established society or trying to survive as aliens in its heartless midst, they set up a numerically and financially minimal society of their own in which love and not law sanctions any ties. The association is consequently precarious, despite its emotional value, and in neither case does it exhaust the imaginative dimensions of the Tramp, who keeps leaving experience, persons and towns behind. The classical ending of many a Chaplin movie in the Charlot cycle, featuring the unforgettable flatfoot in baggy pants, derby hat and pliant cane that plods away towards disappearance on the open road, may recall *Huckleberry Finn*'s conclusion with the announced plan to "light out for the West."

Whether alone or in congenial company, the Tramp must rely on his cunning to escape the many traps of the Establishment (or, in some cases, of the Bad-Guy tramps, like the murderous gold-seeker in *Gold Rush*, and the river pirates, the Duke and the Dauphin, or Pap himself, in Twain's novel). This cunning, being very elemental (like that of children, animals, savages and peasants), fits in with the endearing attributes of goodness, generosity, innocence and wonderment that go into the making of Huck's and Charlot's images as naive heroes. They are both imaginative tricksters, and they had better be, in a world "they never made" . . . . Huck's disguises and lies are of a piece with Charlot's hilarious improvisations when he finds himself in a tight spot; their occasional lawlessness, inherent in the type, is likewise of the comical rather than of the sinister kind: Charlot the itinerant glazier sending his Kid around to break win-

dowpanes so he can stay in business reminds me of Huck when he con-
fesses to "lifting" a chicken that "was roosting uncomfortable."

Laughter has often been a vehicle for social critique, and the comical
note Twain and Chaplin strike can go very far in that direction, though
satire is only one of its aspects, for Huck's verbal mimicry, conveyed
through the rhythms of a colorful dialect, is delightful comedy for its own
sake, too, like Chaplin's ballet-steps and facial mobility. Besides, their
social commentary, when it does not become too explicit (as it often does
in the late work of both), acts just as well in the guise of pathos or tragi-
comedy. The strike scene in *Modern Times*, with its climactic resolution
—the dead man left alone in the deserted street after police have dispersed
the rioters—reminds me somehow of the Grangerford-Shepherdson feud
in Twain's story, particularly on account of its poignant ending: a
bewildered Huck Finn taking leave of his murdered friend Buck. Aimed
as they are at illustrating the urgency of the Depression crisis and, respectively, the tragic absurdity of Southern feudal mores, the two episodes
make their point without preaching, and the result that much more effective. Their "message" is one and the same thing with their poetry.

Tragic pathos and rollicking fun thus constitute the two extremes
between which Mark Twain's and Charlie Chaplin's art moves, with a
marked tendency of the latter extreme to prevail; and in between there
are the intermediate notes of elegy, lyricism, love poetry, which assert
themselves very strongly, for instance, in Chaplin's postwar movie
Limelight. The lyrical breath of Huck's description of a Mississippi dawn
at the beginning of Chapter XIX, or of the Phelps farm in Chapter XXII,
is an unsurpassed feat of literary style which Chaplin never tries to rival
because, unlike Twain, he is interested in man to the exclusion of nature;
but when Huck tries to help Mary Jane and then says goodbye to her for
good, Charlot's clumsy chivalry to his harried blonde heroines comes
to mind.

Being of the naive kind, Chaplin's imagination, like Twain's, is
prone to sentimentality on the one hand and farce on the other. Chaplin's
farce, however, is always redeemed by his virtuoso pantomime, and it
does not spoil our pleasure, aesthetically speaking, because the natural
focus of attention in his case is the character, Charlot as mythical figure,
not the plot or the total structure of one movie in which he appears.
Therefore, if I relate Tom, Huck and Jim in their ludicrous finale to
Charlot's gags, it is only to emphasize certain temperamental affinities between the two humorists, for aesthetic performance is another matter.
Chaplin's vaudeville is no breach of style, while Twain's concession to farcical minstrel-show stereotype mars the otherwise impressive achievement
of a book that can recapture in its *naive Dichtung* the freshness of Homer
and the depth of Cervantes. Homer did have a place for slapstick in his
epic, but he took care not to let Thersites have the last word.

These formal flaws, for all we know, may even have aided Twain's masterpiece to gain its enormous popularity, and to that extent we can forgive them, thinking of the poetry they have smuggled into so many crude minds. Reliance on popular stereotypes isn't always treacherous, though, as Chaplin's repertory of utterly simple fables shows. His Tramp is always having trouble with the representatives of authority and power: the cop, the rich man, and the rich man's clientele. These are frankly popular clichés, but since everything in a Chaplin movie revolves around Charlot, they aren't obtrusive at all; besides, the fairytale atmosphere makes them acceptable as King, Princess, Ogre, Witch and Gnome are in a Grimm story. Charlot's comico-sentimental impersonation of the Blue Prince to a sighing Princess of the slums, Charlot's self-angelization in the surreal escape-dream of *The Kid*, and Charlot's difficult but finally successful treasure-hunt in *Gold Rush* are all deeply rooted motifs of the popular imagination, to be found in so many pre-industrial folktales, and in interpreting them for the modern masses Chaplin instinctively knew he increased his own art's chances of success.

Twain's authority symbols—Aunt Sally, Miss Watson, the Widow Douglas, Judge Thatcher, the perverted Pap—are less stereotypical, but the basic attitude is the same; and he too uses the treasure-hunt motif to give scope to his young heroes' adventures. In defining Twain's and Chaplin's art as "naive" I have in mind two different but related meanings, i.e., Schiller's conception of spontaneous art, having the traits of wholeness and immediacy, and the more current use of the word to denote candor or crudity. Candor certainly radiates from everything our two artists do, and it explains their popular appeal along with their occasional lapses. It was a candid mind which could set the sentimentalized child-savior story of *Saint Joan* above the matchless impishness of *Huckleberry Finn*; it is a naive mind which has abruptly broken the unity of an initially promising film like *A King in New York* to employ a little child (Chaplin's own son) as a solemnly vociferous mouth-piece of the author's heartfelt pacifist beliefs.

The myth of the Tramp, which writer and actor have brought to life in their different media, is itself a naive archetype of romantic ancestry, having in its blood the genes of Wordsworth's Wanderer (and Seer Child), of Blake's Innocent, of Scott's Outlaw-Knight, of Rousseau's Natural Man & Noble Savage. The anarchic dream expresses the recurrent longing of society for regeneration, along with the protest of the disinherited against entrenched privilege; but Twain's and Chaplin's naive idyll has nothing in it of the mystique which characterizes the primitivism of a Lawrence, a Faulkner, a Hamsun. Hart Crane, in a partly great poem, identified Charlot with Parsifal, and something of the Pure Fool forever seeking the unattainable Grail of happiness, love and goodness is to be sensed in Chaplin's filmic creature as well as in Twain's imaginary child.

Chaplin's radical ideas parallel Twain's social protest, but I don't know that the tireless moviemaker now living in Switzerland would be at home in a totalitarian Communist society, or meet with tolerance there. His is the naive yearning for a utopia of pure goodness, and the shattering blows this undying dream of man received in our century finally found their repercussion in the dark disenchantment of *Monsieur Verdoux*, Chaplin's first postwar movie in which the fable of Bluebeard serves to bring home the problem of evil as one our tainted society cannot face or solve. "What is evil?" Verdoux ask his judges in the gripping final scene, on his way to execution; and the question, indeed the whole tone of the movie seems to echo Mark Twain's Satan in *The Mysterious Stranger*, which could be called Twain's *Monsieur Verdoux*.

Our two pilgrims' progress from humor to disenchantment and horror is similar, and testifies to their basically naive thinking. In an age which exposes the masses to endless manipulation through political or commercial propaganda their work seems to fulfill, by aesthetically handling a central myth in the language everybody can understand, a countervailing function. As long as there are artists like these around, we have some hope to fight the brutality and stultification which assault us from every side. They have helped the uprooted man of megalopolis to retain or achieve a visage, an identity, a human consciousness. They have done this by collaborating with Queen Mab, Puck, and Ariel, whom they have smuggled back into our midst from where they seemed forever exiled. Charlot's assembly-line ballet in *Modern Times*, besides providing the unifying formal rhythm to his fable, gave us a cry of alarm we cannot easily forget. Since I don't believe in writing or doing anything "impersonal," I shall conclude by saying that my viewing the Charlot movies as a war-tried adult in the last few years detracted nothing from the spell they cast on me in the late Twenties, when I first watched them, eagerly waiting for the luminous message from the screen as a child "sitting in darkness."

Mark Twain and Sholem Aleichem

Edward Field*

Mark Twain and Sholem Aleichem went one day to Coney Island—
Mark wearing a prison-striped bathing costume and straw hat,
Sholem in greenish-black suit, starched collar, beard,
Steelrimmed schoolmaster glasses, the whole works,
And an umbrella that he flourished like an actor
Using it sometimes to hurry along the cows
As he described scenes of childhood in the village in Poland,
Or to spear a Jew on a sword like a cossack.

Sitting together on the sand among food wrappers and lost coins,
They went through that famous dialogue
Like the vaudeville routine, After-you-Gaston:
"They tell me you are called the Yiddish Mark Twain."
"Nu? The way I heard it you are the American Sholem Aleichem."
And in this way passed a pleasant day admiring each other,
The voice of the old world and the voice of the new.

"Shall we risk the parachute jump, Sholem?"
"Well, Markele, am I properly dressed for it?
Better we should go in the water a little maybe?"
So Sholem Aleichem took off shoes and socks (with holes—a shame),
Rolled up stiff-serge pants showing his varicose veins;
And Mark Twain, his bathing suit moth-eaten and gaping
In important places, lit up a big cigar,
And put on a pair of waterwings like an angel.

The two great writers went down where the poor
Were playing at the water's edge
Like a sewer full of garbage, warm as piss.
Around them shapeless mothers and brutal fathers

*Reprinted from *Stand Up Friend, with Me,* by Edward Field (New York: Grove Press, 1963), by permission of Grove Press, Inc. Copyright by Edward Field.

Were giving yellow, brown, white, and black children
Lessons in life that the ignorant are specially qualified to give:
Slaps and scoldings, mixed with food and kisses.

Mark Twain, impetuous goy, dived right in,
And who could resist splashing a little the good-natured Jew?
Pretty soon they were both floundering in the sea
The serge suit ruined that a loving daughter darned and pressed,
The straw hat floating off on the proletarian waters.

They had both spent their lives trying to make the world a better place
And both had gently faced their failure.
If humor and love had failed, what next?
They were both drowning and enjoying it now,
Two old men of the two worlds, the old and the new,
Splashing about in the sea like crazy monks.

Mark Twain, Mencken, and "The Higher Goofyism"

C. Merton Babcock*

Beneath the velvet paw of Mark Twain's amiable humor lurks a cruel fang which on occasion turns heart-warming hilarity into rage. H. L. Mencken's raillery, too, is like the cracking of a whip. Both writers belong to the cantankerous school of American humor, or what Max Eastman has called "the higher goofyism." While there are wide differences in their manner, their aims and purposes were much the same: to strip man of his pretentious robes, his fig leaves, his good conduct medals; to prick his iridescent bubbles of arrogance and pomposity; to puncture his cherished illusions; to hold a loony mirror up to his miserable nature so he can see himself in all his ungainliness.

Judging from the public images created by the two men, one would suppose they belong in quite different leagues. The "wild humorist of the Pacific Slope," on the one hand, radiated warmth and cordiality, despite his rancor and deep-seated bitterness. He possessed a rare knack for making people laugh at themselves: their ridiculous shortcomings and preposterous inconsistencies. When the famous American stepped forward to receive his degree at Oxford University, the Chancellor paid him reverential tribute. "Most amiable and charming sir," he said, "you shake the sides of the whole world with merriment."

The "Sage of Baltimore," on the other hand, posed as "a gay fellow who heaves dead cats into sanctuaries and then goes roistering down the highways of the world." He gained notoriety as a peddler of blasphemy and special agent for the powers of darkness, and his volcanic eruption, during the boisterous years, created a popular image of the man whom Malcom Moos has described as "a dragon slayer poised with a cutlass in one hand and a three-ton blockbuster in the other." Whereas most of Mark Twain's subscribers might willingly have traveled many miles to meet him, Mencken's readers coveted an opportunity to wash his filthy mouth with laundry soap, and they prayed fervently for his demise and damnation.

*Reprinted with permission from *American Quarterly*, 16 (Winter, 1964), 587–94. Copyright 1964, by the Trustees of the University of Pennsylvania.

The differences in the humor of the two men were largely matters of tactics and of timing. Mark Twain usually fooled along, measuring his pauses, slurring his points, stringing incongruities and absurdities together in seemingly purposeless fashion, deriving pleasure from sheer elaboration of detail, camouflaging his deviltry under heaps of tangled verbiage and rhetorical debris. In his piece on "Corn-pone Opinions," for example, he chatted along casually on the subject of American conformity and then dropped this innocent remark armed with a double stinger: "If Eve should come again in her ripe renown and re-introduce her quaint styles, well, we know what would happen." At the end of chapter 39 of *Huckleberry Finn*, in the note signed "Unknown Friend," Mark Twain planted a semantic trap of uncanny ingenuity and covered it up with a misplaced modifier. "I am one of the gang," the note reads, "but have got religgion, and wish to quit it and lead a honest life again, and will betray the helish design."

Such verbal prestidigitation was not in the Mencken manner. Mencken was brief, vivid, villainous. He derived a kind of sadistic delight in burning the witch-burners. Twain used a hangman's rope, in true frontier fashion, and spent a good deal of time preparing the fatal noose. Mencken preferred a switchblade. "This is the United States, God's favorite country," he once wrote to Dreiser. "The fun of living here does not lie in playing chopping block to the sanctified, but in outraging them and getting away with it." Mencken adapted his weapon to the enemy and to the fight. Up to a point it is all laughter, but after that "there is the flash of the knife, a show of the teeth." "Sometimes I try to spoof them," he said, "and sometimes I use a club." His characteristic method was to stir up a witch's brew of high-potency prose with equal parts of incongruity and hyperbole and then use it to toast the simpletons. "No more democrat than a turkey buzzard is an archangel," he said of one politician. He could describe democracy with such outlandish figures as "the loading of a pair of palpably tin cannon with blank cartridges charged with talcum powder" or as "the science and art of running the circus from the monkey cage."

Whereas Mark Twain could take in the whole spectrum of humanity with a cryptic epithet like "the damned human race," Mencken was more specific and, therefore, more insultingly pernicious. He brought down his pigeons with such custom-tailored debunking appellatives as "chamber of commerce witch-hunter," "professional gladiator of prohibition," "upyanker of the downtrodden." William Jennings Bryan he called "the Fundamentalist Pope," and the Ku Klux Klan "Grand Order of the Facial Diaper."

Despite these and other recognizable differences, the two scribblers had much in common. Both were born with a high percentage of sawdust in their blood. Both were practical jokers. Both recognized the "thundering paradoxes" of American life and addressed themselves to the task of turning the sanctified idols into absurdities. In setting forth the essence of Mark Twain's humor, Mencken actually defined his own brand of mirth: "a capacity to discover hidden and surprising relations between apparently disparate things, to penetrate to the hollowness of common assumptions, and to invent novel and arresting turns of speech."[1] The kind of expression that clearly meets these requirements occurs in *Smart Set* and the *Prejudices* as well as in *Roughing It* and *Huckleberry Finn*. While many of Twain's incongruities are contained within the framework of extended yarns, he exhibited on occasion the imaginative vigor, which is Mencken's signature, that can compress a thought into sententious witticism or sparkling metaphor. For example, Mark Twain described a ride over a mountain pass as "spinning around the rings of a whirlwind—a drop of whisky descending the spirals of a corkscrew." Mencken might simply have compounded the absurdity by saying, "We went on all fours like snakes in the grass."

Both Twain and Mencken were adept at composing hymns of dispraise in what the latter called "the key of E flat minor." The Sage spoke of Vachel Lindsay's resounding meters as "Buddha chanting ragtime through a megaphone," "the Twentieth Century Express in a flower garden," "the doxology performed on a steam calliope," and "Billy Sunday and Bert Williams reciting the Beatitudes." Mark Twain berated Cooper's *Deerslayer* as "literary delirium tremens" and John Ruskin's highly-praised Victorian prose as "a cat having a fit in a platter of tomatoes."

Another trick in the repertoire of both humorists is that of taking incidental side-shots at religion and its promoters while aiming directly at other targets. Speaking of a novel by Henry James, Mark Twain said, "I would rather be damned to John Bunyan's heaven than read that." And Mencken, criticizing a Broadway comedian, said, "His work bears the same relation to acting properly so-called as that of a hangman, a midwife or a divorce lawyer bears to poetry, or that of a bishop to religion."

Whether he would admit it or not, Mencken, like the yarnspinner of Jackass Gulch, borrowed models of verbal extravagance for his diabolical purposes from the nineteenth-century frontier and from the ring-tailed roarers of even earlier periods. From Davy Crockett's "half-horse, half-alligator" menagerie, he found the materials for a "political colossus"—a demigod of Paul Bunyan proportions—which he called a *wowser*, and described as "half Bryan and half Billy Sunday, with flashing eyes, a voice of brass, and a heart as big as a wastebasket." *Homo boobiens*, one of his best-known grotesques, might have come out of the nonsensical catalogue of the natural history of the frontier: a kind of hopped-up Chanticleer "stalking the earth vaingloriously, flapping his wings over his god-given rights and his sublime equality to his masters." In deference to his "regal" position in the democratic scheme, Mencken dubbed him "Supreme Worthy Whimwham" and "Grand Exalted Pishposh."

Many of Mencken's caricatures have a barnyard aroma about them. His portrait of a delegate to a national convention, for example, looks like a scarecrow: "a tattered Bible on one shoulder and a new shiny beer seidel on the other." He pictured the New Deal administration as "a milch-cow with 125,000,000 teats," and the standard American citizen as "a high priest in a rustic temple, pouring out his heart's blood on the altar of Ceres, sleeping in his underwear, and dreaming of a Utopia designed from the glossy pages of a worn-out Sears Roebuck catalog." Mencken delighted in antagonizing his country cousins whom he called "the monarchs of the dunghill." His aversion for chicken coops, pig pens and cow pastures was matched only by his distaste for theological humbuggery which he equated with the muddleheadedness of clodhoppers. "What is the effect of making men good in the American sense?" he asked, and then supplied his own answer: "Kansas." "Who would not prefer the society of a few amiable kidnappers, yeggmen, and Follies girls?" he asked. While Mark Twain could crash a Boston tea party dressed as a cowpuncher, swinging a lariat and contaminating the poshy atmosphere with the crude lingo of the West, Mencken, posing as a city slicker, with the profane and lascivious accents of one slightly "splifflicated" on his tongue, could send prohibitionists, pedagogues and tinhorn politicians into what one writer has called "semi-incoherent fits of rage." Mark Twain made good use of every opportunity to insult "royalty." Mencken lavished his attention on the "boobs."

Perhaps this was the most remarkable difference between Twain and Mencken: that, whereas the former felt at home with the verbal patterns of unsophisticated people, the latter consistently depreciated the unintellectuality of homely idioms. Here are examples of their respective uses of the vernacular as a humorous device. In the first passage, Mark Twain is explaining how the Unabridged Dictionary made the popular reading list at Angel's Camp on the mining frontier. Books were scarce, and the cumbersome lexicon went "sashshaying around from shanty to shanty and from camp to camp":

> Dyer can hunt quail or play seven-up as well as any man, understand, but he can't pronounce worth a cuss; he used to worry along well enough, though, till he'd flush one of them rattlers with a clatter of syllables as long as a string of sluice-boxes, and then he'd lose his grip and throw up his hand; and so finally Dick Stoker harnessed her, up there at his cabin, and sweated over her and cussed her and rastled with her for as much as three weeks, night and day, till he got as far as R, and then passed her over to 'Lige Pickerell, and said she was the all-firedest dryest reading that ever *he* struck.

The second passage, from Mencken's translation of the Declaration of Independence into the patois of yokeldom, exhibits no such linguistic playfulness. On the contrary, it is an exercise in innuendo and carefully controlled mockery:

> When things get so balled up that the people of a country got to cut loose
> from some other country, and go it on their own hook, without asking no
> permission from nobody, excepting maybe God Almighty, then they
> ought to let everybody know why they done it, so that everybody can see
> they are not trying to put nothing over on nobody. . . .

At the other end of the lexical keyboard, the two writers disdained all
manner of grandiloquence. Characteristic of Mark Twain's irreverence
for pompous speech forms is his appraisal, in *Roughing It*, of the language
of the Mormon Bible as "an insipid mess of inspiration" and "chloroform
in print." Mencken tried his hand at the same variety of invective. He
started out by attacking the Lincoln idiom, comparing Honest Abe's early
expression with that of a "schoolmaster inflated with helium." On
another occasion, he belittled the "Wilsonian buncombe." *The New
Freedom*, he announced, is made up of "a mass of puerile affectations"
and "a gaudy procession of mere counter-words." He slashed away at one
writer after another, increasing the sting of his vilification at every blow.
Eventually he discovered the cesspool of Veblen's prose and became
positively poetic in his abuse: "an appalling salvo of rhetorical artillery,"
"a cent's worth of information wrapped in a bale of polysyllables," "a sort
of progressive intellectual diabetes," "a leprosy of horse sense." But in his
criticism of the rhetoric of Warren G. Harding, Mencken outdistanced
himself in describing what he considered the ultimate in linguistic
debauchery:

> It reminds me of a string of wet sponges; it reminds me of stale bean-soup,
> of college yells, of dogs barking idiotically through endless nights. It is so
> bad that a sort of grandeur creeps into it. It drags itself out of the dark
> abysm . . . of pish, and crawls insanely up the topmost pinnacle of posh.
> It is rumble and bumble. It is flap and doodle. It is balder and dash.

Twain and Mencken were both wordspinners of unusual ingenuity.
While the former's verbal creations are examples of tall talk in the best
Western tradition, the latter's contributions to the American language,
like his witticisms, contain a snarl. The frontier screamer could throw the
lexicographers into a mental tailspin with words like *hogglebumgullop* or
preforeordestination. Babylon's ring-tailed roarer could incite a riot
among strip-tease artists by calling them *ecdysiasts*, or upset the emotional equilibrium of schoolma'ams with words like *dithrambophobia* or
grammatomaniac. Perhaps his best contribution to a lexicon of wit is
booboisie which contains the essence of his social criticism, that "the
lunatic fringe has begun to wag the underdog." Both writers would com-
pose definitions of existing words that would make a lively supplement to
Ambrose Bierce's *The Devil's Dictionary*. Mark Twain, for example,
defined *puritanism* as "that kind of so-called housekeeping where they
have six Bibles and no corkscrew." Mencken called it "the haunting fear
that someone somewhere may be happy."

Mark Twain and Mencken fired their pieces at almost exactly the same targets: the "chiropractors" of prohibition, the "philistines" of art, the "undertakers" of religion and all manner of phony intellectuals. Both were deeply concerned with the moral depravity evident among those who posed as arbiters of American thought: scoundrels sobbing for prohibition while carrying a flask in their pockets, politicians trying to outlaw cigarettes while puffing away at their cigars, legislators attempting to repeal the law of natural selection by an Act of Congress. "The uplift has damn near ruined the country," Mencken wrote to one of his cronies. Mark Twain said, "When I reflect upon the number of disagreeable people who I know have gone to a better world, I am moved to lead a different life." After reading the morning paper, full of the usual "depravities and basenesses and hypocrisies and cruelties that make up civilization," he put in the remainder of the day, Twain said, "pleading for the damnation of the human race." In one of his attacks on the national mentality, Mencken accused the uplifters of reducing the unknowable to the not worth knowing. Mark Twain concluded that God, having made man at the end of the work week, was obviously tired.

Mencken was well aware that public opinion denounced him, as it had denounced Mark Twain (in some circles at least), as hopelessly uncultured, disgustingly immoral and repulsively immature. He knew that the majority of his readers could find no wisdom in his political criticism, no real sense in his editorials and no genuine humor in his witticisms. He, of course, had helped provoke such opinion and had supplied overwhelming "evidence" in its support. Furthermore, he made no attempt to reverse the popular decision. Upon receipt of the most scathing note of retaliation from one he had insulted with his poisonous pen, he retorted with disconcerting courtesy: "Dear Sir—Perhaps you are right." This was his way of cutting off discussion and of reserving for himself the last and most exquisite laugh.

Mencken was also fully aware, as Mark Twain was probably not, of the low esteem in which even the greatest of our comedians is held—of the truth, so strikingly expressed by E. B. White, that the world "decorates its serious writers with laurel and its wags with Brussels sprouts." In the case of Mark Twain, who strongly influenced the Sage's style, Mencken discovered, after careful inspection of the record, that the "learned authors" (between 1870 and 1900), without exception, had dismissed Mark as a clown "belonging to the lodge of Petroleum V. Nasby and Bill Nye." The thing that bothered Mencken was that Twain, who didn't realize that *Huckleberry Finn* eclipsed all attempts at serious American humor, actually yielded to the apologetic appraisals himself. Mark Twain's humor surpassed that of men like Josh Billings and Artemus Ward, who belonged to the same comic tradition, in its mastery of the homely patterns of an indigenous folk literature compounded of the diverse elements that make up the cultural heritage of the American people. Mencken was one of the few critics of his day who understood what is now almost universally accepted: that Mark Twain was "America's greatest humorist." While the Sage possessed little if any of Twain's intuitive appreciation of the folk mentality, he shared with his literary kinsman a sincere belief that human life is basically a comedy and that happiness, as he himself put it, is "the capacity to detect and relish the comic touches in human tragedy."

Mark Twain and Mencken shared a disdain for the puerilities and pretenses of American life, and both men were severely "moral" in a way that average Americans cannot comprehend. Both men believed that the people Americans admire most extravagantly are the most daring liars, and the ones they detest most violently are those who try to tell them the truth. But Mark Twain had a streak of compassion in his makeup that Mencken did not possess. After heaping "blame after blame" and "censure after censure" upon one of his selected whipping boys, Mark Twain indulged in a moment of penitence for his caustic remarks. When his temper had cooled, he said, "It is my conviction that the human race is no proper target for harsh words and bitter criticisms." "It did not invent itself," he added, "and it had nothing to do with the planning of its weak and foolish character."

Mencken was equipped with a "petrified diaphragm" that was impervious to emotional appeals. He could laugh himself to sleep every night at what he called "the greatest show since Rome caved in." Speaking of a prank he once played on an unsuspecting victim, he said, "I shall recall it upon the scaffold, and so shock the sheriff with a macabre smile."

Notes

1. H. L. Mencken, *Minority Report* (New York, 1956), p. 264.

Hal Holbrook Tonight!

Richard Schickel*

I would like to suggest that all those people who worry about the state and fate of the American theater make a point of seeing Hal Holbrook in his one-man show, *Mark Twain Tonight!*, the next time they get the chance. It is not exactly a play, but if you caught him in the course of his recent, thrice extended Broadway run, or catch him in the course of one of his frequent tours or hear his recordings of the Twain material, you will see that Mr. Holbrook achieves something none of the playwrights of this past season accomplished and something our native dramatic art desperately needs at the moment. He creates, and brings to an almost incredible degree of professional polish, an evening that is both very American and very theatrical.

His impersonation of Mark Twain lecturing in the seventieth year of his life is American not merely because Twain was our most representative writer but because the man Holbrook portrays reminds us of what our national character is ideally supposed to be and rarely is—independent, skeptical, rational, humorous, plagued by demons but coping. It is theatrical in the best sense because, although Holbrook/Twain is alone on stage, he is in constant conflict with the various humbugs "the damned human race" propagates when it gets to thinking about such Very Significant Subjects as politics, religion, culture, civil liberties, war and its own importance.

Moreover—and most important—our playwrights could profit by taking language lessons from the old gentleman who prowls from lectern to book-strewn table, alternately glowering and twinkling at his audience, for he learned long ago precisely how much to expose the essential blackness in his heart, making effective social commentary of it instead of mere self-assertion. They could also learn something about the creation of a character—a full, rounded character—from the shrewd use Holbrook has made of the Twain material to reveal the personality of its author.

In a theater that increasingly resorts to elaborate cruelties and enigmatic symbolic structures to gain our involvement, there is something

*Reprinted from *Holiday*, 40 (August, 1966), 103–05, with permission of *Travel/Holiday*, Travel Building, Floral Park, New York.

salutary in discovering that the theatrical equivalent of plain song still works. Ernest Hemingway thought that American literature began with *Huckleberry Finn*, and Mr. Holbrook's show takes us back to those beginnings at precisely the moment when we most need to be reminded of them. He demonstrates that writing in which style is the servant of meaning, not an end in itself, writing that is utterly unambiguous except when ambiguity serves the purpose of suspense or satire, is not only still valid theatrically but infinitely preferable to the gaudy fancies of a young Albee or an old Williams, disguising mindlessness behind a shower of words. In short, it's always helpful to know what you mean before you say it.

I do not mean to imply that the pleasures of *Mark Twain Tonight!* are purely or even mostly intellectual. It is, however, a good deal more than an exercise in simple nostalgia, or an enterprise that depends for its success on the middlebrow's patronizing delight in discovering that old-time writers still have a message for us. Naturally Holbrook summons up quite a bit of nostalgia (most of it false, considering how few in his audience were around in 1905, the arbitrary date of this lecture). There is his attire—white suit, gold watch and chain, congress gaiters. Then there are his quaint locutions, so resonant of a more leisurely time, when there was no need to telegraph a punch line and one could, instead, circle it and stalk it and study it out in a civilized manner, pausing to comment upon the absurdities one inevitably encountered in the process.

But the truth is that *Mark Twain Tonight!* is much too affecting to be dismissed as a simple evocation of period charm. It is, in fact, an elaborate and cunningly constructed trap designed to ensnare those who unwarily come to view what is admittedly a theatrical curiosity. This is the same trick Twain himself practiced, luring readers along on the premise that they were only reading comic novels—children's books—then slyly introducing the moral complexities of a Huck Finn or the depth of the darkness discovered by Tom Sawyer in his cave.

The way Holbrook works his version of this ploy is worth analyzing, for it seems to me that his creative contribution to the evening has been undervalued. Audiences, struck by the uncanny physical resemblance to the author that he achieves through some three and a half hours at the make-up table before each performance, are convinced that they are seeing a simple impersonation of the real, the historical Twain. Of course, the performance has a veracity that only some thirteen years of research and some 2,000 performances (Off Broadway, on tour at home and abroad) can impart. Holbrook knows almost six hours' worth of Twain material and so may vary his show instantly, depending on his mood and that of the audience, just as if he were, in fact, Mark Twain thumbing through memory and collected works, seeking the joke or anecdote or comment that ideally suits the occasion. But the fact is that Holbrook is offering a selective, artist's vision of Twain, not an impersonation. He is most assuredly true to the known biographical facts about his subject, but his greatness springs from the fact that he is, above all, true to his own vision of the man.

This allows him to cross the line from the particulars of historicism and offer us not just a living Twain but an idealization of old age. We begin to see in Holbrook/Twain the old man all of us aspire to be and few of us will become, a wise, crusty old gentleman who is a marvel of composure. Having lived long and tested himself and his opinions in all manner of circumstances, he knows precisely who he is, what he values and what he despises.

Sure of these matters, he is in no hurry to reveal himself to his audience in order to quickly win its favor. Indeed, he builds a certain amount of suspense over whether he will ever reveal what lies behind a mask he appears to love at least as much as we do, for he comes on very much the public man, the celebrity conceded by his contemporaries to be the greatest writer of his time. For the first act he revels in this identity, exercising the special egocentricity that always seems to accompany the miracle of a vigorous old age (and which may, indeed, be responsible for it). We are forced to wait on his pleasure as he rambles through his history, outrageously embroidering the truth as, he makes it clear, it is the right of age to do. He fumbles with his cigar, trimming its end, licking it and sniffing it in leisurely anticipation, lighting matches and allowing them to burn down to his fingers before flicking them out unused. Once he finally gets the stogie going, puffs of its smoke punctuate his remarks like feathery exclamation points, while the various angles at which it juts from his jaw indicate the responses he desires from us. The whole business rivets our attention as words alone could not, and the old reprobate knows it and delights in his ability to play us.

Nor is he above taking other liberties. In the presence of age we always wonder just how much senility is also present, and Holbrook/Twain builds suspense out of that mystery, too. The old gentleman will, from time to time, stare vacantly off into space, his mind apparently a blank; his hands, which seem too heavy for his wrists, twitch with wayward life, but the rest of him is frightfully still, and we wait, wondering, our sympathies totally engaged by the old man's brave struggle for mastery. How sad, he seemed so spry up to now, younger than his years—and suddenly the eyes glint shrewdly, inviting us to join in his laughter at our misplaced concern. Once again he has gulled us, using our anxiety (and our relief at its end) to win acquiescence in some new assault against our pride or our conventional wisdom.

In the beginning, these assaults are small, no more than one-line gags tossed over his shoulder as he shuffles through his scrappy notes or thumbs his books or fussily scrapes cigar ashes off the table where they have accidentally fallen and neatly deposits them in an ash tray. His principal business, at this point, is entertainment. He acts out an old man's impression of yet another old man telling an incredibly long story about how a third old man got woven into a rug. He may reminisce about newspaper days in San Francisco or about having his hat stolen by an English cleric or about his early attempts to master the horse. It's all simple, old-fashioned, grandfatherly corn, just about what you'd expect from a "beloved humorist."

But in the second act, the mood changes. As if suddenly reminded of literary duty, he decides to read a passage from *Huckleberry Finn*. It is the section where Huck must choose between loyalty to a friend, Nigger Jim, and loyalty to the law which requires him to turn in his friend as a runaway slave. He of course chooses the reality of friendship over the abstraction of a bad law. The piece is a *tour de force* for Holbrook, who must play Twain playing the boy, his father, Jim and assorted minor characters. But more important, it turns the evening in a new and more serious direction: Twain, having recreated Huck's crisis, now seems to feel compelled to deal openly with his own. At seventy, Twain was a deeply pessimistic man, afraid to expose some of the darker products of this mood to a public that preferred him as a comedian and that he judged not ready to receive the bleak message of his maturity. With Huck's example of moral fortitude before him, however, he now decides to experiment with truth-telling. He speaks from the heart—and cuts to the bone. "Man is the only animal who blushes—or needs to," he drawls and then proceeds to enumerate some of the matters he must blush about. "Man is the only animal that has the true religion—several of 'em. . . . He loves his neighbor as himself and cuts his throat if his theology isn't straight—he's made a graveyard of the globe in trying his honest best to smooth his brother's path to happiness and heaven. . . . There's not an acre of ground on the globe that's in the possession of its rightful owner. . . . Man is the only animal who for sordid wages goes forth to exterminate his own kind . . . and in the intervals between campaigns he washes the blood from his hands and works for the brotherhood of man—with his mouth."

There is more in this vein—much of it from the posthumously published *Letters from the Earth*—and its savagery seems to bring the speaker peace. In any case, he returns to the stage in the last act unburdened, free to speak with a new, deeper feeling about his past, in particular contrasting "the haunting sense of loneliness, isolation, remoteness from the worry and bustle of the world" that he experienced as a young pilot on a Mississippi River steamboat with the lust for gain he observed for the first time on his trek to the California gold fields. Now he reaches toward apothegm, his tones saddened as he speaks of a world lost and a world found: "That California get-rich-quick disease of my youth spread like wildfire and it produced a civilization which has destroyed the simplicity and repose of life, its poetry, its soft romantic dreams and visions and replaced them with money fever, sordid ideals, vulgar ambitions and the sleep which does not refresh. . . . Ah, the dreams of youth how beautiful they are, and how perishable."

In this moment, Twain stands revealed—not fully and only briefly (he quickly covers and recovers with a joke). In that instance, we begin to apprehend the intensity of his indictment of man and we recall much that the biographers have told us about him. We know he suffered from the money fever and took to the lecture platform to recover from its ravages; we know that out of vulgar ambition he tempered his artist's vision in order to win the favor of the Eastern cultural establishment; we suspect that the sleep of his later years did not refresh because the celebrity we have seen him enjoy earlier could not compensate for the lost dreams of his youth or his country's youth.

With this revelation, Hal Holbrook completes the arc of his performance. With it, he has taken us as deeply into his chosen character as an actor can go. With it, he goes beyond public image, beyond more or less private thoughts and gives us an indication of the man's emotional wellsprings.

Is this truly Mark Twain? Did he really talk in these twanging tones? Was his timing really as masterful as Holbrook's? Did he always carry himself so erectly but walk with his knees bent in precisely this manner? It isn't important to know, for it is certain that some very few grand old men talk and walk and look like this. Our own shock of recognition tells us that Holbrook is a careful observer of old age; and the integrity of his acting, which never broadens into parody or self-comment, is an earnest of fidelity in deeper matters.

We know, of course, that Holbrook has put no words in Twain's mouth, but has limited himself to the written record Twain left. He has done without the biographer's privilege of drawing supportive material from other sources or indulging in scholarly speculation, and he has not invented to support even the most reasonable supposition about the man's character. That within these tight limits Holbrook's Twain emerges as a perfectly plausible version of the author as he really was, is nothing less than miraculous. That the character who appears before us on stage is so completely unstudied is even more wondrous. It makes the show jump with a kind of life unavailable in productions locked in a fixed script and carefully finished direction.

It is a paradox, but Holbrook, working with material that is in some cases a century old, playing a character encrusted with preconceptions dating back to our childhood and working within the conventions of an old-fashioned lecture, actually gives us the most modern kind of theatrical experience. It is too thoughtful and carries too much rational meaning to be termed a Happening, but certainly it has the unexpected excitement of improvisational theater. Do not be misled by appearances; this is no "reading," no mere exercise in forensics like Gielgud's *Ages of Man*. The tradition in which *Mark Twain Tonight!* belongs is that of cabaret theater or perhaps that which Joan Littlewood has created in England.

It is a tradition in which ideas are animated by taking advantage of the moment's inspiration, but one that always remains faithful to a firmly established basic conception—a tradition that offers us a theater of ideas melded with a theater of life, and creates its best moments out of the resulting inner tension. At its best, as in *Mark Twain Tonight!*, it is a theater that leaves one speculating on the most tantalizing enigmas. Where, one must wonder, does the subject's identity end and the actor's begin? At what point does historical truth cease merely to support the higher truth of artistic invention and actually yield to it? At what points has some eerie transmigration of Twain's spirit and Holbrook's taken place? At what points can such a transmigration never occur? What, in short, is the exact nature of the reality we have witnessed? It is a characteristic of our identity-obsessed playwrights to raise unanswerable questions of this kind, but it is not characteristic of them to get us to join so easily in their speculations. It is ironic that an actor who innocently set forth some years ago to work up an impression of a curious old character who amused him should succeed where so many self-conscious authors have failed. That he involves us so gracefully, so uninsistently in these questions is a good sign that we are in the presence of an authentic artist.

Mark Twain as Proteus: Ironic Form and Fictive Integrity

Maurice F. Brown*

Little of the comment on *Life on the Mississippi* deals effectively with the book itself.[1] The traditional approach points out salient differences between the material and tone of "Old Times on the Mississippi" and the rest of the volume. It admires "Old Times" and follows A. B. Paine in rejecting the rest as "literary journalism."[2] Bellamy calls the additions "Merely good travel reporting,"[3] and Rogers agrees with Andrews that they are "the hack work of a professional traveller."[4] Lewis Leary joins this quartet, providing a compact statement which carries the tone of much of the criticism: "The added material, arduously compiled, recaptures little of the charm of these earlier portions."[5] The position has become a cliché. It is generally propounded as self-evident, unsupported by thorough discussion of the work, guided by irrelevant formalism or by individual taste, and often refers to pressures of research, writing, or publishing on Twain. The casualness of assignment of genre to the additions is obvious if one attempts to view them in the context of other "travel reporting," good or hack.

More favorable reactions to the book are almost useless. DeVoto seems to see significant achievement in the book, although there is confusion as to its nature. In one place he writes that "it is as romance, as the genre of 'Tom Sawyer,' that the book lives"; and in another he lists it as one of the books which "exist as satire and realism to which the frontier humorist attained." He sees its method as that of "narrative interlude . . . organically developed," but does not expand.[6] Dixon Wecter alone finds *Life on the Mississippi* "beyond dispute" one of Twain's three greatest books. Of its method he writes: "Sparse notations spring to life under the hands of a born raconteur, fragments are fitted deftly into the mosaic of the whole." He finds that the book is improvised "in a manner which sheer genius alone could transcend."[7] There is justice in the position, but the assertions are unsupported and seem inflated in the face of the dissenting opinion.

*Reprinted with permission from *Papers of the Michigan Academy of Science, Arts, and Letters*, 51 (1966), 515–27.

words, speaking in a variety of forms and voices. A reader recognizes immediately the voice of the American oral tradition of itinerate yarn-spinner. But Twain has moved far beyond this early mode. At times his voice is that of the genteel man of the world, a straight-faced, generally detached guide. He reports in a condensed, often racy style, and, unidentified with the society and values being examined, he provides comic perspective in the tradition of the gentleman of Southwestern humor. His tone varies from the amused but sympathetic narration of most of "Old Times" to the aloof irony of some of the later passages without jarring the reader's sense of his integrity. But he is often more playful than this, donning a variety of masks in often abrupt shifts of the angle of vision. Twain plays with the roles of historian and geologist of the Mississippi, most notably in the book's early chapters, leering out from behind the masks he assumes. At other times, we find he has somehow become the naive social commentator of the Gilded Age, admiring progress like a Gulliver. Or again he shifts abruptly to the "man from Missouri," undercutting his own extravagance with a sharp cut of terse common sense. Other major roles Twain assumes are those of the poker-faced purveyor of tall-tales, of "end man" drawing out another of his characters, of self-interested, basically immoral, common man, or of sentimental traveler, luxuriating in the picturesque or the sublime.

Not content with this range, Twain interpolates additional points of view by drawing on a variety of supplementary materials and speakers. The supplementary voices testify vividly to the keenness of Twain's ear for dialect, jargon, and cliché, ranging from those of the naive dreaming boy or of the sentimental Southerner to the sharp lingo of the hoaxers, the drummers, the undertakers of the "progressive and cultured" West. Twain uses "verbatim" reports, creating comic perspective in some cases (the reports of Uncle Mumford, of the pilot at the battle of Vicksburg, or of the bartender), dispelling conventional romantic notions in others (the passenger's account of feuding or the story of Vicksburg noncombatants), or supplying ironic contrast (the report on Murel's gang or the excerpts from Southern journalism).

Twain's shifts of character are often deliberately abrupt, jarring the reader into a new perspective. His most common shift is that from an emotive extravagance to a deflating comic juxtaposition. For example, he prepared for a passage describing the effect of piloting science on romantic views of the river[17] by detaching himself. He contrasts pilot and sentimental traveler, slips into the voice of the boy and waxes eloquent, and then contrasts himself as boy and pilot in the deflation which follows. A later sentimental description, complete with "dawn creeping stealthily," "spectral little wreaths of white mist," and "tender young green of spring," ends in the colloquial understatement of a Mississippi boatman: "You grant that you have seen something that is worth remembering." Twain has switched masks and proceeds in the next paragraph to the brief and snappy anecdote of Captain Poe, who by mistake clove his sleeping wife's skull with an ax.[18] Another highly colored description of sunset on the upper Mississippi ends with a lightning switch of voice to that of the man from Missouri: "The sunrises are also said to be exceedingly fine. I do not know."[19] And the chapter ends.

The immediate effect of Twain's disdain of conventions of form and voice seems to have been confusion for critics. This is similar to that effect produced by the Twain personality as early as 15 years before *Life on the Mississippi* in lecture circuit appearances. A Boston reviewer of 1868 remarks that the audience has been put into a " 'queer state' of not knowing 'what to trust . . . where the fun will come in.' "[20] Henry Nash Smith identifies the confusion with a loss of fictive integrity directly related to the variety of Twain's voices. This sense of loss is probably particularly strong because Twain possesses to an uncanny degree that artistic sensibility Keats called "negative capability." As each of his personae struts and frets his hour upon the stage, we feel Twain's total participation in the voice. He *is* his voices in a way in which Browning or Yeats or Eliot are not theirs. For this reason one wonders if the roles Twain plays can be called masks or personae in any conventional sense. Indeed, the presence of the author is felt even in the interpolated tales, the verbatim accounts, and the documents with which he peppers his pages.

Yet to draw the conclusion that Twain is trying to do something he has not done here, or that he should be identified with only one of his voices, would be a mistake.[21] Twain's shifts of voice create rhythms of response, moving from complete imaginative involvement to an ironic detachment from one voice as we become involved in the imaginative response to another. While the effect can range from that of sheer frustration to that of multiple vision, the whole experience is pervaded by the sense of illusion as illusion, of Twain's game as a game. At this level we should be able to recognize the tradition in which Twain is working as that of what I shall call the Protean comic hero. Literary prototypes are to be found in characters like Shakespeare's Falstaff and Prospero, in Ben Jonson's Face, Goethe's Mephistopheles, and Thurber's Walter Mitty. It is an American stage tradition carried on in the 20th century by most of our "comedians"—perhaps most effectively by a W. C. Fields or a Charles Laughton. A dimension of comic irony is created which depends for effect on a secret shared by audience and author: the actor assumes a mask which the audience knows as a mask. Typically the juxtaposition of roles is haphazard, and one has a sense of the actor deliberately parodying himself. The comic ham leers from behind his masks. The tradition itself has a "fictive integrity," the deliberate intent of which is, paradoxically, to maintain the illusory sense of the fiction.

Twain indulges in the leer and in self-parody at times. Brown's monologue[22] is characteristic; and, in its exaggeration of one of Twain's voices and the form of his book, it functions as microcosmic parody of *Life on the Mississippi*. More pervasively, however, our sense of comic irony arises through participation in the rhythms of alternation between immediacy of involvement and successive detachments. The reader becomes aware of purpose in the juxtapositions, of an integrity of vision rising from the tensions among the voices. The point at which lines of tension cross is a point of central ironic vision, the core of the personality Twain developed to come to terms with the public issues of his times. To establish the integrity of this central vision it is necessary to see how it emerges in mediating the major issues of the book.

The issues are those which became involved in the public personality of Twain as it developed, and the value of that personality is a function of the breadth of Clemens' experience, spanning as it did the range of American life in the Gilded Age.[23] Mark Twain was born at least as early as Clemens' riverboating days, and the personality developed through the free-wheeling western experiences, finding early literary projection in Twain's own highly individualistic journalistic career. It was developing in *Innocents Abroad* and *Roughing It*. Twain's personality became more sensitive to the range of concerns and tensions in American life east of the Mississippi as it was molded in response to experience with audiences on his strenuous lecture circuit engagements.[24] In *Life on the Mississippi* for the first and last time, Mark Twain fully emerges to set all his lands in order. In doing so, he orders the experience of his time in his own unique way and creates a major American archetypal personality.

The experience with which Twain deals is the set of conflicts which dominated the Gilded Age. These conflicts are treated in terms of a dilemma, expressed colloquially in the statement with which Twain's bartender ends his tale: "Sounds like poetry, but it's the petrified truth."[25] The range of "poetry" in the book is vast, but it might loosely be termed "the romantic," involving in its permutations an organic view of man and nature, emotional or sentimental distortions of experience, wish fulfillment, metaphysical chicaneries, and subordination of man to nature. The "petrified truth" adumbrates rational, scientific, and technological values; its concern is with cultural and industrial progress and with man's practical conquest of nature. My vagueness in definition of these terms is, of course, a function of Twain's own casualness and his deliberate ironic stance.

The conflict is embodied in Twain's treatment of the Mississippi pilot, which provides the book with its major rhythmic movement. Here he is close to the sources of a personal identity crisis, and his treatment provides the core of Twain's public personality. The boy's early romance with the mystery and beauty of the river and with the godlike stature of the boatman is set against the "science of piloting." But with the pilot's knowledge comes the new romanticism of heroic mastery. Finally the railroads arrive, the technology of government engineers seems to have subdued the river, the pilot becomes a minor functionary, and that heroic romance is gone too. Light treatment in "Old Times" of the destruction and creation of varieties of romance by the science of piloting is balanced by Twain's later consideration of technology in voices sometimes ironic, sometimes naively admiring, sometimes excessively praising.

But Twain's other additions provide full orchestration of the conflicts embedded in this treatment of piloting. He surveys the intricacies of his theme with the engrained intent of the humorist and satirist, never taking either side of the argument for long, exposing folly in the stock responses of blurred popular romanticism on one side and of limited practicality and rationality on the other. His recognition of the values of "science," in his own broad sense of that term, is qualified by a pervasive irony. There is somewhat naive exultation in contemplating human control of nature, the speed of boats, and material and cultural progress along the Mississippi. The naiveté is functional, and Twain's tongue is always more or less in cheek. Chapter LVII begins with fulsome praise of "enlivening signs of the presence of active, energetic, intelligent, prosperous, practical 19th-century populations." And Twain approves: "The people don't dream; they work." But the passage is followed by regrets that Marion City "has gone backward in a most unaccountable way." One senses an ironic undercutting of conventional faith in progress, and suddenly the string of five energetic adjectives in the earlier passage seems a heavy load for even 19th-century populations to bear. More praise of Quincy follows, but Twain then "missed Alexandria; was told it was under water, but would come up to blow in the summer." Lightly ironic treatment of the 1857 real estate boom in Keokuk carries Twain characteristically into the anecdote of Henry Clay Dean, who possessed the talents of his namesake but was without honor in Keokuk until his triumphal if unanticipated performance in the new Keokuk Athenaeum. The Athenaeum is more Keokukian than Athenian, and Twain's reiterated refrain in praise of the westward course of culture and opera houses is touched with irony.[26]

Respect for "science" is further undercut elsewhere. "Old Times" is, among many other things, a parody of how-to-do-it books. It gives very little information on how to pilot a boat, yet Twain keeps up his pretense, making explanations at the beginnings of Chapters X, XII, and XIV to readers who wonder that he deals "so minutely with piloting as a science." There is irony in the practical application of science to the making of oleo and cottonseed oil in order to deceive customers. Religions of fact and measurement among historians and geologists are irreverently spoofed in Twain's treatment of Mississippi history and geology, one geological speculation ending, "There is something fascinating about science. One gets such wholesale returns of conjecture out of such a trifling investment of fact."[27]

Mutations of the romance theme are equally complex. Like Howells, Twain attacks much of romance as distortion of the realities of experience and a perversion of genuine values. Employing humor, satire, and parody, Twain moves in upon the host of conventional attitudes and responses characteristic of popular romanticism. There is the romance of the hero-worshiping boy, with his naive, if charming, dreams of river gloom and glory. The sort of moral conflict which hypnotized Hawthorne is burlesqued in later chapters on the boy's wrestling with guilt. Set attitudes of feudal romanticism which create absurdities of social behavior are the Walter Scotticism of the South and the arbitrary, irrational code of honor in Southern feuding. Pretensions to beauty and culture along the Mississippi are exposed through fairly direct humor and sarcasm in "The House Beautiful," and through irony elsewhere. Romantic views of war are set against its realities in Twain's Vicksburg chapter, and Southern nostalgia for the past is exposed through anecdote. Many of the longer interlarded tales involve the exposure of popular sentimentalisms or vain dreams, which blur the vision and court folly or manipulation by hoaxers. In these cases, parody of familiar styles gives an edge to the exposure. Offending romanticisms in the tales can be briefly tabulated and identified as religious sentimentalism (the letter hoax); social pretension and conventions of grief (dialogue with the undertaker); superstitions (the sequence on spiritualists); both the romance of gambling and the gambler's conventional response to the apparent gull (the professor's yarn); and the romance of wealth (the sequel to Ritter's tale).

Mediating the tensions of his rich materials are the standards of genuine vision and value implied by the attack and sometimes surfacing in the work. Murel's Promethean romantic achievement dwarfs the chicanery of the petty crook while parodying superficial genteel values. Contemplation of the river is a *true* romance, partaking of "Decline of Empire" moods and motifs: the river is a great brown god, source of life, mystery, and challenge, rolling its mile-wide tide along and sweeping fields and cities away. On the other hand, the human mind is a worthy instrument in the battle of man's will with nature's power, and there is true achievement in the manly science of piloting and in the achievements of society in spite of its dreaming, prideful folly. As the true science of piloting provides the true romance of the pilot's life—the nature of which was unsuspected by the dreaming boy—so the two approach union for Twain in their integrity and immediacy as human experience and are mutually supporting values. Twain envisions romance resting firmly on the genuine possibilities for human experience, and science and technology on a pervasive but immediate sense of the power and mystery of nature. The resolution is implicit in the comic and satiric handling of sentimental conventions, illusions, and dreams—the "poetry" which makes suckers of thinking human beings—and in the attack on petrifaction of thought in the illusions of human power and progress. This central ironic vision is the still point from which the reader moves out into illusion, and back to which he is drawn by the juxtaposition of other voices.

The sources of problems Twain was dealing with in *Life on the*

Mississippi may be located in an intensive role conflict precipitated for Clemens by the reorientations forced upon him and upon the nation by the Civil War, and by the dislocations inherent in technological change and urbanization. Role conflict was inevitable in the increasingly open society of the Gilded Age. There is nothing startling in the observation that the possibilities of mobility and the paradoxes of social status on the Western frontier, together with the inevitable reverberations in more established patterns of American life, are basic to Twain's problem as they are to the larger problem of American personality. 19th-century formulations of conflict in role and values by Cooper, Thoreau, Emerson, Whitman, Twain, and others are but a prelude to contemporary concern with technology, the urban community, class structure and mobility, role play, identity crisis, and the existential predicament. The conflict is our collective American fate.

The personality of Mark Twain, established through this conflict, moving between immersion in immediate experience and ironic detachment, recalls that curious double-vision characteristic of the American personality, one result of which has been its intensity. Whitman shares it; he is now immersed in a range of immediate experience—"I am the man, I suffer'd, I was there."—and now detached, observing himself and "the game":

> Apart from the pulling and hauling stands what I am,
> Stands amused, complacent, compassionating, idle, unitary, . . .
> Both in and out of the game and watching and wondering at it.

The stance in "Song of Myself" is that of the Puritan and Quaker journals, of William Byrd's diary and Franklin's autobiography, of Ralph Ellison's invisible man and Wallace Stevens' man with the blue guitar, as much as it is that of the Transcendentalists or of Twain. One remembers further that somehow the integration or establishment of the American personality—even at its most intense and concentrated in Thoreau or Dickinson—has involved diffusion of the personality in a need to encompass some envisioned total role. It is a personality in rebellion against conventional and inorganic forms, seeking its own form—a personality which, like Twain's or Franklin's or Emerson's, can tolerate much apparent disorder, preferring with P. T. Barnum the three-ring to the one-ring circus.

That Twain's particular response should be that of the comic Proteus is unique but not strange. He stands at the beginning of our era, literary responses to which have involved the rejection of voices of omniscience in favor of experiment with either limited point of view or with new and vital forms of drama. The first response provides for an integrated personality which asserts its independent integrity on the basis of immediate experience in a society of multiple value structures. The second allows the writer to mediate the larger experience of the society, and he finds his integrity in the tensions among his many voices. *Huckleberry Finn* and *Life on the Mississippi* represent Clemens' greatest achievements in these two forms of literary response. Both forms, of course, mirror familiar personality patterns. Contemporary Americans spin out absolute personal value systems, denying or ignoring questions of their general relevance. Or second, the paradoxical detachment of the American personality from the variety of roles it plays—each with great involvement and intensity—is a common phenomenon. Such detachment becomes ironic when understood, anxiety-arousing when it is not.

If the range of Mark Twain's vision precludes the imaginative intensity and focus of *Walden*, and if the pseudo-dramatic mode precludes the analytical depth of *The Education of Henry Adams*, the virtues of *Life on the Mississippi* more than right the balance for the student of American life. Because of its unique form and its central problem in personality, the book is our richest introduction to American experience in the Gilded Age. Some of the gilt of that experience and personality, to be sure, has tarnished; the rewards of Twain's inclusiveness of details have their costs in minor irrelevancies and dead issues. But the book comes to its own good terms with pervasive problems of the American character, mediating perennial conflicts through creation of a modern ironic mode of personality which finds its integrity in tensions among its roles and in the perception of the false, the illusory, and the automatic in human experience.

Notes

1. I am indebted to James Cox of Dartmouth College for useful comments on an earlier draft of this paper.

2. A. B. Paine, *Mark Twain: A Biography*, in *The Writings of Mark Twain* (New York, 1922–25), XXXI, p. 746.

3. Gladys Bellamy, *Mark Twain as Literary Artist* (Norman, 1950), p. 275.

4. Franklin R. Rogers, *Mark Twain's Burlesque Patterns* (Dallas, 1960), p. 90, quoting Kenneth Andrews, *Nook Farm: Mark Twain's Hartford Circle* (Cambridge, Mass., 1950), p. 290.

5. Lewis Leary, *Mark Twain* (Minneapolis, 1960), p. 21.

6. Bernard DeVoto, *Mark Twain's America* (Cambridge, 1932), pp. 110, 240, and 246.

7. Dixon Wecter, "Introduction," *Life on the Mississippi* (New York, 1950), p. x.

8. DeVoto, *op. cit.*, p. 110.

9. Walter Blair, *Mark Twain and Huck Finn* (Berkeley, 1960), p. 294, quoting Edward Wagenknecht, "Introduction," *Life on the Mississippi* (New York, 1944), p. vii.

10. See Walter Blair, *op. cit.*, and Dewey Ganzel, "Twain, Travel Books, and *Life on the Mississippi*," *American Literature*, XXXIV (March 1962), 40–55. Ganzel finds Twain's use of travel literature more sophisticated and thoughtful than earlier criticism of Twain for padding, borrowing, and hasty writing under pressure of time would indicate.

11. Albert E. Stone, Jr., *The Innocent Eye* (New Haven, 1961), p. 143. The italics are mine.

12. Rogers, *op. cit.*, pp. 90 and 94.

13. Henry Nash Smith, *Mark Twain: The Development of a Writer* (Cambridge, Mass., 1962), p. 113.

14. My treatment of the public personality of Mark Twain has been influenced by Erik H. Erikson's suggestive approach to personality in *Young Man Luther* (New York, 1962).

15. Edward Wagenknecht, *Mark Twain, the Man and His Work* (Norman, 1961), pp. 44–45, citing A. B. Paine (ed.), *The Writings of Mark Twain* (New York, 1922–1925), Vol. XII, p. 304. All further references to *Life on the Mississippi* are to this edition.

16. *Writings*, XII, pp. 94 and 107.

17. *Writings*, XII, pp. 78–80. Smith bases much of his argument on a lengthy analysis of this passage. (See *op. cit.*, pp. 77–81.) My own thought is indebted to his subtle definition of issues.

18. *Ibid.*, XII, p. 259.

19. *Ibid.*, XII, p. 468.

20. Quoted by Paul Fatout, *Mark Twain on the Lecture Circuit* (Bloomington, Ind., 1960), p. 128.

21. Smith is repulsed by the "absolute moral authority" and "conventionally derisive attitude" to the lower class in the voice of the gentleman-narrator, finding him often a mere mouthpiece for the author. (*Op. cit.*, p. 77.) I find ironic deflation of the gentleman common enough to be pervasive.

22. *Writings*, XII, pp. 110–112.

23. See the treatments of Smith, *op. cit.*, pp. 71–81, and of Kenneth S. Lynn, *Mark Twain and Southwestern Humor* (Boston, 1959), pp. 227ff, for suggestions of the book's significance as cultural history. Roger B. Salomon, avoiding literary value judgments, treats the book thoroughly and often perceptively in the context of his interest in Twain's attitude to history. See his *Twain and the Image of History* (New Haven, 1961), pp. 74–94.

24. The detailed information on Clemens' response to audiences and on the relation of his written work to his lecture material in Paul Fatout's book, cited above, offers invaluable suggestions for study of the development of the public personality.

25. *Writings*, XII, p. 292.

26. Salomon quotes the praise which opens Chapter LVII as evidence for Twain's "vociferous assent" to and "celebration of historical progress." (*Op. cit.*, p. 74.) The attempt to treat Twain's ideas without taking sufficient account of voice and context is perilous, especially in a book like this one. Salomon's proposal that Twain's allegiance switched impulsively from the idyllic past to the industrial present by 1883 is unacceptable even if it were not an oversimplification.

27. *Writings*, XII, p. 156.

The Theology of Mark Twain:
Banished Adam and the Bible

Stanley Brodwin*

On March 25, 1887, when Mark Twain was fifty-two years old, affluent and famous, and still living in Hartford, Connecticut, he wrote the following letter to Mrs. Boardman (née Jenny Stevens), a childhood acquaintance, who had first written to him reminiscing about the early years in Hannibal:

> You have spirited me back to a vanished world & the companionship of phantoms. But how dear they are, & how beautiful they seem!—so graced and spiritualized in the far stretch of time, whose mellowing perspectives hide all their faults & leave visible in them & rememberable only those things which made them lovely then & holy now. But I thank you for carrying me back to that old day, for in thinking of it, dreaming over it, I have seemed like some banished Adam who is revisiting his half-forgotten Paradise & wondering how the arid outside world could ever have seemed green & fair to him.[1]

This letter crystallizes a dominant factor in the emotional and imaginative life of Mark Twain: the myth of the fall of man and the archetypal characters who are inextricably part of it. Though he claimed to "detest . . . theology,"[2] he remained a kind of cracker-barrel folk theologian throughout his career as he explored this most significant of biblical stories. Not only did the myth give him characters to be reinterpreted theologically, or satirized, or made into subjects of both pathos and humor, but it was also a controlling force in shaping his view of humanity and, therefore, much of his creative work. His pessimistic determinism and the black satire of the later years drew artistic strength and meaning from the basic moral and ontological assumptions implicit in the fall, especially as seen from the Presbyterian point of view prevalent in the American South and Southwest of the early and mid-nineteenth century. "The damned human race," an utterance of Mark Twain's attributed to his later "misanthropy," has rarely been interpreted theologically. Yet even a cursory reading of his works shows that, for Twain, "damned" was not simply an angry curse, but a theological con-

*Reprinted with permission from *Mississippi* Quarterly, 29 (Spring, 1976), 167–89.

demnation and judgment. Man is a banished Adam, Mark Twain most thoroughly so:

> Every man is in his whole person the human race, with not a detail lacking. I am the whole human race without a detail lacking; I have studied the human race with diligence and strong interest all these years in my own person; in myself I find in big or little proportion every quality and every defect that is . . . in the mass of the race. . . . The human race is a race of cowards; and I am not only marching in that procession but carrying a banner.[3]

For Mark Twain, all men were morally alike; all men were caught in a single web of destiny in which evil predominated, preventing real moral progress. And for those individuals like Joan of Arc, who Mark Twain thought transcended the inherent depravity of man, only the dubious destiny of martyrdom remained. Huck Finn, who likewise transcends evil in saving Nigger Jim, is rewarded ironically with guilt and confined to a world of restriction and hypocrisy from which he must finally escape.

But Mark Twain's view of man as a banished Adam was not established entirely on his awareness of his own loss of innocence. The nature of the God he was taught to believe in as a child, and the gap between Christian ideals and Christian practice that he was able to observe early in life, are inextricably linked to his identification with Adam's destiny. Throughout his works Mark Twain agonizes over these themes. Ultimately, Christianity failed to give him the spiritual sustenance he needed, and the God of both Old and New Testaments evoked from him vicious philosophical attacks. Emotionally and intellectually he tried to emancipate himself from a background and a training that had struck deep roots. Still, Mark Twain's relationship with the Bible, and the Adamic myth in particular, was too ambivalent for any simple affirmation or rejection and Mark Twain, himself by training and disposition, too questioning and, indeed, skeptical of dogmas and orthodoxy, to come to quick solutions.

Orthodox Christian ideas did have their ironic effect upon him as a youth. "For we were little Christian children and had early been taught the value of forbidden fruit,"[4] writes Mark Twain in explaining why, as a boy, it was more delightful to swim in a prohibited waterhole. Then there is the amusing incident that shows Mark Twain, Huck Finn-like, testing the text expounded by his Bible teacher, Mrs. Horr:

> . . . she dwelt upon the text, "Ask and ye shall receive," and said that whosoever prayed for a thing with earnestness and strong desire need not doubt that his prayer would be answered.
>
> I was so forcibly struck by this information . . . that was probably the first time I had heard of it. I thought I would give it a trial. I believed in Mrs. Horr thoroughly and I had no doubts as to the result. (p. 32)

The young Sam Clemens prays for gingerbread and, sure enough, sees a piece he can filch from the baker's daughter who sat next to him. "I was a convert," he exults. But the inevitable "fall" or disillusionment takes place, recounted here with laughing irony:

> But this dream was like almost all the others we indulge in, there was nothing to it. I did as much praying during the next two or three days as any one in that town, I suppose, and I was very sincere, . . . too, but nothing came of it. I found that not even the most powerful prayer was competent to lift that gingerbread again, and I came to the conclusion that if a person remains faithful to his gingerbread and keeps his eye on it he need not trouble himself about your prayers. (p. 32)

These incidents from his *Autobiography*, however embroidered or reshaped by the perspective of his old age, nevertheless reveal a pattern evident in Mark Twain's major works from *Innocents Abroad* (1869) to "The Mysterious Stranger" stories (1897–1908). The pattern is one of constant promise—the promise of moral goodness and its rewards of health, wealth, and peace—and the even more constant betrayal of such promise by an aggressively backsliding Man and a treacherous Universe or God, both of whom destroy the possibility of innocence. God's world is reduced to a meaningless and unreal nightmare because innocence and truth are illusions. The essence of Mark Twain's complaint is centered in the fantasy he had about correcting the biblical God:

> He would not be a jealous God—a trait so small that even men despise it in each other. He would not boast. . . .
> There would not be any hell—except the one we live in from the cradle to the grave.
> There would not be any heaven—of the kind described in the world's Bibles. He would spend His eternities in trying to forgive Himself for making man unhappy when he could have made him happy with the same effort. . . .[5]

But the fact that, for Mark Twain, such a "revised" God could not exist reveals how seriously he took the Bible, even if with deep revulsion for its God and miracles. His despair in later life was compounded by his inability to completely shake off the cosmic and moral view of life projected by both the Testaments. Near the end of the nineteenth century, he constantly dwelled on the figures of Adam, Eve, and Satan, in a series of "Diaries," showing the First Couple as totally unable to understand and obey God's prohibitions, and Satan a compassionate, but helpless advisor to them. And in his last published piece, "The Turning Point of My Life" (1910), he traced his whole destiny to Adam, his "kin." But in "Extracts from Adam's Diary" (1893, 1897), "Eve's Diary" (1905), and "That Day in Eden (A Passage from Satan's Diary)" (1923), Twain also developed his deepening conviction that the very nature of humor is theologically bound up with the idea of man's fall. For humor, derived as it is from the incongruities and absurdities inherent in the human condition and "reality" itself, is a sign of man's fallen world and reveals an aspect of God's "absurd" creation which can be perceived as a cosmic practical joke. This is the meaning of Twain's famous epigram, "Everything human is pathetic. The secret source of humor itself is not joy but sorrow. There is no humor in heaven" (XX, 101).[6]

Thus, instead of drawing further and further from the Bible's concepts and characters, he mined them more deeply. Even the language he used to convey his basic attitudes remained biblical and theological rather than secular.[7] In 1900, after returning from abroad, he had this to say to the Society of American Authors at Delmonico's:

> It seems to me a most difficult thing for any man, no matter how well prepared, to say anything that is not complimentary. Sometimes I am almost persuaded that I am what the Chairman says I am. As a rule the Chairman begins by saying something to my discredit . . . and then begins to compliment me. Nothing bites so deep down as the facts of a man's life. The real life that you live is a life of interior sin. Everyone believes I am a monument of all the virtues. Someday there will be a Chairman who will be able to give the true side of my character.[8]

Despite the humor of these remarks, the tone is thrown off balance by the statement, "The real life that you live is a life of interior sin," and the suggestion that the ultimate "Chairman" to find out the sin will be God. The idea is presented with epigrammatic finality. Though man may have surface virtue, good material for after-dinner speeches, he is at bottom sinful. That Mark Twain was aware of this tenacious religious element in himself there is little doubt. In his *Autobiography* he refers to the incident in which he felt guilt for having given some matches to a drunken tramp in jail, who then burned himself to death:

> I was *not* responsible for it, for I had meant him no harm but only good, when I let him have the matches; but no matter, mine was a trained Presbyterian conscience and knew but one duty—to hunt and harry its slave upon all pretexts and on all occasions, particularly when there was no sense nor reason in it. (p. 41)

And to William Dean Howells he wrote concerning some literary project that "Its hidden motive will illustrate a but-little considered fact in human nature; that religious folly you were born in you *die* in, no matter what . . . reasonabler religious folly may seem to have taken its place meanwhile & abolished & obliterated it."[9] This conviction makes it clear that Mark Twain's involvement with the Bible was more than "literary." There was in him a dark strain of religious anguish and intellectual conflict with the Bible as it shaped his "Presbyterian conscience." This conflict would have to be coped with in the images of his creative fantasies. And this is what occurs. Significantly, there are more biblical references in his collected works than references to any other literary work or figure.[10]

But references and allusions, important as they may be, only suggest the deeper aspects of a work of art, its style, structure, characterization and the imaginative patterns that control the vision presented. And the pattern most conspicuous in Mark Twain's work, amounting almost to a mythic structure, is the pattern of promise and betrayal, the inevitable fall of human innocence as it chooses or is forced to spoil itself. The determinism of *What is Man?* (1906) is merely a philosophic surrender to the theological truth of man playing and replaying Adam's inevitable fall. The idea also occurs in a darkly comic way in one of Pudd'nhead Wilson's epigrams: "Adam was but human—this explains it all. He did not want the apple for the apple's sake, he wanted it only because it was forbidden. The mistake was in not forbidding the serpent; then he would have eaten the serpent" (XVI, 8).[11]

But to understand more clearly Mark Twain's involvement with Adam, it is necessary to examine his concept of God, and his views on the relationship between God's justice and human suffering. In these matters, Mark Twain was always explicit.

In his "revised" idea of God, Mark Twain writes that the Deity would "recognize in Himself the Author and Inventor of Sin and Author and Inventor of the Vehicle of Application for its commission; and would place the whole responsibility where it should of right belong: upon Himself, the only Sinner" (*N*, p. 301). Yet Mark Twain was aware of shifting the burden of responsibility and making God his scapegoat: "There are many reasons for our blunders, but the most popular one is Providence" (*N*, p. 347).

Mark Twain fulminated against the God in the Old Testament whom he characterized as "jealous, trivial, ignorant, revengeful" (*N*, p. 361). He called the Bible the most "damnatory biography in print" (P, III, 1354).[12] For Twain, God was an Infinite Creative Power, pure Spirit that knows not man and cannot therefore be prayed to or bargained with. His God is a God of Nature whose Universe is an aspect of His eternality:

> To trust the God of the Bible is to trust an irascible . . . fickle . . . master; to trust the true God is to trust a Being who has uttered no promises, but whose beneficent, exact, and changeless ordering of the machinery of his colossal universe is proof that he is at least steadfast to his purposes; whose unwritten laws, so far as they affect man, being equal and impartial, show that he is just and fair. . . . (P, I, 412)

And again: ". . . one cannot put the modern heavens on a map, nor the modern God; but the Bible God and the Bible heavens can be set down on a slate and yet not be discommoded" (P, I, 412).[13]

Mark Twain here pits his deistic conception of the "true God" against the anthropomorphism accepted usually at face value in the pulpits of his age, an anthropomorphism from which he struggled to free himself. He wished for a more viable concept of God to enter man's spiritual life. The force of this desire is demonstrated by the fact that the above passage was written as his apologia to his wife, "Livy," in order to soften the blow his refusal to listen to her Bible-reading gave her soon after their marriage. But though he was striving toward some more metaphysically acceptable concept of God, Mark Twain continually turned back to flog what should have been a "dead horse" for him, but which surprisingly stayed alive. He never ceased berating and satirizing biblical concepts, from the illogical nature of its God, in his long-suppressed *Letters from the Earth* and "Reflections on Religion,"[14] to its harps-and-angels idea of Heaven in *Extract from Captain Stormfield's Visit to Heaven* (1907). He fulminated throughout his whole work on the hypocrisy of Christians and the failure of Christianity itself to fulfill its promise of a more moral world:

> Christianity will doubtless still survive in the earth ten centuries hence—stuffed and in a museum. (*N*, p. 346)
> There has been only one Christian. They caught Him and crucified Him early. (*N*, p. 344)
> If Christ were here now, there is one thing he would *not* be—a Christian. (*N*, p. 328)

While these epigrams were written in the late 1890's, Mark Twain thought in essentially the same way in such early works as *Innocents Abroad* and other productions of its period. His views persisted to such an extent that Twichell could chide him for being "too orthodox on the Doctrine of Total Human Depravity."[15]

Mark Twain could not suppress his involvement with the Bible, its God and His followers. Apart from Adam, Eve, and Satan, he was attracted to Noah and his Ark, and, as early as 1870, began "Shem's Diary," which he left incomplete. He made thorough use of Joseph in puncturing over-inflated biblical figures.[16] For Mark Twain, Joseph was no child of grace; rather, he was a shrewd buyer who "skinned" his neighbors during the famine of "every last acre they had, of every last animal they had. . . ."[17] This was written in 1906 and at the expense of John D. Rockefeller, Jr.'s widely publicized Bible Class, which Twain saw being used to justify "Robber Baron" methods. Years earlier, in 1898, Mark Twain had attempted to "explain" anti-Semitism by deriving it from the hatred engendered by Joseph's brutal capitalistic methods.[18] But he also thought the Joseph story the most "beautiful of all biblical tales" (III, 220), and very likely saw himself, in part, as a Joseph figure, i.e., born to success as well as "exile."

Such ambivalence shows that, despite his overt rejection of the Bible and its theology of a fall, repentance, sacrifice and redemption, it remained a dynamic force to which he responded on many levels. This ambivalence stems largely from the tension between the fundamentalist cultural upbringing he received early in life and the later intellectual influences of his manhood. For the Bible played a vital role in the cultural development of all frontier areas in the nineteenth century,[19] either as the source of religious values and inspiration, or the center of the intellectual war between Science and Religion. And while fundamentalism is no longer the religious stance of American society, a good deal of it still exists in the South and Southwest today. It must be remembered that as late as 1925 fundamentalist influence was strong enough to defeat Clarence Darrow in the famous Scopes Trial involving the freedom to teach evolution in the schools.[20] Not until the 1880's, when Mark Twain was a middle-aged man, did biblical fundamentalism come under the attack which was at last to defeat it. This was the Higher Criticism of Julius Wellhausen and Christian Baur. The Higher Criticism, however, met strong opposition from theologically conservative forces who refused to accept the possibility that the Bible was man-made and had developed over many centuries by four strands of authorship, each with its own theology, historical emphasis and literary style.[21] Interest grew, nevertheless, in such questions as the Hebrew debt to other civilizations and the inter-relationships of culture. Many thoughtful individuals faced genuine spiritual crises as they were forced to choose between their sacred Bible and the commitment to intellectual "truth" and "progress." Though the Bible had a tenacious hold on Mark Twain's imagination, he chose to reflect the influence of the Higher Criticism, though somewhat crudely:

> There is a curious poverty of inventions in Bibles. Most of the great races have one, and they all show this striking defect. Each pretends to originality. . . . We went back to Babylon for the Deluge . . . whereas we now know that Noah's flood never happened—not in that way. The Flood is a favorite with Bible-makers. (P, III, 1354–55)

He then goes on to accord the same treatment to the idea of the Immaculate Conception, confusing it with the Virgin Birth, in which, he claims, all ancient civilizations believed.

Although Mark Twain often reduced the complexities of mythic and theological interpretation to simple, sometimes wrong-headed, generalizations, he consistently embraced any "new" thought that would help free him from his youthful fundamentalist background, as a brief review of the intellectual influences on his views of religion should indicate.

It is probable that Mark Twain's deistic conception of God either began with or was stimulated by his early reading of Tom Paine's *The Age of Reason* when he was still a cub pilot.[22] Paine's central idea, that Bibles are man-made fables which actually denigrate God, reflects Mark Twain's own ideas. What is central to both of them is their rejection of anthropomorphism and orthodox Christian theology in favor of a more rational, scientifically oriented view. Both appreciate the purely literary greatness of the Bible. Indeed, Mark Twain loved to read aloud from the

Bible, and Charles W. Stoddard recounts how he impressed an audience in London with a beautiful reading of *The Book of Ruth*.[23]

Another important influence was John Fiske, a leading American thinker of the latter half of the nineteenth century, whose main task was to reconcile Evolution and the Bible. In his *Outlines of Cosmic Philosophy* (1874), Fiske presents the view that "evolution is God's way of doing things."[24] A. B. Paine says that Mark Twain planned to use the study of American flora and fauna that Fiske had made in his *Discovery of America* for a story of the Quaternary epoch, a story which was never written. But God's ultimate product, Man, was an evolutionary failure because his "intellect was a depraving addition to him, which . . . placed him . . . below the other beasts" (P, I, 115), an idea that found its way into the biblical *Letters from the Earth*.[25] In this work the intellect becomes identified with the Moral Sense which, in enabling man to choose evil over good, is the cause of the fall of man and his depravity. Animals become morally preferable to human beings.

It is likely, then, that when Mark Twain turned to scientifically oriented philosophers like Fiske, or the equally admired and influential Andrew D. White, he sought in them support for ideas already planted, but which needed intellectual nourishment. Mark Twain called White's *A History of the Warfare of Science with Theology* a "lovely book" (P, III, 1506), for it forcefully attacked fundamentalism using the standards of contemporary knowlege of geology and paleontology. Mark Twain thought White had shown that "those old theologians never reasoned at all" because they were unwilling to appreciate the significance of fossils. Finally, White's book supported his conviction that God was not concerned with the affairs of men. For Mark Twain, God's concern for man would be akin to the "President of the United States wanting to impress the flies and fleas . . ." (P, III, 1507).

But perhaps the most important intellectual influences occurred during the Hartford years, when Mark Twain lived in the new climate of religious liberalism dominated by thinkers such as Horace Bushnell, Harriet Beecher Stowe, and a superior group of clergymen. In the sermons of his clergymen friends, he encountered a theology in which love, rather than fire and brimstone, was emphasized. Living in the atmosphere created by ministers like Joseph Twichell, who was to become his closest friend, Mark Twain was able, for a brief time at least, to come to terms with the Christian world. Kenneth R. Andrews tells us that at this time Mark Twain "was not contemptuous of Christianity as a basis for an equitable society," in spite of his rejection of its theology. With clergymen like Nathaniel Burton, Edwin Pond Parker, and Twichell, men of high personal qualities, Mark Twain found a sympathetic and tolerant ear for his complaints and questions about the nature of God, interpretation of the Bible, and life in general. Andrews and Leah A. Strong, Twichell's biographer, show that Mark Twain and Twichell often disagreed on theological issues but respected each other's views and discussed them over and over again.[26] And it was in this period, in 1878, that Mark Twain (with W. D. Howells) made explicit his denial of the divinity of Jesus.[27] Very likely the Unitarian influence at Nook Farm confirmed a long-growing conviction. But such rationalistic influences could not abate the deep-seated anger he often directed at the New Testament and the character of Jesus. In *Letters from the Earth* (p. 45), he writes that the "palm for malignity must be granted to Jesus, the inventor of hell." How Twain arrived at such a theological idea is not too difficult to grasp. Curiously, he was fond of using the Hebrew word *sheol*—hell—in his works. But he probably did not distinguish between the rather inchoate, Hades-like conception of hell in the Old Testament and the more graphically punitive one deriving from the New Testament and early Christian tradition. His logic was that if Jesus is God, and God created hell, then Jesus was the "inventor" of hell. By the same logic, the central theological drama of the New Testament, Christ's sacrifice, was not only horrible, but also absurd. In his *Notebook* (p. 290), he wrote: "There seems to be nothing connected with the atonement scheme that is rational. If Christ were God, he is in the attitude of One whose anger against Adam has grown so uncontrollable . . . that nothing but a sacrifice of life can appease it, & so without noticing how illogical that act is going to be, God condemns Himself to death . . . and wipes off that old score." The complex distinctions of Trinitarian theology were not for Twain; reflecting an unsophisticated, fundamentalist cast of mind nourished by his frontier experience, he drew large generalizations from biblical texts and stories, only to subject them to his own iconoclastic logic.

During this period Mark Twain was reading his favorite book of history and ideas, Lecky's *History of European Morals* (1869), finding in it support for his own belief that Man was essentially a corrupt hedonist, seeking pleasure and avoiding pain as a motive for action and standard for conduct. As for Lecky's thesis that human cooperation is necessary for survival, Mark Twain retorted that Man has "proceeded from unreasoned selfishness to reasoned selfishness. All our acts reasoned and unreasoned are selfish" (P, II, 511). This was written in 1874 during the writing of his novel of genuine "innocence," *Tom Sawyer*. Years later the idea emerges virulently in *What is Man?* and defines a basic attitude concerning the damned human race.[28] For "reasoned selfishness" makes "true" morality impossible since there can be no morally disinterested act. Moreover, such "selfishness" necessarily hidden by each man tends to isolate him morally from others, so that each person works in a vacuum of self-concern, unable to relate to another person's concerns. People, therefore, act on false knowledge, illusion and partially understood self-concern. The possibilities for moral, tragic, and comic irony in such situations are self-evident, and Mark Twain consistently explored these possibilities in works as far apart in time and mood as *Huckleberry Finn* (1884) and *The Man*

That Corrupted Hadleyburg (1899). In both works the problem of unreasoned and reasoned selfishness leads to a fall. At least Huck *thinks* he has fallen after saving Jim, an act of "selfish" rather than social concern. The town of Hadleyburg suffers a genuine fall because its people are hypocrites, morally isolated from one another, who fail to understand their own motives. All in Hadleyburg are guilty of both kinds of selfishness.

Studies of the influence of Lecky on Mark Twain, including a record of Mark Twain's marginal notations,[29] have revealed his intellectual debt to the historian to be greater than that to any other single thinker he read. These notations expose Mark Twain's complaints against Christianity, his interest in the Stoics and their capacity to face death with philosophic calm, and his concern with the influence that religious ideas have had on mankind. He underscored this passage of Lecky's: "The [philosophers] taught that death is a law and not a punishment; the [fathers] taught that it is a penal affliction introduced on account of the sin of Adam, which was also the cause . . . of all convulsions in the material globe. . . ."[30] Then he underlines Lecky's explanatory passage on this problem which stated "that the first [the philosophers] represented man as pure until his will had sinned; the second [the fathers] represented him as under a sentence of condemnation at the very moment of his birth."[31]

These underscorings are extremely significant, for Lecky placed before Mark Twain the two basic alternatives Western thought had developed to explain human suffering and death. Mark Twain accepted the second view, the view of the fathers, Original Sin.

Mark Twain's determinism sprang essentially from those strands of Protestantism that deny free-will. The Lutheran and Calvinistic emphasis on "Faith Alone" (*Sola Fides*) and the belief that all human history has a predetermined course, making it ultimately impossible for man to cross the Will and Plan of God, were the theological principles he must have been exposed to during his youth. But it was determinism and not predestination which Twain finally affirmed. What he also came to reject—if he ever believed it—was the Protestant reliance on the Grace of God. Thus, Mark Twain was burdened with the belief in the ultimate sinfulness of man which derived from an innate defect created by God, unreformable and incorrigible, but without the possibility of Divine Grace "saving" him. Such a view leads to an unrelieved pessimism, for it holds to the belief in Damnation without the consolation of Redemption. For Mark Twain, the only hope was that, through satire and laughter, man might reform, but the growing futility of this hope only made his satire increasingly black. The despair of Mark Twain's later years, laced with dark laughter, may therefore be seen as a form of religious *angst*, in which God, sin, temperament, and environment prevent man from rising above himself.

Yet this did not stop Mark Twain from trying to effect reform through satire. Obviously he felt that satire could touch man's political and social nature, and he continued to lash out in this fashion in novels and short pieces. But what satire could not touch or change was man's cosmic destiny: ultimate evil and death and the possibility that "reality" was nothing but a dream, anyway. Against this inevitability he fashioned his own release. Death became a positive mood. In 1903, using Adam once again in order to give universal import to his words, he wrote this epigram in his *Notebook*: "Adam, man's benefactor—he gave him all he has ever received that was worth having—Death" (*N*, p. 381).

The Lecky notations and comments show how deeply Mark Twain was distressed by the burden of his theologically shaped despair. Lecky had written that "man is not only imperfect but a fallen being, and this . . . exercised an influence of the most serious character upon the moral history of the world." Mark Twain crossed out the word "serious" and substituted "rotten."[32] In another part of his copy of Lecky, he wrote that "Plainly God never knew anything about human beings, or he would not have trusted the idiots with so dangerous a thing as a Bible."[33]

There is a curious kind of brute logic in Mark Twain's views about the Bible. To a perceptive man living in the nineteenth century, a century in which the social order, morality, and even the most intangible aspects of civilization were shaped by biblical authority, there would be no escape from the problem that the Bible had seemingly created more suffering than good. The religious wars of history, the bigotry and hatred inspired by different readings of the same biblical text, could not be casually overlooked. White men could use the Bible to justify the slavery of the Negro, and one Christian sect to persecute another over such matters as baptismal rites, or the question of whether salvation lay in "works" or "faith." The stark fact was that Christianity and the Bible had failed to effect a morally better world, and indeed, had created a more disunited one. Since "the devil could quote Scripture to his own purpose," which aspects of biblical thought could an independent mind accept? Darwinism and the Higher Criticism had shattered the "miracles" for many people, though the Ten Commandments and the character of Jesus were almost beyond criticism. But what of the supreme Sermon on the Mount that even a John D. Rockefeller, Jr., could rationalize away, arguing that his money was not an "obstruction" to salvation?[34] Despite the healthy corrective of an authentic Christian like Joe Twichell, seen in the context of his time, a thoughtful person like Mark Twain might well conclude that the Bible was "dangerous."[35]

The effect of the intellectual influences on Mark Twain's mind was to free him from the simplistic anthropomorphism he learned in his youth, and to make him see the double-edged role the Bible played in Western culture. In short, he felt he had emancipated himself from "traditional" Christianity, its uses and abuses, to become part of the progressive scientific thought of the nineteenth century. Yet the image of the banished

Adam and man's innate sinfulness, of the Adamic myth as a whole, persists throughout his work. It would seem that if Mark Twain thought he had emancipated himself intellectually, he was still emotionally and psychologically a captive of the Bible's influence. Mark Twain tells us that he was "compelled" to read the Bible "unexpurgated" before he was "15 years old," adding with comic ruefulness, "None can do that and ever draw a clean, sweet breath again . . ." (P, III, 1281). Having been exposed to the violent images of sinful passion—often sexual—in the Bible, and the demanding, harsh nature of the God who punished man for the slightest moral error, the young boy is made to feel temptation and guilt before he has sufficiently developed, psychologically or morally, to be able to cope with these moral problems. He is made to feel sinful even before he knows the meaning of sin. Punishment seems cruel, inevitable, and just. The Sacred Book that is supposed to shore him up spiritually, only succeeds in intensifying his sense of sin and obsessive need to reform in order to be saved. As his emotional identification with Adam develops and filters into his work, the moral experiences of his own youth are used to provide the core of his explanation of Adam's fall. But it was in all probability the fundamentalist way the Bible was taught that either created or powerfully stimulated Mark Twain's preoccupation with the Adamic myth.

Van Wyck Brooks's thesis should be considered in this context. For Brooks, it was Jane Clemens who "wounded" his creative force by putting an intolerable burden of guilt on him, a thesis that recent critics have revised.[36] It appears that Jane Clemens was actually "quite liberal for her day. . . . She never was one whose life centered in the Church; she was not a steady Churchgoer; . . . she did not read the Bible a great deal."[37] This, plus the fact that both his father and his uncle, John Quarles, had been called "freethinker" and "Universalist" respectively, mitigates the idea that Mark Twain's sense of religious guilt derived from his parents. Rather, the evidence seems to point to the general culture of Hannibal and his education in the Sunday schools as the source of his Calvinistic attitudes. The incident of young Sam Clemens cringing in bed during a thunderstorm ready to be struck down by the wrath of God, and his obsession with reforming himself[38] reveal such an attitude.

A final anecdote from the *Autobiography* seems especially relevant to this analysis. It is the chilling experience of being haunted by a murder which took place in Hannibal when he was still a boy:

> The shooting down of old Smarr . . . at noonday supplied me with some dreams; and in them I always saw again the grotesque closing picture—the great family Bible spread open on the profane old man's breast by some thoughtful idiot and rising and sinking to the labored breathings and adding the torture of its leaden weight to the dying struggles. We are curiously made. In all the throng of gaping . . . onlookers there was not one with . . . sense enough to perceive that an anvil would have been in

better taste than the Bible, less open to sarcastic criticism and swifter in its atrocious work. In my nightmares I gasped and struggled for breath under the crush of that vast book for many a night. (p. 41)

While Mark Twain was not given to double meanings and obvious symbolism as a rule, it would be hard not to interpret the final line of this passage as symbolically significant. Indeed, its meaning becomes immediately intriguing and suggestive when we realize that, according to Dixon Wecter, there was no formal eyewitness account that validates the detail about the use of the Bible.[39] All we know is that Twain wished to recount a traumatic event of his youth and may have been compelled, psychologically, to introduce the Bible into it. In any case, whether the event took place in the exact way Twain described it or not, there is the implication that he *was* spiritually crushed by that "vast book." Therefore I see no reason why the critic, with full knowledge of the Bible's effect upon Twain's spirit, cannot so interpret the line. Though we can never be sure what the unconscious meaning of the event was for him, whether the Bible had become a symbol of all that was oppressive with its call to reform and guilt and punishment, the event itself, and the role the Bible played in his life on a literal level, are meaningful enough. This incident was so deeply etched into his mind that he used it for great dramatic and moral effect in *Huckleberry Finn* in the Boggs-Sherburn episode.

Such events demonstrated, in ways that the intellectual influences of later life could not, the terrible effects of fanaticism and ignorance. The combination of his own searching mind, his friendships with people like Twichell and Howells and other "modern" thinkers, his reading in history, science and philosophy—all these influences enabled him to transcend the "dangerous" aspects of the fundamentalism of his youth. Yet, ironically, his experience with man's inhumanity buttressed the Bible's pictures of man as a fallen creature. The Bible's moral codes appeared ever more noble and ideal as man revealed the impossibility of living up to them. The biblical figures of Adam, Eve, and Satan embodied for him the personally felt experience of his own banishment from the Eden that was Hannibal. Translated and explained in terms of his comic art and folk imagination, these archetypal characters personified his loss of innocence and his oppressive sense of guilt. Thus, in works like *Innocents Abroad, Roughing It*, and *Tom Sawyer*, there are persistent patterns of promise and failure, innocence stumbling over experience, evil challenging, but not quite overwhelming good. Yet the largest pattern of all is the portrayal of young Adam-Mark Twain attempting to return to an Eden imagined or real—the Holy Land, the Far West, the Hannibal of his boyhood.[40] It is the quest of the naive innocent who is not yet aware of the banishment. The quest discovers Evil, but the passion for innocence and psychic health is so strong, the implicit faith in the New World so intense, that the quester triumphs over any disenchantment. Perhaps most significantly, the prohibitions that perpetually restrain the free comic spirit of Twain's Adamic figures—the narrators of *Innocents Abroad* and *Roughing It*, Tom Sawyer and Huck Finn—are there to be dramatically circumvented in one way or another. One thinks of Mark Twain, the innocent abroad, slipping secretly into the quarantined port of Athens to see the Acropolis by moonlight, and Tom's whitewashing trick, to name only two outstanding instances.

In a work like "That Day in Eden (A Passage from Satan's Diary)," Adam and Eve eventually, inevitably, transgress the prohibitions they cannot even understand, prohibitions that are only words without experiential content. For Mark Twain, their fall is inevitable, but it is also a deceit of God, and their banishment by God is an unsurpassed act of absurd cruelty. In the fullness of his life, Mark Twain began to see himself as a banished Adam, too, and his anger at God and the unfairness of the fall grew steadily more violent throughout his life. Yet, during the 1880's and the writing of *Life on the Mississippi* and *Huckleberry Finn*, he retained his spirit of freedom and challenge, and was willing to accept exile or "lighting out" as a meaningful response to a fallen world. At the same time, however, that his Adam-Huck persona was escaping gleefully into the territory, his Adam–Tom Sawyer persona was seeking identity with that fallen society in an act of acceptance and compromise. These two responses are perfectly balanced in *Huckleberry Finn*.

But the final period shows what happens to a freedom preserved in exile. Surrounded by a disgraced and fallen humanity, the exile tries to carry his dream of freedom and Eden to man, and fails miserably, as does Hank Morgan in *A Connecticut Yankee*. Pudd'nhead brings humor and intelligence to Dawson's Landing, but he too is forced into exile and ironic bitterness. His court victory does not negate his judgment that all men are fools. And these same fools, in French and English fifteenth-century dress, burn that spiritual exile, Joan of Arc. The exiles have become strangers, and in their estrangement begin, by and large, to develop Satanic characteristics.

It was not long before the pattern took its final turn in "The Mysterious Stranger" stories. Banished Adam became banished Satan. If, indeed, there was any salvation for Mark Twain, this metamorphosis provided it. For banished Adam by himself was proven to be a helpless, embittered creature, finally useless. But banished Satan, unaware of human suffering, could survive where Adam could not. Mark Twain's admiration for Satan is more than an attempt at ironic humor. The Satan of "The Mysterious Stranger" stories, as well as the exiled Satan of *Letters from the Earth*, is a dynamic figure who is unfallen, outspoken, and completely without sham or hypocrisy. The Satan of the *Letters* judges God and man as Mark Twain judged God and man, and the Satan of "The Mysterious Stranger" fables embodies the creative power that Mark Twain reveled in. Both Satans, moreover, provided Mark Twain with masks[41] through which the nature of man, God, and Universe could be comprehended. The grand irony is that Satan, the apostle of dreams and determinism, is the final Adamic image Mark Twain took to himself. Weaving all the major strands of the Adamic myth, dream psychology, and determinism together in the famous dream-passage (1904) of "No. 44, The Mysterious Stranger," Twain confronted the "reality" of an Absurd Universe in which "Nothing exists but You. And you are but a Thought . . . wandering forlorn among the empty eternities!" (p. 405). But to free oneself from the "nightmare" of history and nihilism implicit in Satan's solipsistic idealism, one would have to dream oneself, actually become a God. As I have argued in my study of Twain's Satan-figures,[42] Twain turned the theology of Genesis upside down. Adam becomes Satan and Satan becomes a "new" Adam, glorying in his release from corrupting flesh with its burden of conscience, and exulting in his unlimited creative powers. Unaware of or indifferent to all human pain and limitations, Twain's mysterious stranger is released from those conditions by which both Judaic and Christian theology define the tragic, but not hopeless nature of the fallen human condition: that man is created in mere flesh that decays, and trapped in a world of moral ambiguities where faith in Absolute values often disintegrates. But it seems reasonable to assume that, in formulating his theological protest through his native humor and art, Twain was not only seeking release from the mortal conditions of the fall, but also from the very weight of the Bible itself with its call to repentance and the acceptance of God's creation, regardless of how mysterious and unjust that creation may appear to be.

Notes

1. Letter to Mrs. Boardman, March 25, 1887. Berg Collection, New York Public Library.

2. A. B. Paine, *Mark Twain: A Biography* (New York, 1912), I, 512. Hereafter referred to in my text as P. And for a good study of Twain's Adamic references and allusions, see Allison Ensor, *Mark Twain & the Bible* (Lexington, 1970). Also Minnie Brashear, *Mark Twain, Son of Missouri* (Chapel Hill, 1934), pp. 207–209; and Kenneth Lynn's "Huck and Jim," *Yale Review*, 47 (March 1958). Lynn shows how important the Moses-freedom theme is to the form and meaning of *Huckleberry Finn*. Indeed, there are so many references and allusions to biblical characters and themes, and the influence of the Bible is on the whole so powerful on Twain's thought and art, that I can explore only a few key aspects of them in this paper.

3. *Mark Twain in Eruption*, ed. Bernard DeVoto (New York, 1940), epigraph, unpaginated. The statement is dated September 4, 1907.

4. *The Autobiography of Mark Twain*, ed. Charles Neider (New York, 1959), p. 5. All references to the *Autobiography* will be placed in the body of my text. Though this is not a definitive, scholarly text, it is easily available and is reliable for the few incidents I have cited.

5. *Mark Twain's Notebook*, ed. A. B. Paine (New York, 1935), pp. 301–302. The idea of God's contradictory and absurd Universe is dramatized in "The Mysterious Stranger" com-

plex, particularly in "No. 44, The Mysterious Stranger." See *Mark Twain's Mysterious Stranger Manuscripts*, ed. with an Introduction by William M. Gibson (Berkeley, Calif., 1969), p. 405. Reference to "The Mysterious Stranger" will be from this edition.

6. *The Writings of Mark Twain*, ed. A. B. Paine, 37 vols. (New York, 1923–24), the Stormfield Edition. Unless otherwise specified, all further references to Mark Twain's work will be to this edition. And for a full analysis of Twain's theology of humor, see my study "The Humor of the Absurd: Mark Twain's Adamic Diaries," *Criticism* (Winter 1972), 49–64. See also Richard Boyd Hauck, *A Cheerful Nihilism: Confidence and "The Absurd" in American Humorous Fiction* (Bloomington, Ind.: Univ. of Indiana Press, 1971), Chapter 5.

7. On the question of the Bible's influence on Mark Twain's style, there is no clear consensus. Minnie Brashear emphasizes the biblical influence on many of his titles, such as *What is Man?* and "To the Person Sitting in Darkness" as well as on the cadences of his sentences. See *Mark Twain, Son of Missouri*, pp. 207–208. Gladys Bellamy in *Mark Twain as a Literary Artist* (Norman, Oklahoma, 1950), p. 84, writes that his "style reveals Mark Twain's habit of dropping into Biblical language and Biblical rhythms, a device he would use until the end of his days." However, DeLancey Ferguson in his biography *Mark Twain, Man and Legend* (New York, 1963), p. 126, dissents: ". . . Mark's mature style is anything but biblical. Not from the Bible did he learn the art of building up a phrase with meticulously chosen adjectives, his vivid images, his skillfully contrived anti-climaxes. These were the result of learning to write as he talked."

On the face of it, Ferguson seems to be right, because Mark Twain's style does pattern itself more on an oral tradition of tall-tale telling than on biblical rhetoric. Yet Mark Twain greatly admired biblical style, as he testifies in *Innocents Abroad* (III, 220): "Who taught those ancient writers their simplicity of language, their felicity of expression, their pathos, and above all, their faculty of sinking themselves out of the sight of the reader and making the narrative stand out alone and seem to tell itself?" Mark Twain could admire and burlesque biblical style at the same time, as, for example, in *Innocents Abroad*. Very likely biblical cadences did occasionally shape his style. Far more important is the consideration that biblical images and thought inhere in his style as an epiphenomenon, a dimension of sensibility that informs and expands his basically indigenous, Western oral qualities.

8. Quoted in *Mark Twain's Letters to Mary*, ed. Lewis Leary (New York, 1961), pp. 18–19.

9. *Mark Twain—Howells Letters*, ed. Henry Nash Smith and William M. Gibson (Cambridge, Mass., 1960), II, 461.

10. But see Minnie Brashear, p. 204. Miss Brashear cites the original study by Henry Pochmann of Mark Twain's literary allusions. But obviously there are countless more in recently published works by Twain as well as in a great deal of unpublished material. Biblical allusions and images simply saturate Twain's writings.

11. See my article "Blackness and the Adamic Myth in Mark Twain's *Pudd'nhead Wilson,*" *Texas Studies in Literature and Language*, 15 (Spring 1973), 167–176.

12. But see Paine, Chapter CCLII, *passim*. For Twain, the Biblical God was, in fact, a portrait of "a man, if one can imagine a man with evil impulses far beyond the human limit" (III, 1354).

13. For a fuller treatment of Mark Twain's God, see Paine, III, 1356–1365. Mark Twain invokes the study of geology and evolution to suggest the infinity and grandeur of his God of Nature and to further belittle the anthropomorphism of the God of Genesis. He never seems to have noticed the conception of God in the Psalms, for example, particularly Psalm 104, in which God is imagined on a vast scale.

14. Ed. Charles Neider, *Hudson Review*, 16 (Autumn 1963), 329–352.

15. Joseph Twichell to Mark Twain, September 5, 1901, as quoted in Kenneth R. Andrews, *Nook Farm: Mark Twain's Hartford Circle* (Cambridge, Mass., 1950), p. 253.

16. See *Mark Twain in Eruption*, p. 91.

17. *Ibid.* But see Louis J. Budd, "Mark Twain on Joseph the Patriarch," *American Quarterly*, 16 (Winter 1964), 577–586. And see also Maxwell Geismar, *Mark Twain: An American Prophet* (Boston, 1971), Chapter Twelve, for a good account of Twain's attitudes toward the Robber Barons, both friend and foe.

18. See "Concerning the Jews," XXII, 262ff.

19. For accounts of the influence of the Bible on frontier life see, for example, C. Olmstead, *Religion in America, Past and Present* (New York, 1950), as well as Louis B. Wright, *Culture on the Moving Frontier* (New York, 1961), pp. 190ff. Wright says that "The constant reading of the Bible helped to shape the language patterns of countless Americans and its rhythms were reflected in the oratory, not only of preachers, but of politicians and statesmen. The King James version of the Bible exerted a greater influence on American imagination and thought than any other book" (p. 190).

20. See Olmstead, pp. 140–141.

21. For a good summary of Higher Criticism scholarship see Robert H. Pfeiffer, *The Books of the Old Testament* (New York, 1957), particularly the introduction *passim*.

22. See Brashear, pp. 162–164, 204, 214, 244–248, *passim* for the influence of Tom Paine on Mark Twain. For another source of Twain's ideas about God and the Bible, see Alexander E. Jones, "Mark Twain and Free Masonry," *American Literature*, 26 (January 1955), 363–373.

23. See E. Hudson Long, *Mark Twain Handbook* (New York, 1957), p. 302.

24. As quoted in Olmstead, p. 118. A good treatment of Fiske's work and influence is to be found in Philip P. Weiner, *Evolution and the Founders of Pragmatism* (New York, 1965), pp. 129–151. Weiner writes that Fiske wished to extend "the harmony portended by his cosmic doctrine of evolution into religion and politics at a time when both were undergoing the . . . travails of 'the Higher Criticism' of Christianity and the social upheaval signalized by the Paris Commune of 1871" (p. 148).

25. In *Letters from the Earth*, ed. Bernard DeVoto (New York, 1962), pp. 239ff. Mark Twain wrote that, after studying mankind, he had to "renounce my allegiance to the Darwinian theory of the Ascent of Man from the Lower Animals" to the truer one of the "Descent of Man from the Higher Animals."

26. Kenneth R. Andrews develops this notion in his *Nook Farm: Mark Twain's Hartford Circle*, pp. 25–77. Leah A. Strong's *Joseph Hopkins Twichell: Mark Twain's Friend and Pastor* (Athens, Ga., 1966) also demonstrates this in full. Though Twain could not accept Twichell's view of man as having free-will and developing through Christ, to a supreme spiritual manhood, he attended his Old Asylum Congregational Church for many years and never allowed theological differences to interfere with his basic respect for the kind of "progressive" Christianity Twichell represented. Twain's relationship with Burton and Parker was equally one of tolerance.

27. Mark Twain to Orion Clemens, March 23, 1878, *Letters*, I, 323.

28. Howard G. Baetzhold's *Mark Twain & John Bull: The British Connection* (Bloomington: Univ. of Indiana Press, 1970), *passim*, contains an excellent account of Twain's "discussion with Lecky." In *What is Man? And Other Philosophical Writings*, ed. and with an Introduction by Paul Baender (Berkeley, 1973), we see how Twain revised *What is Man?* until he finally clarified it. Baender writers: "The revisions expressed what Mark Twain meant all along: men were selfish in the sense that they had to satisfy their consciences and temperaments, regardless of consequences" (p. 14).

29. Chester L. Davis has edited Mark Twain's notations and marginal comments in his copy of Lecky in *The Twainian*, 14 (May 1955, December 1956). Davis gives 1906 as the date of these notations, although Walter Blair in *Mark Twain & Huck Finn* (Berkeley, 1960), p. 401, fn. 6, suggests they were written earlier, perhaps in the late 1870's and early 1880's.

30. *Twainian*, 14 (May–June 1955), 4.

31. *Ibid.*

32. *Twainian*, 14 (May–June 1955), 3.

33. *Twainian*, 15 (December 1956), 44.

34. See *Mark Twain in Eruption*, p. 81.

35. Mark Twain spells out his complaints against Christianity and the abuse of the Bible in his "Bible Teaching—Religious Practice" (XXIX, 387–93).

36. For the whole Brooks-DeVoto controversy see *Mark Twain's Wound*, ed. Lewis Leary (New York, 1962), a selection of essays on the subject from varying points of view.

37. In Philip Foner, *Mark Twain: Social Critic* (New York, 1958), p. 127. Also Dixon Wecter, *Sam Clemens of Hannibal* (Boston, 1952), writes that Jane was an "espouser of almost any religion" (p. 86). Wecter also feels that young Sam's Sunday School, "The Old Ship of Zion," had much more to do with creating his Calvinist attitudes than did his family.

38. Chapter LIV in *Life on the Mississippi*. The more comic aspect of young Sam's training is of course the famous Bible-lesson scene in *Tom Sawyer*.

39. A full reconstruction of the event is given by Wecter, pp. 106–109.

40. See H. N. Smith, "Mark Twain's Image of Hannibal: From St. Petersburg to Eseldorf," *Texas Studies in English*, 37 (1958), 3–23.

41. But see Coleman O. Parsons, "The Devil and Samuel Clemens," *Virginia Quarterly Review*, 23 (Autumn 1947), 582–606; John S. Tuckey, *Mark Twain and Little Satan: The Writing of the Mysterious Stranger* (Lafayette, Ind., 1963); Roger B. Salomon, *Twain and the Image of History* (New Haven, 1961), Chap. 9; William M. Gibson's Introduction to *Mark Twain's Mysterious Stranger Manuscripts, passim*; and my study "Mark Twain's Masks of Satan: The Final Phase," *American Literature*, 45 (May 1973), 206–27.

42. In my "Mark Twain's Masks of Satan: The Final Phase," esp. pp. 217–227.

"Tears and Flapdoodle": Point of View and Style in *The Adventures of Huckleberry Finn*

Janet Holmgren McKay*

Mark Twain's *The Adventures of Huckleberry Finn* is one of the most stylistically significant works in American literature. T. S. Eliot is not alone in his evaluation of Twain as "one of those writers, of whom there are not a great many in any literature, who have discovered a new way of writing."[1] Literary critics have praised Twain time and again for creating a narrative style in *Huck Finn* which uses vernacular or colloquial American English to revitalize the imaginative representation of reality. However, few critics have actually examined the way in which Twain fashioned a consistent literary style for an apparently nonliterary form of discourse.[2]

To say that Twain created Huck's voice by copying the speech patterns of a young boy is factually inadequate, as any student of language knows. Spoken and written modes of discourse can never be identical, particularly in literature where the language must be highly conscious and compactly organized. What Twain actually does in *Huck Finn* is to use certain strategically placed vernacular and colloquial features[3] to create the impression of an untutored narrator, while simultaneously developing a sophisticated, innovative literary style which uses a full range of standard English constructions and literary devices.

The success of this stylistic *tour de force* depends upon the consistency with which Twain maintains Huck's narrative point of view. If Huck's language convinces the reader of his innocence, his perceptions and actions must support this impression. This essential interdependence of form and content further requires that Huck's style be rigorously coherent. However, after bringing the reader to accept the illusion of naive narration, Twain is free to play with both language and the related point of view for imaginative effects.

To understand this complex interaction we need both the linguist's attention to language structure—his knowledge of the social and cultural implications of particular linguistic forms—and the literary critic's awareness of the artistic significance of language devices in the individual

*Reprinted by permission from *Style*, 10 (Winter, 1976), 41–50.

context. Above all, however, we need substantiation of our stylistic perceptions with actual textual analysis. What linguistic devices establish Huck's voice and simultaneously achieve poetic effects in a particular context? Are these devices apparent elsewhere in the work, and if so, what artistic variations within them are evident here? A wide-ranging analysis of individual passages can then lead to an examination of the relationship of the individual passage to the work as a whole and to the larger literary stylistic context. Only then can we make convincing claims for "simplicity," "innovativeness," and "consistency."

A passage from the central section of the novel offers some interesting insights into the complexity of Twain's *Huck Finn* style and into the subtle narrative irony that Twain creates through the style. In the course of their journey down the Mississippi River, Huck and the runaway slave Jim are set upon by two con men who claim to be dispossessed aristocracy. Although Huck resolves to get along with the King and the Duke as long as they are around, he becomes increasingly disgusted with their antics. His aversion reaches a peak in the Wilks family incident when the King and Duke contrive to rob three defenseless girls, hiding their deceit in the trappings of familial love and Christian fellowship. The moment when the King, posing as both preacher and grieving brother, bursts forth in his "soul-butter and hogwash" speech provides Huck with an opportunity to vent his anger. The description which follows is a stylistic masterpiece—a subtle blending of Huck's and the King's voices balanced for the maximum satiric effect.

> Well, by and by the king he gets up and comes forward a little, and works himself up and slobbers out a speech, all full of tears and flapdoodle, about its being a sore trial for him and his poor brother to lose the diseased, and to miss seeing diseased alive after the long journey of four thousand mile, but it's a trial that's sweetened and sanctified to us by this dear sympathy and these holy tears, and so he thanks them out of his heart and out of his brother's heart, because out of their mouths they can't, words being too weak and cold, and all that kind of rot and slush, till it was just sickening; and then he blubbers out a pious goody-goody Amen, and turns himself loose and goes to crying fit to bust.[4]

A number of literary scholars have noted that in the original draft of this section Twain used direct quotation to present the King's speech, but in revision he shifted to indirect discourse.[5] In fact, however, the discourse here is only partially indirect—a fact masked by one of the hallmarks of Huck's style, the run-on sentence.

Huck frequently uses run-ons, like the one here which constitutes nearly the entire paragraph. Within them he employs few overt marks of subordination, although many of his coordinate major clauses function as subordinate clauses.[6] While the relationships among the parts of this sentence are not always clearly defined, the structure is essentially cumulative—to borrow a descriptive term from Francis Christensen. In a cumulative sentence the main clause, which Christensen numbers "one," establishes the topic and subsequent clauses and sentence modifiers elaborate it with increasing specificity. These elaborations have a narrower focus than the main clause and are therefore assigned a lower level of generality.[7] Both the cumulative structure and the loose coordination are typical of the conversational style in English.[8] Furthermore, they contribute to the reader's impression of Huck's naiveté and lack of linguistic sophistication.

In the compound/complex sentence of this paragraph, an important variation on the cumulative structure creates a narrative frame for the King's discourse. The sentence follows a pattern of decreasing levels of generality up to the absolute, "words being too weak and cold." In the next phrase, "and all that kind of rot and slush," Huck returns to the level of general description he used at the beginning of the sentence. Thus Twain begins with Huck's introduction, moves into Huck's rendition of the King's words ("its being a sore trial for him and his brother"), and finally, in the middle of the sentence, gives us the King himself speaking ("it's a trial that's sweetened and sanctified to us"). From this point on, we move gradually back to Huck's voice, passing once again through the intermediate stage of Huck's account of the King ("because out of their mouths they can't"). The sentence's structure can be represented roughly as follows:[9]

HUCK	[2]Well, by and by (adv)
	[1]the king he gets up and comes forward a little,
	and works himself up and slobbers out a speech,
	[2]all full of tears and flapdoodle, (reduced RC)
HUCK/KING	[2]about its being a sore trial . . . (Abs as object of prep)
	[3]after the long journey . . . (PP)
KING	[3]but it's a trial that's sweetened and sanctified
	to us . . . (Major C)
HUCK/KING	[3]and so he thanks them out of his heart . . .
	(Major C)

[4]because out of their mouths they can't,
(SC)
    [5]words being too weak . . . (Abs)

HUCK	[2]and all that kind of rot and slush,
	[3]till it was just sickening; (SC)
	[1]and then he blubbers out a pious goody-goody Amen. . . .

Twain accomplishes the changes in narrative perspective by contrasting Huck's style to the bombastic posturings of the King, although he incorporates the latter into Huck's narration. The passage's lexicon reveals the major distinctions between Huck's narrative voice and his recounting of the King's speech. In the frame clauses at the beginning and the end of the sentence, an element of disdain marks Huck's key lexical choices and constitutes one thread of lexical cohesion. Thus the King "slobbers" and "blubbers"; his speech, which Huck finds "sickening," is "rot," "slush," and "flapdoodle." The verb phrases Huck uses to encompass the King's entire act—"works himself up," "turns himself loose"—also clearly reflects Huck's scorn for the King's histrionics in this fraudulent scene.

Phrasal verbs, which play a prominent role in Huck's casual style, are numerous in the frame elements—"gets up," "comes forward," "works up," "slobbers out," "blubbers out," "turns loose," "goes to"; however, none occur within his presentation of the King's discourse. Furthermore, most of Huck's vernacular syntactic constructions occur in the frame elements, where, in addition to the ambiguity of syntactic relations which we will examine below, we find tautology ("the king he," "all full of"). Finally, lexical choices and constructions which the reader has come to associate with Huck through constant repetition are prominent in the opening and closing. Two of Huck's favorite adjectives of disdain are "sickening" and "goody-goody." Structurally, "goody-goody" exemplifies a pattern in Huck's style of forming slang adjectives by adding a -y suffix to other adjectives and nouns.[10] Semantically, it reflects Huck's persistent skepticism about people who try to be good by "sivilized" standards.

When Huck records the King's speech, he adopts the King's ostentatiously pious vocabulary. The clichéd phrases, such as "sore trial," "poor brother," "sweetened and sanctified," and "holy tears," force the reader to focus on the pretense of genteel mourning. Tearfulness becomes a dominant theme, linking the paragraph to the surrounding descriptions where the King, the Duke, the Wilks sisters, and the townspeople carry on excessively. Huck's term "slush" effectively captures the mental and physical sogginess of the scene.

All of this "sobbing and swabbing" (p. 227) contrasts sharply with Huck's own understated emotional expressions. For instance, during the Shepherdson/Grangerford feud when Huck's friend Buck is killed, Huck says, "I cried a little when I was covering up Buck's face, for he was mighty good to me" (p. 160). The contrast resides in the language, and the reader's perception of Huck develops from the contrast. Huck's actions and the language he uses to describe them are Twain's most powerful indictment of the "pretended or misguided piety" (Smith, 118) and the maudlin sentimentality of the pre–Civil War South. However, in striving for the maximum satiric effect Twain was not content to rely on irony—a fact which accounts in part for his decision to shift from direct to indirect discourse in this passage. Huck's scathing denunciation becomes the angle from which we view the sham and adds to his moral authority. Outrage reinforces satire. Notice that with the adjective "pious"—a lexical choice not suitable to Huck's colloquial vocabulary and made unnecessary by Huck's own "good-goody"—we sense Twain pushing beyond the limits of Huck's narration to make his point.

Another interesting example of authorial control occurs in the "diseased/deceased" pun. Throughout the Wilks episode, the King in the role of Harvey Wilks, noted English minister, attempts to introduce terms of learning and gentility into his speech—a linguistic impersonation which allows Twain to characterize the King while mocking the genteel values which the King mimics. In the process the King comes up with some ludicrous malapropisms, like his confusion of "orgies" and "obsequies" (p. 233). In this passage, because Twain uses the frame of indirect discourse, it is not clear whether the King actually uses "diseased" for "deceased" or whether Huck mixes the two up. The error thus serves two purposes. The King's subsequent "orgies/obsequies" error makes it likely that this one is his, too. As such, it plays a part in Twain's satire, for it focuses on the King's ignorance and on the ignorance of those who hear him and still believe his ruse. However, Huck uses "diseased" again a few pages later ("Well, then, pretty soon all hands got to talking about the diseased again . . ." pp. 232–33). As Huck's error, it adds to the ironic distance between Huck and the implied author. In both the "orgies/obsequies" and the "diseased/deceased" confusions Twain is playing on the macabre logic of the substitutions—a rhetorical manipulation that would be beyond Huck.

Although the changes in narrative perspective are indicated primarily by lexical devices, some important syntactic variations also play a part. Huck normally uses the active voice in his clauses and sentences, the majority of which follow the subject-verb-object pattern. The consistency with which Twain maintains this pattern makes variations on it all the more striking. Thus in this passage a single passive construction is strategically located in the clause wholly attributable to the King ("it's a trial that's sweetened and sanctified to us"). This one small shift has multiple functions. It adds a pompous note to the King's speech; it contrasts the King's evasiveness with Huck's habitually straight-forward style; and it permits Twain to play on the repetition of "it's a trial," with its sermon-like rhythm (reminding us of the King's ministerial impersonation). Finally, the passive construction makes the change from third person (him, his) to first person (us) pronouns less noticeable—an important linguistic function. Twain scrupulously avoids any features that might make Huck's style obstruct rather than support the reader's involvement with the story.[11] Thus, for instance, although many of Huck's sentences are run-on, their cumulative, right-branching construction makes them easily comprehensible. Here the pronoun shift might constitute a potential impediment, so it is subtly obscured.

Huck generally begins his sentences and clauses with their subjects, as I noted above, occasionally prefacing those that begin new paragraphs with a simple transition like the "well, by and by" we find here. One clause in this sentence, however, violates this pattern with its opening—"because out of their mouths." The variation heightens the satire by drawing the reader's attention to what *is* coming out of the

King's mouth and by providing an ironic contrast to the maudlin repetition "out of his heart and out of his brother's heart."

Finally, Huck's phrase "and all that kind of rot and slush," which begins the closing frame element, has an ambiguous relationship to the sentence. Although it functions as a disdainful comment on what the King has said, structurally the phrase is either a coordinate object with "speech" or more likely another modifier of "speech." Thus it reminds the reader of the connection between this concluding part of the sentence and the opening. Ambiguity is a typical colloquial feature of Huck's style, but as with all of Huck's idiosyncratic features Twain rarely uses it without a larger structural purpose.

Other features of Huck's which have a rhetorical function include his usual conjunctions "and," "and then," "and so," which tend to move the passage along at a rapid pace, adding to what Ferguson calls the sense of "compression" (p. 222). Huck frequently uses repetition and parallelism, and here these features are concentrated in the King's simulated sermon style—"to lose the diseased"/"to miss seeing diseased alive," "its being a sore trial"/"but it's a trial," "this dear sympathy"/"these holy tears," "out of his heart"/"out of his brother's heart"/"out of their mouths." Finally, Huck's narration constantly benefits from an apparently guileless alliteration and sound symbolism—part of his innate feeling for the play of language. Although not obtrusive, the plosives /p/, /b/ and the hard /g/, /k/ sounds pervade the frame elements while smoother sibilants /s/ highlight the King's speech.

While most of the linguistic features I have discussed thus far have tended to distinguish Huck's voice from his account of the King's speech, in one area Twain minimizes the distinction to capitalize on the dramatic potential of the scene. Throughout the passage Twain has Huck use what Martin Joos in *The English Verb* labels the narrative actual present tense.[12] As with the French "historical present," to which Joos compares the English construction, the reader is aware that the event described took place in the past because of other contextual markers, like Huck's "by and by." However, the shift in tense is both a feature typical of conversation style and a means of showing the narrator's intense involvement. As Joos says, the narrative actual "has a firm basis in speech, where the use of actual tense for past events comes naturally to the lips of a man who gets himself involved in what he is talking about." In addition to characterizing Huck's attitude, the shift in tense here suggests direct discourse. To provide a smooth transition from the preceding paragraph which is in the past tense, Twain concludes that paragraph with two nonstandard preterits which have the same form as the standard present (". . . and *give* the next woman a show. I never *see* anything so disgusting"). Twain's choice of a particular nonstandard feature for its rhetorical value is evident here, since Huck uses the nonstandard preterit "seen" elsewhere as in the fifth sentence of the novel—"I never seen anybody but lied one time or another . . ." (p. 1).

Thus in this paragraph Twain tailors the colloquial features to the literary situation, pulling the inherent opposition of the two into a taut, productive balance. This inquiry into the structure and function of a short passage only hints at the rich linguistic resources of *Huck Finn*. The finest work of an author dedicated to the power and versatility of language, the novel is an outstanding example of the role language plays in creating the reality of a fictional setting.

Through the consistent use of certain linguistic features Twain characterizes Huck and makes the reader believe in the reality of Huck's vision. Huck's style both because of its apparent simplicity and because of the way in which it contrasts with the hypocrisy of acceptable language use comes to represent honesty in a dishonest world. Ultimately, the reader distinguishes truth from falsity by the linguistic contrasts of the text. By putting the more "sivilized" constructions in the mouth of a scoundrel like the King, Twain insures their demise. They are buried by Huck's honest indignation, by Twain's satiric juxtaposition of "tears and flapdoodle."

Notes

1. T. S. Eliot, "American Literature and American Language," *To Criticize the Critic* (New York: Farrar, Straus & Giroux, 1965), p. 54.

2. Notable exceptions to this general tendency are Charles Clerc's article "Sunrise on the River: 'The Whole World' of Huckleberry Finn," *Modern Fiction Studies*, 14 (1968), 67–78, and Richard Bridgman's "Henry James and Mark Twain," chapter three in *The Colloquial Style in America* (New York: Oxford University Press, 1966).

3. Careful distribution of nonstandard and casual features characterizes all of Twain's composition. As Sydney J. Krause notes, "in order that it might *count*, he had to use dialect judiciously, and the same was true of his colloquial diction at large and his illiterate grammar." "Twain's Method and Theory of Composition," *Modern Philology*, 56 (1959), 176.

4. Samuel Langhorne Clemens, *The Adventures of Huckleberry Finn*, Vol. XIII of *The Writings of Mark Twain*, Author's National Edition (New York: Harper and Brothers, 1912), pp. 227–28. Subsequent page references to this work will appear in the text. No thoroughly accurate edition of *Huck Finn* is presently available; therefore, I have chosen this edition because it is the same as the Definitive Edition and much more readily accessible. The few punctuation differences in the 1885 American version as reproduced in the Norton Critical Edition (*Adventures of Huckleberry Finn: An Annotated Text*, ed. Sculley Bradley, Richmond Croom Beatty, E. Hudson Long [New York: W. W. Norton & Co., Inc., 1972]), are not significant for the analysis of this passage.

5. DeLancey Ferguson, *Mark Twain: Man and Legend* (New York: Russell & Russell, 1966), pp. 221–22; Henry Nash Smith, *Mark Twain: The Development of a Writer* (New York: Atheneum, 1967), p. 121.

6. David Crystal and Derek Davy in *Investigating English Style* (Bloomington: Indiana University Press, 1969) label such structures "dependent coordinate," a pattern in which" the coordinate component is functionally as much dependent on the preceding clause as a subordinate clause in the same position," p. 59, n. 9.

7. *Notes Toward a New Rhetoric* (New York: Harper & Row, 1967), pp. 5–9.

8. For a general analysis of conversational English see Crystal and Davy, chapter 4, "The Language of Conversation," particularly the discussion of sentence types, p. 110.

9. The numbering system within the diagram is based on Christensen's analytical model as are the grammatical labels for types of phrases and clauses. Christensen (p. 9) uses the following abbreviations of "free-modifiers"—sentence modifiers that are nonrestrictive: SC-subordinate clause; RC-relative clause; Abs-absolute; PP-prepositional phrase. I have added the two designations adverbial (adv) and major clause (Major C) to account for some typical patterns in Huck's sentences.

10. I use the designation "slang" based on the findings of Hans Marchand, *The Categories and Types of Present-Day English Word-Formation*, Alabama Lingustic and Philological Series, No. 13 (University of Alabama Press, 1966). Marchand notes that "beginning with the 18th c., the sf [suffix-*y*] has shown a tendency to form words of a colloquial, slangy character," p. 288.

11. Thus, for instance, Robert Lowenherz notes that Twain restricts "dialect spelling to less than one percent of Huck's narrative speech . . . consistently throughout the novel." "The Beginning of 'Huckleberry Finn'," *American Speech*, 38 (1963), 197.

12. *The English Verb: Form & Meanings* (Madison: University of Wisconsin Press, 1968), p. 131.

Mark Twain and His Times:
A Bicentennial Appreciation

Arthur G. Pettit*

I warn the reader that if he leaves out of the account an indignant sense of right and wrong, a scorn of all affectation and pretense, an ardent hate of meanness and injustice, he will come infinitely short of knowing Mark Twain.

William Dean Howells

It is by the goodness of God that in our country we have those three unspeakably precious things: freedom of speech, freedom of conscience, and the prudence never to practise either of them.

Mark Twain

In the year just passed of bicentennial backslapping, we witnessed several ambitious stage and screen tributes to our nation's past, many of them in the form of television specials which attempted to answer Crèvecoeur's famous question, "What then is the American, this new man?" in terms of biographies of famous past Americans.[1] We are no longer so new as we were in Crèvecoeur's time, but the notion that we are a peculiar people with a unique destiny is still very much with us. That the notion itself seems indistinguishable from nonsense does not alter the fact that such self-congratulatory phrases as American Destiny, American Experiment, American Mission, and American Dream still command the allegiance of a good many Americans, especially during an election year.

Yet now that 1977 has brought release from the twin burdens of bicentennialism and the election, it is apparent that most of the popular media's attempt to hold a bicentennial mirror to the American face have gone the way of other well-intentioned spurts of national introspection. Indeed, the only current show business tribute to a famous American that is bound to survive well beyond 1976 is the only impersonation which predates the bicentennial by almost two decades: Hal Holbrook's *Mark Twain Tonight!* This reflects not only the presentation's intrinsic quality but also the fact that of all our present historical favorites, Mark Twain alone seems both timeless and contemporary. His writings and stage

*Reprinted with permission from *South Atlantic Quarterly*, 76 (Spring, 1977), 133–46. Copyright © 1977, Duke University Press.

posturings exude a sweaty odor of fallibility and vulnerability that the televised Founding Fathers, or the martyred Lincoln, or the recently whitewashed Truman, or even the semi-tarnished Kennedy lack. No famous figure of our past—certainly no famous figure who rests outside the pantheon of the presidents—speaks more forcefully and personally to the sins and virtues, the triumphs and debacles of our own time. While Washington, Adams, and Jefferson lecture from the grave to tell us how much we have changed, Mark Twain sits on his tombstone, chomping his cigar, to tell us how much we remain forever the same.

Mark Twain's candidacy as our most "contemporary" historical figure is based in part on his colorful personality, in part on his imperishable writings, in part on the fact that he managed to give voice to most of the issues and problems that still plague us six decades after his death. Several recent biographers and critics have needlessly reminded us that this man might almost as well be living and writing in the last half of the twentieth century as in the last half of the nineteenth. Justin Kaplan, in his popular biography, *Mr. Clemens and Mark Twain*, shows us how fashionably similar Clemens's eccentricities were to our own. Maxwell Geismar repeatedly reminds us in *Mark Twain, American Prophet* and *Mark Twain and the Three R's* that we need only substitute Vietnam for the Philippines, Southeast Asia for the Congo, and the suppression of blacks in our own time for the suppression of blacks in Mark Twain's time to hear how much he indeed proved his claim as "God's Fool," and how much the self-assigned epithet simply enhances his candidacy as the Representative American. Finally, and most important, the volumes of writings pouring out of the Mark Twain Papers at Berkeley, containing everything from petty personal vanities to timeless tirades against the wicked human race, once again remind us how much Mark Twain was like the rest of us, only more so.

From the vantage point of history, it is easy to discredit Mark Twain's boast that he was the representative man. He was an American original; the country had never seen the like, and doubtless never will again. Yet for all his peculiarities, Mark Twain's self-promotion as the representative American had to be based on a solid list of biographical credentials. Eccentricity and genius were not enough. To qualify as the country's mouthpiece, he had to experience, personally and vividly, the main historical events of his time. He did so in a manner equalled by few of his countrymen and surpassed by none. In part through sheer luck in happening to be in the right place at the right time, in part through shrewd talent in stage-managing his public and private affairs, Mark Twain touched on more celebrated episodes in his country's history than any famous American rival. The list of his personal experiences reads like a table of contents for a textbook in nineteenth-century American history: Slavery in the Border South; Life on the Mississippi; The House Divided; The Civil War; The Frontier West; Reconstruction; The American Innocent Abroad; The Industrial Revolution; The Politics of Business; The Gilded Age.² His biographical claim to the title of Representative American began with his birth and childhood in the border South and ended with his "conversion" and death as a Connecticut Yankee. Born to a poor but proud slaveholding family in border Missouri, young Sam Clemens was raised on the notion that he was a half-southern aristocrat and a half-midwestern democrat. His mother, Jane Lampton Clemens, was a fiery Kentuckian who boasted a wondrously exiguous connection to English feudal lords and Virginia slaveowners, but her corncob-puffing style made her more at home in Hannibal, Missouri, than she would have been in the drawing rooms of Savannah or Charleston. Clemens's father, John Marshall Clemens, was a poverty-stricken storeowner who considered himself an authentic throwback to the ethos of a previous generation—a leftover Whig stranded in the backwater of Missouri who sought to improve his status by owning a few black "household servants." Mark Twain remembered as a boy watching his father "cuff" a slave boy named Lewis who became the model for Aunt Polly's "small colored boy" Jim in *Tom Sawyer*, and flog an "uppity nigger wench" named Jenny who became the model for the rebellious slave woman Roxana in *Pudd'nhead Wilson*. At age nine, standing on Hannibal's main street, Sam Clemens watched an overseer crush a slave's skull with a piece of iron ore. Two years later, while rowing around the foot of the island in the Mississippi that became Jackson's Island in *Tom Sawyer* and *Huckleberry Finn*, he happened upon a black corpse, disembowelled and sunk in the river by slavehunters. When he was fourteen, a slave who was accused of raping a white woman was lynched on the outskirts of Hannibal, before one of the largest crowds ever assembled for a social function in that part of Missouri.

If these boyhood memories of slavery provided Mark Twain with nightmares that lasted a lifetime, they also echoed the memories of a good many Americans raised in the antebellum South. Indeed, to trace Mark Twain's shifting views of slavery, blacks, and race relations over fifty years of writing and lecturing is to plot the evolving attitudes and opinions of a good many Americans, North and South, in the half-century after slavery. We have Sam Clemens's word for it that as a southern teenager he accepted the South's peculiar institution without moral reservations. Later, during his steamboating years on the Mississippi, he favored secession; and when the lower South left the Union, so did Clemens, serving briefly in a Confederate guerilla unit. Through the 1850's and into the 1860's, he ranted against "niggers" and told a long series of popular jokes about "nigger odor," fried "nigger" steaks, black sexual promiscuity, and the evils of miscegenation. Yet from the 1880's to his death, he befriended Frederick Douglass and Booker T. Washington, financed several black students through Yale Law School, wrote blistering essays about atrocities committed against blacks, and created two of the outstanding black characters in American literature: Nigger Jim and Roxana. As a native southerner, Mark Twain began his public career as a segregationist and Negrophobe. As a self-professed "reconstructed" Yankee, he turned himself into a champion of interracial brotherhood in *Huckleberry Finn* and ended his life as a prophet of racial war and the complete extermination of black and white alike.

These experiences as a native southerner, however "reconstructed," placed Mark Twain in the ranks of a sizable minority of Americans. His five and a half years in the Far West, however, greatly enlarged his qualifications as a national rather than a regional spokesman. At a time when Horace Greeley was advising young men to go West, Clemens deserted the Confederacy and travelled to Nevada and California, where his experiences as a miner and a journalist established his early reputation in the East as a wild and wooly westerner, and added "The Jumping Frog of Calaveras County" and *Roughing It* to the list of imperishable tall tales about the Far West. Coming east in 1866 on the laurels of the jumping frog, Mark Twain signed up for the Gilded Age's first elitist charter tour of Europe and the Holy Land. Posing as the Innocent Abroad, he told the folks back home what they wanted to hear: Lake Como was smaller than Lake Tahoe; the storied Danube was dirty and lacked the size and charm of the muddy Mississippi; and the Great Masters of Italian art were better off dead. More than any travel book of the age, *The Innocents Abroad; or, The New Pilgrim's Progress*, is an implicit commentary on, and an unmistakable product of, nineteenth-century America.

It was as a spokesman for the Gilded Age that Mark Twain finally transcended his reputation as a native southerner, a sometime westerner, and an adopted Yankee to become the country's foremost national man—a legend in his lifetime, a protagonist of the American experience who was expected to record, and to reflect, certain widely held opinions of his time. Setting out to be both participant and critic in that gilded age that bears the title he gave it, he was pulled in so many directions at once by his enormous energies and diffuse interests that he became, curiously, the country's "united" man only by experiencing the most profound and disquieting sense of personal and philosophical disunity. Part of the problem was brought on by his sudden rise to fame and fortune. Between 1867 and 1874 he married into eastern respectability and a quarter-million dollars, built a lavish mansion in Hartford, Connecticut, and rose spectacularly in financial, social, and literary status—altogether an intoxicating experience that left Mark Twain himself a little giddy, and more than a little uncertain about his permanent status. Though probably the most colorful and conspicuous American of his time, he felt the need to search out a long list of politicians, tycoons, ministers, and men of letters to admire, emulate, or pit himself against: Ulysses S. Grant, Theodore Roosevelt, steel magnate Andrew Carnegie, Standard Oil mogul Henry H. Rogers, clergymen Henry Ward Beecher and Joseph Twichell, Bret

Harte, George Washington Cable, William Dean Howells. A man of many faces who never achieved a unified personality, Mark Twain was a great tangle of tensions and dualities. The most vain of men, he acknowledged his vanity with a childlike innocence that became a vital part of his appeal. A self-dramatized misanthrope who ranted tirelessly against the damned human race, he loved a few people with an intensity that was downright discomfiting. A master of invective who spewed forth a great stream of venom and kept a "Hate List" for years which recorded enemies as "eunuchs," "missing links," and "sexless tapeworms," he followed up many of his public and private scurrilities with deep remorse and prolonged self-flagellation. Proud of his reputation as a liar, he was probably the most completely honest man of his time and was surely his own most severe critic, censor, and tormentor.

Much of Mark Twain's charm—and much of his personal agony— was based on the fact that he could be counted upon to support and oppose, attack and defend almost every conceivable subject of his day—and reverse himself within the fortnight. His boast that he was "the whole human race compacted and crammed into a single suit of clothes"—a man housing in his person "every quality and every defect that is findable in the mass of the race"—was not intended altogether as a joke. No man of his time zigzagged more widely across the full spectrum of what foreign critics flattered themselves to be distinctly "American" traits of character. If we are to measure Mark Twain's full importance to his times, we must play his life and personality against the backdrop of the mind and mood of nineteenth-century America. Foreign observers had long charged that Americans were the least philosophical of all people, that they were bothered by theories and speculations, and that they listened to their foremost philosopher, Ralph Waldo Emerson, only when Emerson stopped prattling about the Soul, the Ego, and the "spermatic man" and started talking common sense. That most Americans failed to understand Emerson most of the time disturbed them not at all; the fault, they suspected, was Emerson's and not theirs, and they may have been right. No philosophy that got much beyond common sense commanded the American's interest for long, and he ruthlessly transformed even the most abstract metaphysics into practical ethics. His favorite native philosophies and religions—instrumentalism and pragmatism, Mormonism and Christian Science—were "practical" in theory and in application. And so too with Mark Twain, who detested theories, worshipped "facts," ignored Emerson, and dabbled for years in pragmatism and Christian Science. As a self-acknowledged "philosopher" of sorts, he held protean opinions that offered a little something for everyone. Fancying himself a level-headed thinker in the tradition of Franklin and Jefferson, he usually relied on snap judgments, to be abandoned later if they didn't hold up under criticism or if the initial enthusiasm wore off. Fascinated by pragmatic logic in the mode of William James, he reached most conclusions by impulse, argued in support of self-evident propositions, and showed little patience for sustained inquiry. Untroubled by inconsistencies, he was alternately a determinist or a nondeterminist, a realist or an idealist, a pessimist or an optimist, an eccentric or a conformist, a hard-boiled pragmatist or a starry-eyed romantic. Like those of many of his countrymen, his philosophical sympathies and personal affections oscillated between Europe and America, East and West, North and South, the past and the present, aristocracy and democracy, solitude and society, indolence and industry, the intellect and the heart, dream as reality and reality as dream.

Nowhere was Mark Twain's boast that he housed "every quality and every defect" of the race more embarrassingly accurate than in his energetic participation in the rush and clatter, the chink and heft of Gilded Age moneymaking. Nothing in all history had succeeded like late nineteenth-century America, and Mark Twain joined his countrymen in celebrating the fact. Nowhere on the globe had nature been at once so generous and so hospitable, and her unbounded riches were available to all who had the enterprise to take them and the good fortune to be white. The self-made man was still the hero in Gilded Age America, as he had been in Jacksonian America, and by "made" most Americans meant enriched rather than cultivated or educated. Foreign critics who thought this vulgar had little conception of its connection with the realities of American life. Long accustomed to watching even their most visionary blueprints for expansion outstripped by reality, nineteenth-century Americans showed a collective passion for facts and figures to measure and quantify their country's astounding progress: farm acreage, population statistics, stock market averages, wheat and corn production records, tons of steel, bales of cotton, miles of railroads. Long accustomed to watching their temporary economic setbacks resolved by practical ingenuity, they showed a high regard for technology and for mechanical inventions: the cotton gin, steamboat, harvester, steel-tipped plow, Westinghouse brake, McCormick reaper, hydraulic steam-drill, vulcanized rubber, the telegraph and telephone.

And so too with Mark Twain, the prototypical self-made tinkerer of the Gilded Age. As entrepreneur, impresario, inventor, speculator, and publisher, busily pouring thousands of dollars into schemes and squabbles of all sorts, he was his own Colonel Beriah Sellers, the hapless booster who boasts and bribes his way through the best-selling exposé of the era, *The Gilded Age*. The central dilemma of Mark Twain's career as a businessman was that his distress with the era he named and satirized was proportionate to his complicity in it. Like several prominent Americans of the time, he was not entirely pleased with the direction the country was taking: men as philosophically incompatible as Henry Adams, Henry George, Henry James, Carl Schurz, Clarence Darrow, Eugene Debs, Edwin Godkin, and George Curtis decried the materialist cast and financial distemper of the times. The Gilded Age had its prophets of pessimism as well as its preachers of progress—and no man served both camps more feverishly than Mark Twain. Out of patience with the moneymaking phobia of the times, he nonetheless enthusiastically embraced the "sivilization" that Huck Finn lit out from. Given to ranting over Rockefeller's oil monopoly, Carnegie's steel empire, and Vanderbilt's crooked railroads, he tried for thirty years to become a millionaire monopolist himself. Deeply distraught over the shady business ethics of the Gilded Age, he considered several questionable enterprises, including fire extinguishers that worked like hand grenades and a concoction of kerosene and cheap perfume to be marketed as a cure for "Chilblains." Infuriated over the speculative madness of the Era of Get Rich Quick, he invested in an engraving company, a publishing company, an insurance house, a watch factory, a carpet manufacturing firm, a health food called Plasmon, a diaper agency, a scissors manufacturing firm, and the Paige typesetter that bankrupted him. Fascinated by gadgets of all sorts, he was one of the first writers to use (and discard) a newfangled typewriter and a dictating machine, and one of the first Americans to install (and grow to despise) a telephone in his home. Fond of recalling Huck Finn's simple existence on raft and river, he personally had more in common with another character of his creation: Hank Morgan, the showy mechanic of *A Connecticut Yankee in King Arthur's Court* who coins the term, the "New Deal," to characterize his career as developer of machines and attitudes that bring progress and destruction to Arthurian England. To the end of his life, Mark Twain remained torn between the niceties of his wealthy existence and a nostalgic fondness for prewar, agrarian America. He had lofty conceptions about the simple life but no gift for living it.

In matters of education and refinement, no less than philosophy and business, Mark Twain took on the air of a common cultural property of the country who was expected to act out certain national mannerisms and cultural prejudices. Much of his charisma was based on the same combination of personal eccentricities and folksy mannerisms which made up the appeal of several of the country's second-generation heroes. When Americans heard that Andrew Jackson had spelled poorly and smoked a corncob pipe, or that Lincoln was largely self-educated and told earthy jokes, or that Grant issued monosyllabic war memos and chewed his cigars to shreds, they took these gestures as self-reflecting symbols of democracy in action. And so when Mark Twain, the drawling, corncob-puffing humorist, mussed his hair before a photograph, or played upon his humble origins and lack of education, he was perfecting a plain-folks image that—for all his private flirtings with royalty and aristocracy—placed him squarely in the social mainstream of nineteenth-century America. And when he confessed that he had trouble with "high" culture, he earned the enduring affection of his countrymen. European critics had long criticized Americans for practicing cultural chauvinism; that is, for enjoying Robert Browning, Stephen Foster, and Currier and Ives while pretending to fancy the Continental poets, the Great Masters, and the compositions of Old World musicians long dead. Mark Twain, echoing his country's split-level mood, began his cultural "career" as a brassy young Innocent Abroad who preferred the "shiny" reproductions of famous Old World paintings to the originals and declared that he was glad the Great Masters were no longer alive to make mischief. Later, as a member in precarious standing of the eastern establishment, he faithfully made Old World pilgrimages to moldy cathedrals and dank museums, and he tried for years to listen to opera without visible signs of agony. Finally, with a string of undeleted expletives, he gave it all up, echoing the sentiments of a good many Americans when he confided that he preferred Browning to Shakespeare, "nigger" minstrels to opera, and no art at all to "high" art. But perhaps the most revealing glimpse into Mark Twain's bifocal view of the culture of the Gilded Age is the half-respectable, half-heretical mansion he built outside Hartford, Connecticut, in 1874. For all his grumbling about the garishness of the Gilded Age, Mark Twain's gaudy, polychrome-gingerbread "castle" at Nook Farm is a classic of the era—a bewildering mixture of traditional decor and outlandish trimmings. Old World furniture and Oriental rugs cohabit with a tropical indoor garden and a bright red bedroom. Delicate outdoor towers and turrets clash with a forest of chimneys which, for a brief time, were strapped with lightning rods that gave a dazzling pyrotechnic display during summer thunderstorms—a sis-boom-bah sideshow that might have made Tom Sawyer green with envy.

In matters of political and sexual morality, too, Mark Twain straddled his times—sometimes teetering on the edge of public propriety, sometimes balancing toward the center of acceptable conduct. Despite his fondness for what William Dean Howells tactfully called "Elizabethan parlance," Clemens voluntarily suppressed most of his private jokes and jottings about scatology, masturbation, onanism, and animal intercourse; and he was genuinely stunned when it was rumored that Henry Ward Beecher, the era's foremost man of the cloth and a family friend, had committed adultery. Yet Mark Twain saw nothing wrong with Beecher's accepting several thousand dollars worth of stock from banker Jay Cooke for puffing the Northern Pacific railroad in a sermon. Indeed, while he fired irate broadsides at the era's numerous equivalents of Watergate, he was hardly a consistent champion of political rectitude or of democratic liberalism. At once the idol of the common man and the pet and protégé of the plutocracy, Mark Twain endorsed labor unions and hobnobbed with Standard Oil moguls, supported the Russian Revolution and feared the "mob," denounced Tammany Hall and received several "professional" favors of his own in the publishing world. Fond of championing the common man and denouncing Congress as the only "distinctly native American criminal class," he flirted with royalty and held private sessions in Speaker Czar Reed's chambers to lobby for a more equitable copyright law. An ardent advocate of liberal immigration laws, he privately felt so direly threatened by the wave of new eastern Europeans that he proposed a sweeping (and anonymous) solution to the danger of mob-rule in America. Instead of restricting the suffrage, which would be unconstitutional, why not expand it by giving men of education and property (such as Clemens) five or even ten votes apiece—thus blending meritocracy and oligarchy?

If America refused accommodation to his terms, Mark Twain would prefer to leave it. Between 1872 and 1907 he spent more than eleven years abroad. First England and then Germany stood for the hallowed virtues of thrift and stability that his own country had lost in the frenzied getting and spending of the Gilded Age. The United States was going mad; and if he did not wish to expatriate himself permanently because it was not profitable, the least he could do was to withdraw as much as possible from the stink and corruption of the present by retreating aesthetically into the past. Convinced that his anger was too great to be unleashed into imaginative literature about the American present, Mark Twain increasingly turned to the Old World past and to an earlier America for his literary material—the farther back, the better. Except for *The Gilded Age*, written early in the era, all of Mark Twain's major books were to be tales of yesterday: the frontier West, the South before the War, the England of King Arthur and the Plantagenets, the France of Joan of Arc, the Germany of medieval times, the Austria of the Middle Ages. Indeed the central drama of Mark Twain's life as a man of letters was his discovery of a series of usable pasts which enabled him to escape the day-to-day business and political harassments of the present. More than any other factor, it was the moral and mercenary decadence of the Gilded Age—by whose standards Mark Twain lived and whose values he alternately embraced and loathed—that drove him to seek refuge in the dream world of times and places other than his own.

The last two decades of Mark Twain's life veered into a dead-end despair that he did not hesitate to read as an omen for the entire country and, finally, the world. He was always subject to seizures of remorse and self-recrimination, and his sense of guilt and his paroxysms of rage and bereavement about almost everything—his family, his public life, the books he had censored, the ideas he had suppressed—grew in the 1890's to the point that he began to question his sanity. Beneath the public image of the crotchety old sage, parading in his white suit, walrus mustache, and black cigar, lay a bitter and neurotic cynic who believed, he said, in nothing. Life had no dignity or meaning. The mass of men were cowards, and he was in the front row, carrying a yellow-streaked banner. Man was a slave of circumstance, his mind a mere machine, his body a mangy museum of diseases rotting in the intestine of God. The human race began as dirt, departed as stench, and was useful in between as a breeding place for bacteria, a repository for worms, and a urinal for dogs. The world, "the true one," was odious and horrible. It would have been better if Noah had missed the boat. If sheep had been created first, man would be a plagiarism.

Much of Mark Twain's despair grew out of the crushing financial and family misfortunes that struck him in the last fifteen years of his life. In 1894 his private publishing company was shut down, its capital too quickly siphoned off to feed the Paige typesetting machine, that "baby with a Gargantuan appetite" that devoured most of his earnings and his wife's inheritance for nine long years. The diabolical typesetter finally failed, and Mark Twain declared bankruptcy, with his wife holding the humiliating position of largest legal creditor. The gilded house in Hartford, symbol of the distance he had traveled from Hannibal, Missouri, was sold. The family idyll was destroyed. In 1896, on the last leg of his global debt-paying tour, Mark Twain received word that his favorite daughter Susy, aged twenty-four, had died in delirium at home, slowly and painfully, from meningitis. His wife Livy declined into invalidism and death in 1904. His youngest daughter Jean, an epileptic, died on Christmas Eve, 1909. Of the six members of the family (a son had died years before as an infant) only one daughter, Clara, married and living in Europe, survived Clemens.

In the midst of personal tragedy there was public triumph. Outwardly, the popular folk figure Mark Twain remained much the same, dictating his memoirs, reading his fan mail, emerging from seclusion to receive the accolades of a doting public, recouping his fortune, and building a less eccentric mansion at Stormfield in Connecticut. Inwardly, however, he changed a good deal. Fearing madness if he became enslaved by family guilt, he worked, as he said, like a madman. Aware that he had reached the age when he could no longer afford to be prodigal, he also found that the literary luck he had always counted on had finally run out. The late piles of skimpy manuscripts, sometimes ending in mid-sentence, reveal a man poisoned with self-loathing and consumed with a well-grounded fear that he was losing his creative powers. When the time seemed ripe to speak what his friend Howells called "the black heart's-truth," to lay his soul bare, to write the final indictment of the damned race that he kept promising the public and himself, it was too late. Like the derelict steamboats he had seen rotting on the great river when he returned to his childhood home in old age, his spark was quenched, his fire out. No sooner would he start a story about the pristine, prewar Mississippi Valley, with the mile-wide river shining in the summer sun, than the currents of his mind would veer toward some dark vortex of horror—toward caves, tombs, red-hot oceans, and Antarctic wastelands in which phantom ships are consumed by sea monsters and the ocean boils down into a molten lunar landscape. Even the cozy, all-white village of St. Petersburg, hugging the ever-summer banks of the

Mississippi, failed him. In one of his last, pitiful efforts to recall the magic valley of his youth, Mark Twain reprised Huck, Tom, and Nigger Jim as toothless old men and placed them atop Holliday Hill, there to call the roll of their long-dead boyhood companions before dying themselves. Finally, even the sun-lit river that had flowed through *Tom Sawyer* and *Huckleberry Finn* froze on him.

Whatever the metaphor, these late visions have in common utter despair. Clutched by turn-of-the-century anxiety, Mark Twain felt that time and history were passing him by. The old century—*his* century— was a part of the past, booted into history by rough-riding Teddy Roosevelt ("the Tom Sawyer of the political world"), as he charged up San Juan Hill and promised fresh military "excursions" in the Philippines and the Orient. Enraged over the extraterritorial escapades of new-century imperialism, Mark Twain lent his tired voice to those of a good many of his countrymen who, like himself, had lived through the Mexican War and the Civil War only to see the flag further tarnished in the nation's first overseas engagements. The country was going to hell in a basket; and if the mass of Americans did not follow their foremost "humorist" into deepest despair, Mark Twain nonetheless echoed the feelings of a growing minority of Americans who began to question the purpose and direction of the new century. That he was no longer representative of the majority mind and mood of his countrymen by the time of his death in 1910 actually enhances rather than diminishes his importance. For what Mark Twain viewed as the decline and fall of his country, followed by the entire world, amounts almost to a national cliché in our own time. In the twilight of his life—having enlarged on his role as the representative American by appointing himself Ambassador At Large For The Human Race—Mark Twain saw the history of his country as a parable of man's tragic but richly deserved lot around the globe: America was simply the world in microcosm. To take his last writings and remarks seriously is to hear Mark Twain saying that there had been, after all, no noble New World experiment, no unique American destiny, no fulfilled mission, and no realistic American dream. Furthermore, there was to be no cleansing or catharsis of the American conscience, no purging of national guilt for the sins of the past, and no new chapter in American history: no new deal, no new frontier, no great society. With this message, Mark Twain played the final act in his one-man role as a national stagepiece. Like other writers who followed him a half-century later, he cursed his country; and in doing so he decried a part of himself and remained the quintessential American to the end.

Notes

1. *Alistair Cooke's America*, the Hallmark Hall of Fame's *Ben Franklin*, *The Adams Chronicles*, *Sandburg's Lincoln*, *Clarence Darrow*, the *Autobiography of Jane Pittman*, *The*

First Woman President (Woodrow Wilson's wife), *Eleanor and Franklin, Give 'Em Hell, Harry!*, and Henry Fonda narrating the American Revolution's *Decades of Decision*.

2.   Most of these titles are taken from a well-known textbook in American history, *The National Experience*, ed. John M. Blum and others (New York, 1963).

Mark Twain and the Pope

Anonymous*

There's a lot we still don't know about the new head of the Roman Catholic Church, Pope John Paul I. But, from what we do know, we can't help feeling good about him.

It's not just the winning benevolence of the smile. It's the Mark Twain connection.

It has come out that the former cardinal from Venice is given to writing open letters to great spirits from the literary world who have captured his imagination, and one of his favorites is Mark Twain.

It is easy to see how Pope John Paul must have been moved by the way Mark Twain, the frontier skeptic of a Protestant culture, fell so in love with the idea of Joan of Arc that he wrote a worshipful book about her. That was before she was officially a saint, but the qualities never depended on the title.

A man who identifies himself as a peasant, the new pope must also have felt a certain empathy with everything in Mark Twain that was provincial and gauche and undazzled and determinedly not taken in by the treasures he saw when he first came, an innocent abroad, to Europe. So many of them are church treasures which the new pope himself may have first seen with not too different emotions.

We suspect that Pope John Paul must have been equally responsive to the Mark Twain who was forever questioning the relics and legends he encountered as a tourist. How he did enjoy saying he had seen the five stones David used to kill Goliath and knew for a fact that they were the real thing! Real stones, that is.

There was always in Mark Twain a strong element of the child who not only notices that the emperor has nothing on but says so. What could be more appealing to a man whose business is truth and truth-seekers? The debunker in Mark Twain is, of course, an aspect of his enormous zest for life—for every encounter with reality from the snags, the challenge of

*Reprinted from Durham Morning Herald [N.C.], 16 September 1978, p. 4A, which reprinted this editorial from Washington Star.

the Mississippi River pilot to the pursuits and dangers and escapes Mark Twain invented for Huck Finn.

Yet we like to think that part of Pope John Paul's feeling for Mark Twain is for the tragic old man he became when doubts and disappointments had soured his ebullience. The man sitting in darkness.

It is a familiar enough human condition, but in Mark Twain scaled large to fit the spirit afflicted. It is good to feel that Pope John Paul has the compassions of an equally large spirit.

Mark Twain and the Anxiety of Entertainment

Judith Fetterley*

Toward his "alternate career" as a professional entertainer, Mark Twain was consistently ambivalent. From his triumphant note to Livy on the success of his toast to "The Babies" at the Grant reception to his grovelling recantation after the "fiasco" of the Whittier Birthday speech, the arcs of his emotional pendulum swung between the twin poles of exultation and disgust. As Lorch, Fatout, and others have demonstrated,[1] Mark Twain was highly self-conscious about the art of public performance, more so than he was about the art of writing. Often sloppy when it came to revising manuscripts, he would spend hours polishing a lecture or analyzing a performance down to the last detail, and "How To Tell A Story" is perhaps his major aesthetic document. It is not, therefore, surprising that while his fictions present virtually no portraits of the artist as writer, they are filled with portraits of the artist as performer, entertainer, showman, storyteller. Indeed, seen in this light, they present a complex and interesting study of the artistic self, analogous in some respects to that provided by the works of that most self-conscious of artists, Henry James. By and large, the portrait of the entertainer that emerges from Mark Twain's fiction is a negative one: it is a portrait flooded with anxiety, rage, contempt, and disavowal; one which works in constant counterpoint to the tone of exultation and triumph frequently revealed in the autobiographical dictations and letters; and one which illuminates the sources of his ambivalence.

Despite the air of detachment, permitted by virtue of his speaking from the grave, Mark Twain's autobiographical projection of himself as the sole survivor in the "cemetery" of American humor reveals considerable anxiety about the profession of entertainer and suggests that the central quality which defined that profession for him was the sense of risk.[2] That risk should characterize entertainment is not surprising for, although Mark Twain describes his failed contemporaries as "merely humorists" and attributes his survival to his seriousness, in fact successful entertainments are more difficult to accomplish than successful sermons.

*Reprinted with permission of the author from *Georgia Review*, 33 (Summer, 1979), 382–91.

The expectation of pleasure is a harder taskmaster than the promise of information, and the fear of failure in the service of pleasure is aggravated by the knowledge that proof of success or failure is immediate, tangible, and irrefutable: the audience laughs or it doesn't. Further, success at entertainment, while it brings a momentary triumph, generates a demand for ever greater effects. The achievement is fragile; it cannot survive repetition or competition—a perception reflected in the fact that all of Mark Twain's entertainers are solitary figures.

In Mark Twain's work, however, the anxieties surrounding the failure of entertainment are equalled, if not exceeded by, the anxieties attendant upon success. If the entertainment is successful, then the entertainer is forced to confront certain fears about the nature of entertainment. Primary among these is the fear that the entertainment is without substance and that the entertainer is a fraud, an imposter, a thief (Mark Twain often "jokingly" referred to lecturing as robbery)—a taker rather than a giver. The autobiographical explanation of his success as a humorist reflects this fear of not being sufficiently serious, of not providing the audience with "food for thought." However, the most interesting treatment of this particular performance anxiety is the infamous Whittier Birthday speech. In this sketch, Mark Twain implicitly accuses Emerson, Holmes, and Longfellow of imposing on the public and getting food, lodging, and clothing for nothing. The poets are robbers who steal the miner blind; in return for his beans and boots, they offer only words. While on one level the sketch makes a distinction between the value of the serious genteel New England poets and the wild Western humorist (in favor, of course, of the latter), the complexities of impersonation which provide its structure link Mark Twain with the poets under the larger aegis of entertainer, one who makes a living playing with words. Thus, at the end of the speech, Mark Twain puts to himself the question which not only the speech itself but the lavish *Atlantic Monthly* dinner given in honor of entertainers could not help but raise: "Ah! impostors, were they? Are you?" What return for *your* beans, Mark Twain?

A second fear attendant upon the successful entertainment is the logical corollary, given the nature of anxiety, of the first—not that entertainment is without substance but that its substance is suspect. That entertainment is aggression and the entertainer engaged in an act of hostility against the audience was a perception both close to the surface of Mark Twain's consciousness, as is evidenced by his remarks on the response to his toast at the Grant reception or on the proper delivery of "The Golden Arm"[3]; and finally unavailable to him for analysis, as his frantic apologies for and denials of the Whittier Birthday speech make clear.[4] In his fictions, however, Mark Twain could undertake this analysis; the hostile relationship, whether implicit or explicit, of the entertainer and the audience is a constant element in his portraits of entertainments. His books are filled with aggressive entertainers: the returned crusader of the spoof on legends in *Innocents Abroad* who enters the castle disguised as a harlequin and exterminates his audience; Tom Sawyer whose staging of his own funeral involves the potential humiliation of all of St. Petersburg; the Duke and the King whose Royal Nonesuch is a common rip-off; Hank Morgan whose entertainments cause his audience to collapse by platoons; Dave "Pudd'nhead" Wilson who enters his world with a hostile joke whose intention he ultimately fulfills by killing his half of the social dog. And they are filled with "sold" audiences: the narrator of "The Jumping Frog," the "innocent" abroad, the attendants at Tom Sawyer's "funeral," the viewers of the Royal Nonesuch. And they are filled with entertainers under attack: the aging singer in *Innocents Abroad* whom the audience torments mercilessly; the Duke and the King, tarred and feathered and ridden out of town on a rail; Hank Morgan sold into slavery as a result of one of his entertainments; Tom Driscoll kicked into a crowd of drunks and tossed from row to row because of a joke. Clearly, the impulse to entertain has its dangerous side, and entertainment is, not surprisingly, associated with anxiety.

Tom Sawyer is central to St. Petersburg because he is an entertainer. Tom's centrality defines his world: in St. Petersburg entertainment is the most significant human activity. The human condition in St. Petersburg is boredom; thus entertainment is not simply relief, it is survival. The Widow Douglas is saved from the vengeance of Injun Joe by reading. In St. Petersburg everything is converted to entertainment—funerals, murders, trials; the need for entertainment takes precedence over justice, even safety—Tom risks his life and the lawyer risks Injun Joe's escape in order to make theatre of Tom's testimony.

Tom is the power in St. Petersburg because he is a genius of entertainment. He is defined through the whitewash scene as the one truly able to convert *everything* into play; he has the imagination and the irreverence necessary to free people from their boredom and to provide them with the opportunities for acting out their secret fantasies. In a world whose concept of entertainment is suggested by the annual "Examination Evening," Tom is a gift; and he is amply rewarded by attention, glory, and power.

This portrait of the entertainer is remarkably free from anxiety. Tom's entertainments are all successes; they are substantive and liberating; and the relation between Tom as entertainer and St. Petersburg as audience is remarkably symbiotic. They need him and he needs them and everybody gets to be Robin Hood or at least have a nice part in the play.

But there are negative undercurrents to this relationship that derive from what must inevitably be Tom's attitude toward his audience. His power, after all, results from their *lack* of it, and they lack power because they are cowardly and hypocritical. They are as bored in church as he is and are delighted when his bug gets them out, but they submit to church and pretend to like it because they are supposed to. In addition, Tom's entertainments are exposures and as such come perilously close to being acts of aggression. This tension culminates in Tom's appearance at his own funeral, which is timed to produce the maximum exposure, and consequently humiliation, of the audience as sentimental hypocrites. Tom backs off from the hostility implicit in his entertainment and after his "funeral" is reborn as a thoroughly conventional good boy who protects women, accumulates capital, and enforces conformity on rebels such as Huck Finn. But he is no longer an entertainer. When he reemerges as an entertainer in *Adventures of Huckleberry Finn*, Tom is completely aggressive and his concept of fun is cruelty. In his handling of Tom Sawyer, Mark Twain has subtly bonded entertainment and aggression; and the entertainer's contempt for an audience that craves entertainment and then attacks those who provide it—for not being serious or substantial, for being "merely" entertainers—is implicit in this portrait.

Since Huck Finn is in so many ways a reaction against Tom Sawyer, it is not surprising that *Adventures of Huckleberry Finn* reflects a revulsion against viewing life from the perspective of entertainment. Despite his adulation of Tom's style and his enjoyment of the circus, Huck is singularly free from the desire to be either entertainer or entertained. Huck's position outside the drama of entertainment has several implications. It suggests, for instance, that being an entertainer is incompatible with a whole range of significant human qualities—kindness, compassion, humility, innocence; indeed, one might say that the heaviest indictment Mark Twain ever made of entertainment was to define Huck in opposition to it. In addition, Huck's position suggests a radical revision of the functional value of entertainment. Entertainment is salvation in St. Petersburg because it handles boredom, but it can't handle the loneliness and fear which are Huck's conditions. Huck handles his loneliness by joining up with Jim, but the bond between them is threatened when Huck tries to entertain Jim or to entertain himself at Jim's expense. The King Sollermun exchange produces an interaction between Jim and Huck that is palpably different from their previous or subsequent relation; each one concludes that the other is a fool, incapable of reason, and impervious to a differing point of view or frame of reference. It is just possible that Huck's decision in the fog episode shortly thereafter (to act like Tom Sawyer and have fun at Jim's expense) derives from the contempt implicit in the conclusion he drew following his attempt to entertain ("you can't learn a nigger to argue"). Certainly, it is clear that entertainment and companionship are incompatible in *Huckleberry Finn.*

Nor can entertainment handle fear. In *Huckleberry Finn*, entertainment is perceived as the luxury of the safe. The encounter with the wrecked "Walter Scott" (which Huck says Tom would call an "adventure" and would undertake "if it was his last act") and the final "evasion" (note the significance of the title in this context) elaborately staged by

Tom amply demonstrate that entertainment is defined by an absence of risk for the entertainer. When Huck tries to convince Jim that landing on the "Walter Scott" was a grand adventure, Jim replies "that he didn't want no more adventures . . . because he judged it was all up with *him* anyway it could be fixed." And at the end of the novel, Tom is safe in bed, but Jim is "in that cabin again, on bread and water, and loaded with chains, till he's claimed or sold." Indeed, the centrality of entertainment to *The Adventures of Tom Sawyer* is closely correlated with the utter safety of a world in which all dangers are magically sealed up in a cave; entertainment cannot answer to Huck Finn's nightmare world in which all the caves are open. (That entertainment may involve no real risk at all is, perhaps, the ultimate anxiety of the entertainer who thinks of entertainment as risky.)

The denigration of entertainment implicit in Huck's lack of interest in it is made explicit by the portraits of entertainers and entertainments in the novel. In *Adventures of Huckleberry Finn*, the human need for entertainment is embodied in the instantaneous conversion of the shooting of Boggs into theater, with the actor being generously "treated" for his performance. In this context, it is one of the major items in the indictment of the damned human race. In *Tom Sawyer*, the Widow Douglas is saved by entertainment; in *Huckleberry Finn*, Boggs is killed by it, for it is the need for entertainment that makes possible the original performance by Sherburn. The need for entertainment also supports people like the Duke and the King, portraits of the entertainer whose fulfilling of that need simply denigrates it further. The fear that entertainers are imposters and entertainments are "sells" is thoroughly expressed in *Huckleberry Finn* through the Duke and the King and the Royal Nonesuch. Equally explicit is the vision of entertainment as aggression. The audience, which receives because it demands the "sell," gladly turns on the entertainer, and the hostile relation between them is carried to its ultimate conclusion as Huck and Tom encounter the audience of the Royal Nonesuch having fun with the old tar, feather, and rail routine. As Huck says, "human beings *can* be awful cruel to one another." In *Huckleberry Finn*, cruelty is entertainment and entertainment is cruelty: tying pans to dogs' tails; soaking them in turpentine and setting them on fire; screaming at drunks in circuses—"knock him down! throw him out!"; shooting old men; tarring and feathering; acting out in the name of fun the slave's horrified vision of what it means to be sold down the river, deaf to the cry of "but what kine er time is *Jim* havin'?" Only a sadist would take part in it; "it was enough to make a body ashamed of the human race."

A Connecticut Yankee in King Arthur's Court continues the denigration of entertainment by associating it with the world of sixth-century Britain, the world which Hank Morgan is bent on reforming and transforming. There are more explicit references to entertainers and entertainments in *A Connecticut Yankee* than in other books—Merlin, Sir

Dinadan, the musicians whom Morgan Le Fay hangs, the numerous after-dinner scenes involving dog fights, joke swapping, story telling; but the cumulative effect of these references is to identify entertainment with the primitive. In Hank's republic of the future, built on the patent and the paper, there is no place for—because there is no need for—entertainment. The fear that entertainment is insubstantial is here reflected in the conviction that it has no part to play in the serious business of converting the sixth century into the nineteenth. In fact, Hank is always dreaming up entertainments to keep the knights occupied and out of the way while the real work goes on.

Entertainment is big in Arthur's Britain because the people are ignorant, superstitious, and mentally and physically enslaved. Entertainment is the signature of a corrupt world based on the system of monarchy, an unjust hierarchy which provides power for the few and slavery for the many. The knights, symbols of that system, are devoted to entertainment; in isolating them as the enemy, Hank defines his attitude toward entertainment. Merlin, another entertainer, is another enemy. Merlin is a fraud who exploits the ignorance of the people and their superstitious need for the sensation of miracles to achieve and maintain a position of power in the kingdom. To the power and attraction of Merlin's entertainments Hank wishes to oppose the power and attractions of technology—the opportunity to change the conditions of one's life. That Hank must disguise his offering in the trappings of entertainment is one of the major ironies of his situation and one of the major sources of his ultimate failure. Hank's performances as a showman are atavistic; they are imitations of the primitive undertaken to gain the power to transform it. But the degree to which he enjoys the role suggests the extent of his own identification with the primitive. The pleasure he takes in being a showman is part of the web that finally traps him in sixth-century identity. The dangers inherent in entertainment and the anxieties attendant upon success at it are succinctly dramatized in our final view of Hank, dying in the attempt to get up one last "effect."

The desire to be free of the anxieties of entertainment may well be one of the reasons why it has no place in Hank's brave new world. Hank rapidly discovers the fragility and instability of the performer's triumph. One miracle demands another, and Hank finds himself under pressure to produce more and greater sensations. When he responds to this pressure and provides one of his greatest shows, the "miracle" of the Valley of Holiness, its effect is short-lived. Out of commission briefly due to a cold contracted in the line of duty, he reemerges to find that his audience has deserted to a rival and that if he wishes to remain the center of attention, he must quickly come up with yet another "miracle." The fickleness of the public asserts the essential hostility of the relation between audience and entertainer. In a world which responds to Merlins, Dinadans, dog fights, and knights, how can an expert showman find adequate appreciation?

When Hank hangs Sir Dinadan for his volume of stale jokes, he is expressing his rage at a public that supports such entertainers and that, by its
support, allows Sir Dinadan to assume Hank as *his* audience. The particular joke that produces Hank's rage is revealing; it is the old story
"about a humorous lecturer who flooded an ignorant audience with the
killingest jokes for an hour and never got a laugh" because "it was all they
could do to keep from laughin' right out in meetin'." The entertainer's
performance fails because of the stupidity of his audience. Hank's final
act of massive aggression, his blowing up of his entire world, is in part the
act of a frustrated performer who feels he has not been sufficiently
appreciated. This is truly primitive. Freed from the plague of entertainment, the new world might indeed be brave.

The original impulse behind *A Connecticut Yankee in King Arthur's
Court* was the desire to transform; annihilation was the court of last
resort. By the time of Mark Twain's later works—*Pudd'nhead Wilson,
The Mysterious Stranger*—annihilation is the original impulse. This shift,
however, provides the context for a restoration of the status of entertainers and a framework for resolving the anxieties attendant upon entertainment. Entertainment is no longer a way into power and therefore
suspect to the audience and unnerving to the performer, as it was in *The
Adventures of Tom Sawyer* and *A Connecticut Yankee*; rather, power
manifests itself as entertainment. And entertainment is transformed from
the personally invested and potentially hostile act of exposure into the
cosmically transcendent act of revelation—of the status of the entertainer
and of the nature of reality. Dave Wilson enters Dawson's Landing with a
joke that defines the essence of that community and identifies Wilson as
one who sees through to that essence. The "comprehensively disagreeable" dog is a metaphor for Dawson's Landing, which kills one half of
itself and foolishly believes that the other half can live. Invisible to the
community, the dog is visible to Wilson, who proceeds in the course of the
novel to reveal his vision. While the community rejects both seer and vision and isolates Wilson by calling him a "pudd'nhead," Wilson's isolation
signifies not the anxiety of an entertainer unappreciated by his audience
but rather his power over them. And that power derives from his knowledge of who they are, systematically acquired through the collection of
their signatures in the form of fingerprints. In *Pudd'nhead Wilson*, it is
not the entertainer who is an impostor—he is the only one whose identity
is what it appears to be; the impostor is the audience, the town of
Dawson's Landing, whose communal identity is built upon the myth that
black and white are different and distinguishable. Wilson's courtroom
performance, reminiscent of Tom Sawyer's, is a revelation of reality that
has the potential for reuniting and revivifying the social dog. That it does
not do so is the result of the severe pessimism which informs the novel,
and it reminds us that the restored status of the entertainer is the result of
his role as an agent of a cosmic despair. Ironically, entertainment

becomes positive at precisely the moment when Mark Twain becomes most negative about the value of human existence.

In *The Mysterious Stranger*[5] this conjunction is even more clearly articulated. *The Mysterious Stranger* is more pessimistic than *Pudd'nhead Wilson*, yet the vision of entertainment is the most positive since *Tom Sawyer*. Satan's appearance in the role of entertainer reasserts that centrality of entertainment which organized *Tom Sawyer* but it validates it as Tom Sawyer could never do. The thirst for entertainment still springs from and indicates the limitations of human existence, but in *The Mysterious Stranger* Satan's entertainments do not simply reiterate or intensify those limitations. Rather they suggest the possibility, however dim, of transcending them. In contrast to the connection established in *A Connecticut Yankee*, the villagers' responsiveness to Satan's entertainments manifests their link with divinity. Indeed, Eseldorf's preference for Satan's performances over the pale human shadows of it provides one of the few good things that can be said about the human race.

Satan is a major assuagement of Mark Twain's anxieties about entertainment. It is highly significant that Satan, who is Mark Twain's dream self, so consistently presents himself as an entertainer: musician, poet, storyteller, joker, creator of fantastic theater, supreme performer of vanishing acts, and provider of creative games. When Satan assumes the identities of others, dull village folk become instantly transformed into superior performers. Satan's entertainments cannot fail and he cannot bore. His very presence, even when invisible, enlivens his audience, and they are invariably worshipful. In addition, his entertainments are substantial; he is a feeder and the food he gives is both pleasure and knowledge. And finally, the fear that entertainment is a secret act of aggression and the relation between entertainer and audience one of hostility is cancelled out by the simple fact that aggression and hostility are meaningless in relation to Satan. Satan feels no hostility toward his audience because they are utterly unlike him, the distance between being cosmic. He needs nothing from his audience—*he* never eats and nothing they do affects him. On the other hand, their hostility toward him is obviated by the realization that the aggression apparent in his entertainments is only the product of their limited human vision. When Satan eliminates without a qualm one of his first entertainments, the boys are horrified by his lack of feeling for the little world he has created. Later they learn, through the example of Nikolaus, that, given the nature of human existence, death is in fact a gift and Satan's "cruelty" is revealed to be kindness.[6]

God has revealed himself as an entertainer, but in the last analysis entertainment becomes a cosmic weapon. Satan exhorts the human race to laugh and by so doing to blow the world to bits. The supreme entertainment of the ultimate entertainer accomplishes that goal by dissolving the world into nothing. Mark Twain's anxieties emerge from the assuasive fantasy: in the final show, the audience realizes that the entertainer is a bad dream; nevertheless, his performance leaves them appalled.

Notes

1. See especially Fred W. Lorch, *The Trouble Begins at Eight: Mark Twain's Lecture Tours* (Iowa City: Univ. of Iowa Press, 1968), and Paul Fatout, *Mark Twain on the Lecture Circuit* (Bloomington: Indiana Univ. Press, 1960).

2. *The Autobiography of Mark Twain*, ed. Charles Neider (1959; rpt. New York: Washington Square Press, 1961), pp. 296–98.

3. See Justin Kaplan, *Mr. Clemens and Mark Twain* (New York: Simon and Schuster, 1966), pp. 226–27, 309–10.

4. See Henry Nash Smith, *Mark Twain: The Development of a Writer* (1962; rpt. New York: Atheneum, 1967), pp. 97–100.

5. For the purposes of exploring Mark Twain's fictional presentation of entertainers and entertainments, I have chosen the version edited and in some part "composed" by Albert Bigelow Paine. While the discovery of the various manuscript versions of this story constitutes one of the major achievements of recent Mark Twain scholarship, defining the essential fact about Mark Twain's final work as his inability to complete it, nevertheless I cannot accept the blanket condemnation of Paine's process or product delivered by William M. Gibson in his Introduction to the California edition of *The Mysterious Stranger* (Berkeley and Los Angeles: Univ. of California Press, 1969). Paine's changes were not as massive, not as significant, and not as contrary to Mark Twain's "intention" as Gibson claims. As James M. Cox puts it in *Mark Twain: The Fate of Humor* (Princeton: Princeton Univ. Press, 1966): "In the last analysis, Mark Twain discovered in Paine the editorial intention which he had lost; thus Paine's posthumous edition of Mark Twain's last work is the closest thing to Mark Twain's intention that we shall ever have." (Cox's entire discussion of *The Mysterious Stranger* and Paine's relation to it is most illuminating; see pp. 266–72.)

6. It is interesting to note that the manuscript of this version of *The Mysterious Stranger* breaks off at precisely the point where Satan's cruelty is no longer kindness but is recognizably human aggression. Satan's punishment of the foreign imperialist who denies the Indian natives the fruits of "his" tree evinces in its carefully designed and systematic torture a personal investment and vindictiveness that is noticeably different from his previous actions. The tension involved in seeking to damn the human race without thereby becoming like it has proved too much for even this most subtle of Mark Twain's balancing acts. Nothing remains but to retreat to the final position and dissipate the accumulated rage by asserting that nothing is real.

Mark Twain Fights
Sam Clemens' Duel

Leland Krauth*

One of the oddest episodes in a life more than commonly filled with the unusual is the duel Sam Clemens did not fight. Clemens' challenges to James L. Laird, one of the owners of the Virginia City *Daily Union*, were never accepted; there was no confrontation on the field of honor. Yet the proposed duel precipitated Clemens' departure from Nevada and became in the retellings of Mark Twain an event of some consequence. The duel and Mark Twain's later accounts of it are worth examining again for several reasons. First, they help us understand Clemens' state of mind during a crucial transition in his life and career, a moment that Henry Nash Smith and Frederick Anderson have termed a "crisis."[1] Second, the differences between the duel and the later tales of it illuminate the processes whereby Mark Twain characteristically purged through his art that which was painful and humiliating in Sam Clemens' past.[2] For Clemens' real fight was not with Laird but with recollections of his own conduct. And finally, in considering Sam Clemens' handling of the duel, a peculiarly Southern institution, we can glimpse the buried outline of his Southern character.

In August of 1863 while employed both as a regular writer for the Virginia City *Territorial Enterprise* and as the Nevada correspondent for the San Francisco *Morning Call*, Sam Clemens posted with apparent glee the following notice to the *Call*: "The Virginia Union and the Territorial Enterprise have been sparring at each other for some time, and I watched the contest with great satisfaction, because I felt within me a presentiment that somebody was going to get into trouble."[3] Ultimately that somebody was Sam Clemens. The trouble began in May of 1864 when he served as acting editor of the *Enterprise* in the absence of the regular editor, Joseph Goodman. Clemens' actions leading up to the abortive duel, long familiar in scholarship, can be briefly summarized.[4] In the editorial columns of the *Enterprise* he anonymously issued two charges. He accused the ladies of Carson City who had raised money at a formal ball for the Sanitary Fund of diverting the money to a Miscegenation

*Reprinted with permission from *Mississippi Quarterly*, 33 (Spring, 1980), 144–53.

Society; he ambiguously added that the imputation was "a hoax, but not all a hoax" (*MTEnt*, p. 200). At the same time he charged the workers on the rival *Union* with defaulting on their pledges to the Sanitary Fund. Both charges were groundless, as he probably knew. The ladies and the *Union* immediately demanded retractions. Clemens tried to appease the ladies through Mollie Clemens, Orion's wife and one of the sponsors of the ball, and through Mrs. W. K. Cutler, president of the women's group that had organized it. When his attempts to placate failed, he apologized for the article in print without signing his name. However, when the *Union* defended itself in strongly worded replies by Laird and J. W. Wilmington, a printer on the paper, Sam Clemens chose to play the part of the hot-blooded Southern gentleman.[5] He immediately issued a series of notes challenging Laird to a duel. Laird persistently declined (referring Clemens to Wilmington, an experienced ex-military man, as the offending party) while vigorously denouncing Clemens, and Clemens (shrewdly ignoring Wilmington) then published in the *Enterprise* all the correspondence that had passed privately between him and Laird, thereby making public his sense of personal affront as well as his demands for gentlemanly satisfaction. One other letter, possibly another challenge, came to Clemens from Mr. Cutler, the husband of Mrs. Cutler, at which point Clemens, who had taken to wearing a gun around town, cleared out on the stage to San Francisco, either fearing he might actually have to fight a duel, or else fearing that, to his embarrassment, he would not be able to.

Outwardly Clemens remained belligerent up to the time of his departure. He assured Orion that he was ready to fight either Laird or any representative of the offended women: ". . . if there is any chance of the husbands of those women challenging *me*, I don't want a straw put in the way of it. I'll wait for them a month, if necessary, & fight them with *any* weapon they choose" (*MTEnt*, p. 203). There is more than a touch of bravado about his declaration here, and Clemens reveals in the same letter a contradictory desire for evasion rather than fight: "We have thoroughly canvassed the Carson business, & concluded we dare not do anything, either to Laird or Carson men without spoiling our chances of getting away" (*MTEnt*, p. 203).

Sam Clemens' motives in making his original accusations have remained so obscure that one recent critic has called some of his conduct "incomprehensible."[6] Clemens himself explained his insult to the Carson ladies as the combination of his own drunken "jest" and a printer's mistake (*MTEnt*, p. 190). Although no one seems to have suggested it, there is one apparent cause of his suddenly active hostility toward the *Union*. Just before he charged the *Union* of reneging on its pledges, Clemens confided to his mother and sister that he was vying with that paper to see who could pledge the most to the Sanitary Fund:

The other day the *Daily Union* gave $200, and I gave $300, under instructions from the proprietors always to "go them a hundred better." To-night the *Union* bid $100, and I bid $150 for the *Enterprise*. I had to go to the office to make up my report, and the *Union* fellows came back and bid another $100. It was provoking, because I had orders to run our bid up to $1,000, if necessary, and I only struck the *Union* lightly to draw them on. But I guess we'll make them hunt their holes yet, before we are done with them. (*MTEnt*, pp. 188–189)

Clemens is obviously uneasy about his failure to keep his paper ahead of the *Union*. At stake for him is both personal pride and by his own admission professional responsibility. He is clearly chagrined. One way of defending himself was to attack the *Union*, to claim, as he finally did, that it would not pay its pledges. But if this was his tactic he failed. Eventually it was Sam Clemens who took to his hole by heading over the mountains.

Although no one has pointed it out, Clemens was caught by his dual offense, as he himself seems to have perceived. When he wrote privately to Mrs. Cutler, he explained that he was not able to "publish an ample apology" at a time when he was "in the midst" of a "deadly quarrel with the publishers of the Union." He could not, he said, "make public apologies to any one at such a time."[7] Clemens' explanation of his silence has at least implicit in it an accurate sense of his dilemma: he could not apologize in print (in his own name) for a tasteless, ungentlemanly slur upon the ladies of Carson at the very moment he was staunchly demanding of Laird "the satisfaction due to a gentleman" (*MTEnt*, p. 193). Clearly the first admission would invalidate the second claim.

Most commentators have seen Clemens' problem as "the danger of being ridiculous and ridiculed" as he claimed grievous insult on shaky grounds and demanded a duel without getting it.[8] Equally at stake for him was, I think, his own propriety, his sense of himself as a gentleman. "I cannot," he told his sister-in-law, "submit to the humiliation of publishing myself as a liar" (*MTEnt*, p. 191). Although he published all his lofty challenges to Laird along with Laird's reasoned refusals, he struggled to keep his culpability with the ladies hidden. So desperate was he to conceal his ungentlemanly behavior that he confessed to Mollie and Orion that if the ladies' protest "were from a man" he would "answer it with a challenge, as the easiest way of getting out of a bad scrape," even though he knew he was "in the wrong & would not be justified in doing such a thing" (*MTEnt*, p. 190). This is exactly what he had done with Laird. Yet even stranger than his desire to save face was his need to feel—somehow—triumphant. His persistent denunciations of Laird and the act of publishing them were not only designed to cover up his own error but also to show his superiority as the injured party whose high standards were lost on the unprincipled. Even more revealing is his bizarre statement to Orion four days before he finally extricated himself by leaving town:

> I consider that I have triumphed over those ladies at last, & I am quits with them. But when I forgive the injury—or forget it—or fail to set up a score against it, as opportunity offers—may I be able to console myself for it with the consciousness that I have become a marvellously better man. (*MTEnt*, p. 202)

Here is a complete reversal of roles, as Clemens transforms himself from maligner to injured victim—the same reversal he attempted to effect with Laird by challenging him. Clemens' bitterness is apparent in his facetious suggestion that the future consolation for his ordeal will be the awareness that he has become a "marvellously better man." Most striking of all, however, is the angry urge to retaliate. Clemens toys with vindictiveness in the very act of disavowing it. In reality he could find no consolation, and retaliation proved as impossible with Laird as it was with the ladies. Clemens thus passed his crisis in a state of frustrated outrage, worried over public exposure, but even more, craving not just vindication but triumph. His escape to the coast soothed his anger by removing him from all its objects except himself, but there was no triumph in the affair for Sam Clemens. Only Mark Twain could achieve that, years later, when he came to write his fictive autobiographies.

Miscegenation cropped up occasionally in Sam Clemens' dreams and eventually made its way directly into Mark Twain's fiction in *Pudd'nhead Wilson*.[9] But Clemens apparently never felt the need—or perhaps more accurately, could never bring himself—to face again his slanderous charge against the Carson ladies. He never mentioned it in any of the various accounts of his Nevada days; he was, as he had said, "quits" with those women. Dueling, on the other hand, became one of Mark Twain's obsessive themes. He returned to it in one form or another in *Roughing It*, *A Tramp Abroad*, *Life on the Mississippi*, the unfinished *Simon Wheeler, Detective*, and *Pudd'nhead Wilson*, as well as in minor short stories and essays. His recurrent interest is undoubtedly more personal than sociological, a manifestation of unresolved conflicting emotions. Mark Twain reconstructed the specific conflict with Laird three times. He retold the story of the abortive duel first as a part of his "Roughing It" lecture, given during 1871–72 (an abbreviated version, little more than an allusion, appeared in the book *Roughing It*), then as a tale, "How I Escaped Being Killed In A Duel," published in *Tom Hood's Comic Annual* for 1873, and finally—and most importantly—as an incident in his autobiographical dictations of 1906.

Not surprisingly, the three versions differ somewhat in detail, and the final autobiographical account is notably different from the first two. Yet the three accounts have important things in common. Perhaps the most striking is simply the fact that, although any actual exchange of shots is averted, in all three tellings the challenge to duel leads Mark Twain and his opponent out onto the field of combat. In his fictive accounts Mark Twain comes a lot closer to fighting a duel than Sam Clemens ever did. The duel is avoided in all three accounts when Mark Twain's opponent is duped into believing that a small bird shot at thirty paces by his second was brought down by Mark Twain himself. This apocryphal story makes Mark Twain something less than a hero and other than a coward.[10]

The three accounts of the duel are all designed to exonerate Sam Clemens. The agent of absolution is of course Mark Twain's humor, and it plays over the entire episode, dissolving everything into the ludicrous. The potential danger of death, for instance, emerges in the prospect—itself hyperbolic—of being riddled by "thirteen bullets" only to disappear in the idiotic suggestion that thus perforated Mark Twain could have "pegs" put in "the holes" and become a useful "hat-rack."[11] In shaping his humorous narrative Twain approaches some vexed aspects of the past entanglement, issues of cause and accountability. Twain takes upon himself a measure of responsibility in all three versions by acknowledging himself as the provoker of the duel. But in not one version does he come close to the facts: there is no mention of the Sanitary Fund, no indication of personal bitterness toward the *Union*, no hint of the compounding difficulties provided by the ladies. Mark Twain tends to acknowledge his guilty part by saying of a rival editor (who is nameless in the first account, called "Lord" in the second, and only given his real name in the third) something like the following: "He got touched at something I said about him—I don't know what it was now—I called him a thief, perhaps."[12] In fact, following the curious etiquette of the duel, Sam Clemens had called Laird in the course of their exchanges a "cowardly sneak," a "craven carcass," an "unmitigated liar," an "abject coward," and a "fool" (*MTEnt*, pp. 192–196). Mark Twain's telling masks the depths of Sam's bad temper and mitigates his culpability. Even so, he needs a scapegoat, someone upon whom ultimate blame may be cast.

Predictably perhaps, Mark Twain seizes as scapegoat his lifelong antagonist: society itself. In his lecture he points only briefly at society as the cause of his own misdoings. He simply says that in Nevada if a man took offense at something he wrote he "had to challenge him, and shoot him" because, as his publisher explained it to him, "it was the custom—society must be protected."[13] In "How I Escaped Being Killed In A Duel," however, he elaborates the social constraints he labors under, the pressures to conform or suffer loss of face:

It was the old "flush times" of the silver excitement, when the population was wonderfully wild and mixed: everybody went armed to the teeth, and all slights and insults had to be atoned for with the best article of blood your system could furnish. . . . Duelling was all the fashion among the upper classes in that country, and very few gentlemen would throw

tion (*Auto*, p. 114). (Although a steely-eyed brave man is a cliché, Mark Twain is wholly serious, citing his friend Bob Howland, the one-time marshal of Aurora, as another man who possessed the "mysterious" eye.) Mark Twain betrays in all this a genuine admiration of conventional masculine bravery that is notably absent from the other two accounts of the duel. The elevation of conventional bravery places his own conduct in an ironic light. For of course he evades his duel through a ruse and decamps rather than prosecute his own campaign.

The emotional and psychological bearing of Mark Twain's digression is further revealed by its arrival at the figure of the elder Gillis. (After escaping from his own duel Sam Clemens had lodged for a time in the Gillis home in San Francisco.) Had he reminisced of Steve Gillis, the second in the abortive duel, his remarks would have been natural enough. But he focuses instead on the father, creating this emotion-charged tableau:

> The father made the campaign under Walker, and with him one son. They were in the memorable Plaza fight, and stood it out to the last against overwhelming odds, as did also all of the Walker men. The son was killed at the father's side. The father received a bullet through the eye. (*Auto*, p. 113)

Courage thus becomes in Mark Twain's final account a matter of a son emulating his father. Looming behind the array of valorous men—except for Goodman, all proud Southerners—and specifically embodied in the elder Gillis (who served, as Sam Clemens' landlord, *in loco parentis*) is no doubt the real father, John Marshall Clemens. John Marshall Clemens, known in his life as "Judge" Clemens, was a lawyer, a storekeeper, and eventually a Justice of the Peace. The "product of inherited Virginia pride and straitened circumstances," he was a firm man of high principle, rigid discipline, impeccable honor, and irascible temper, a judge who was not averse to keeping the peace in his courtroom by swacking brawlers over the head with a mallet.[21] Mark Twain's most extended fictional representation of him is in *Pudd'nhead Wilson* where he appears as Judge Driscoll. Significantly, in that novel when the false, cowardly Tom shirks a duel, Judge Driscoll, his *de facto* father, not only denounces him but also takes his place. Mark Twain seems to have felt that Sam Clemens betrayed some part of his heritage when he evaded his duel.

But that is only half of Mark Twain's feeling. If he is guilty over Sam's failure to fulfill the manly role assigned by fathers to sons, to risk death with equanimity, he is also angry and resentful about the role itself—in fact, rebellious. (He mocked as well as admired Judge Driscoll, and of course one way of carrying out his rebellion was to desouthernize.) When he describes the stand of the Gillis father and son, he mentions that the father "received a bullet through the eye," and adds, the "old man—for he was an old man at the time—wore spectacles, and the bullet and one of the glasses went into his skull" (*Auto*, p. 113). Mark Twain's tone here is respectful. The mutilation—tantamount to castration, since the eye has been singled out as the sign of manliness—is presented as a part of the general picture of the father's bravery. In all published versions of the autobiography the account of the wounding ends at this point. But in the original dictation Mark Twain continued, and his tone changed radically: "—but often, in after years, when I boarded in the old man's home in San Francisco, whenever he became emotional I used to see him shed tears and *glass*, in a way that was infinitely moving."[22] Mark Twain himself cancelled this passage (and two additional sentences extending the joke). He suppressed his mockery of the father whose brave conduct was a tacit rebuke to Sam Clemens' own.

Perhaps because he placed dueling in a context of genuine heroes, making it loom as a test of true courage, Mark Twain adds in the autobiography a new twist to the familiar ending of his duel. He inserts into his old narrative a new reason for his departure from Nevada. He says that there was a "brand-new law" against dueling that would entitle him and his second to "two years apiece in the penitentiary" (*Auto*, p. 117). There was in fact no new law, although there was an old one never seriously enforced,[23] yet Mark Twain makes a small drama out of the threat of the bogus new law. As he tells it, a warning comes from a close friend of the governor's advising Mark Twain and his second that they will be searched for but not caught, provided they take the next stage out of Virginia City. All of this is as apocryphal as the new law itself. But Mark Twain makes his need to leave imperative. "Judge North," he explains, "was anxious to have some victims for that law and he would absolutely keep us in prison the full two years. He wouldn't pardon us out to please anybody" (*Auto*, p. 118).

In this last retelling of the duel Mark Twain thus achieves what Sam Clemens had tried to effect years earlier in the course of the actual conflict: he becomes the victim. Having abused the ladies, Sam Clemens had proceeded to imagine himself wronged. Having offended the *Union* and Laird, he had assumed the role of the injured party forced to defend himself with a challenge. So now, in his fantasy, Mark Twain imagines himself the victim—threatened, hunted, even persecuted by a stern law and a remorseless judge. (One recalls again "Judge" Clemens.)

Sam Clemens obviously needed to think of himself as victim rather than aggressor. Though he could, in an unguarded moment, make a sexual and racial joke at the expense of proper ladies, he could never own up to it. And while he could play the fire-eating Southern gentleman who maintains his honor by offering to duel, he preferred not to acknowledge that role either. Mark Twain desouthernized Sam Clemens by reconstructing his warfare, turning it into a necessary act imposed on him by society, turning him into the innocent victim. Mark Twain thus achieved for Sam Clemens the same transformation sentimental writers were to provide for the south as a whole when they re-created the Civil War as the march of Northern aggression over Southern weakness. Both myths, Mark Twain's personal one and the region's general one, were compelling enough to vie in time with reality. The pen has proved mightier than the dueling pistol as well as the sword.

Notes

1. Henry Nash Smith and Frederick Anderson, eds., *Mark Twain of the Enterprise* (Berkeley: Univ. of California Press, 1957), p. 24. Hereafter these documents are cited parenthetically as *MTEnt*. I want to express my gratitude to the late Frederick Anderson and to the staff at the Mark Twain Papers, especially Michael B. Frank, for assistance during my research.

2. I have attempted throughout to maintain the distinction, increasingly common in scholarship, between Samuel Clemens the man and Mark Twain the authorial personality, even though it is imperfect at best.

3. " 'Mark Twain's' Letter," San Francisco *Daily Morning Call*, July 30, 1863, as reprinted in *The Twainian*, No. 2 (March–April 1952), 1.

4. In addition to the careful record provided by Smith and Anderson (*MTEnt*, pp. 24–30), the following studies cover Twain's duel: Ivan Benson, *Mark Twain's Western Years* (Stanford: Stanford Univ. Press, 1938), pp. 106–113; Effie Mona Mack, *Mark Twain in Nevada* (New York: Scribner's, 1947), pp. 307–326; and Paul Fatout, *Mark Twain in Virginia City* (Bloomington: Indiana Univ. Press, 1964), pp. 196–213.

5. For a discussion of Twain's shifting Southern sympathies at this time, see Arthur G. Pettit, *Mark Twain & the South* (Lexington: Univ. Press of Kentucky, 1974), pp. 23–34.

6. Stephen Fender, " 'The Prodigal In A Far Country Chawing Of Husks': Mark Twain's Search For A Style In The West," *Modern Language Review*, 71 (Oct. 1976), 751.

7. *Mark Twain's Letters*, ed. Albert Bigelow Paine, 2 vols. (New York: Harper and Brothers, 1917), I, 97–98.

8. Smith and Anderson, *MTEnt*, p. 29. See also Justin Kaplan, *Mark Twain and His World* (New York: Simon and Schuster, 1974), p. 58.

9. For a vivid instance of these dreams, see *Mark Twain's Notebook*, ed. Albert Bigelow Paine (New York: Harper and Brothers, 1935), pp. 351–352.

10. The apocryphal nature of this tall tale is discussed by DeLancey Ferguson, "Mark Twain's Comstock Duel: The Birth Of A Legend," *American Literature*, 14 (March 1942), 159–161. Citing conversations with those who knew Clemens during his Nevada days, Cyril Clemens—" 'The Birth Of A Legend' Again," *American Literature*, 15 (March 1943), 64–65—has argued unconvincingly that the story was true.

11. Mark Twain, "How I Escaped Being Killed In A Duel," in *Tom Hood's Comic Annual* (London, 1873), p. 91.

12. "Roughing It Lecture," *Mark Twain Speaking*, ed. Paul Fatout (Iowa City: Univ. of Iowa Press, 1976), pp. 60–61.

13. "Roughing It Lecture," p. 60.

14. "How I Escaped," p. 90.

15. "Roughing It Lecture," p. 60; "How I Escaped," p. 90; "Roughing It Lecture," p. 61; "How I Escaped," p. 90.

16. "Roughing It Lecture," p. 62.

17. *The Autobiography of Mark Twain*, ed. Charles Neider (New York: Harper and Row, 1959), p. 112. Hereafter this edition is cited parenthetically as *Auto*. On the subject of the duel there are no substantive differences between Neider's text and that in *Mark Twain's Autobiography*, ed. Albert Bigelow Paine, 2 vols. (New York: Harper and Brothers, 1924).

18. "How I Escaped," p. 91. Except for minor differences in phrasing, the joke is the same in all three versions of the duel.

19. William Dean Howells, *My Mark Twain: Reminiscences and Criticisms* (New York: Harper and Brothers, 1910), p. 35.

20. For Walker's career, see Edward S. Wallace, *Destiny and Glory* (New York: Coward-McCann, 1957), pp. 142–240; and Laurence Greene, *The Filibuster* (Indianapolis: Bobbs-Merrill Co., 1937). For a brief discussion of Clemens' admiration of him, see Margaret Duckett, *Mark Twain and Bret Harte* (Norman: Univ. of Oklahoma Press, 1964), pp. 19–20.

21. Dixon Wecter, *Sam Clemens of Hannibal* (Boston: Houghton Mifflin, 1952), pp. 14–15; 104–105. The best assessment of the father's influence is Louis D. Rubin, Jr., *The Writer In The South* (Athens, Georgia: University of Georgia Press, 1972), pp. 34–81; but see also Irving Malin, "Mark Twain: The Boy as Artist," *Literature and Psychology*, 11 (Summer 1961), 78–84.

22. Autobiographical Dictation, 19 Jan. 1906, Mark Twain Papers.

23. Smith and Anderson, *MTEnt*, pp. 28–29.

INDEX

This index is centered on Mark Twain. A heading such as "anti-romantic" or "autobiography" refers to his own writings. Books, stories, and essays by Twain are also integrated with the main alphabetical listing.